SOCIAL CHANGE AND THE DEVELOPMENT OF THE NURSING PROFESSION

Social Change
and the Development
of the Nursing Profession

A Study of the Poor Law
Nursing Service 1848–1948

ROSEMARY WHITE
MSc, SRN, SCM, OHNC

HENRY KIMPTON PUBLISHERS · LONDON

First published 1978

© 1978 Henry Kimpton Publishers
7 Leighton Place, Leighton Road, London NW5 2QL

ISBN 0 85313 800 1

British Library Cataloguing in Publication Data

White, Rosemary
    Social change and the development of the nursing
    profession
    1. Nursing - Great Britain - History
    2. Nursing - Social aspects - Great Britain
    3. Great Britain - Social conditions
    I. Title
    610.73′069′0941   RT11

Printed in Great Britain by The Anchor Press Ltd
and bound by Wm Brendon & Son Ltd
both of Tiptree, Essex

CONTENTS

FOREWORD BY
MARJORIE SIMPSON, OBE

Since the mid-nineteen-sixties the Ministry of Health (now the Department of Health and Social Security) and the Scottish Home and Health Department have offered fellowships annually to enable nurses under skilled guidance in the universities to carry out research into nursing matters seen by the nurses themselves to be of importance and interest. In this way a growing number of nurses have begun to acquire research skills and a trickle, now becoming a small stream, of research reports on nursing subjects is being published.

The University of Manchester under the imaginative leadership of Professor Alwyn Smith in the Department of Community Medicine was one of the earliest universities to offer places to the Department's research fellows. In addition nurses who were not necessarily graduates were accepted into taught programmes leading to a Master of Science (Public Health) degree, a great boon to a profession many of whose able senior members had had no opportunity when they qualified to acquire a first degree.

Rosemary White is the first research fellow to use documentary research techniques to throw light on the history of the development of the nursing service. She has chosen the Poor Law Nurses as her subject, a group little studied in the past being overshadowed by interest in the nurses of the more prestigious voluntary hospitals. She has used a wide range of primary sources for her material. The result is a fascinating unfolding of a convincing story of the Poor Law Nursing Service with its trials and difficulties, strivings and successes. Over the years 1848–1948, other nurses were winning an established and essential place as contributors to the cure of the sick which scientific developments of the time made possible. The Poor Law Nurses by force of circumstances worked amongst the old, the chronically sick and the insane giving them care when the new, exciting developments were making 'cure' the hallmark of success in the hospital services. They were numerous but not influential. Yet Rosemary White contends that it was these nurses who preserved the unique caring role for nurses.

The history of the Poor Law Nurses is carefully set within a résumé of the social history of the period. The economic, political, demographic and other social factors which were beyond the control of the nurses are examined for their influence on the number of indigent people and the treatment afforded to them. Changes in philosophy and social attitudes are also examined together with the rivalries, anxieties and vested interests which held back reforms.

It is an interesting tale which might be thought to have its conclusion in the National Health Services Acts of 1948 and 1974 which brought all the nurses together into a single national service. But the story is not finished; deprivation in terms of accommodation and staffing ratios are still evident where the old, the mentally ill and the chronic sick are cared for. Many lessons pertinent to today's problems can be learned from this carefully documented study of the patient, persistent effort for reforms in the facilities provided for the care of the underprivileged group served by the Poor Law Nurses. The unique caring function of the nurse is today being accorded higher recognition and is beginning to be practised with pride and not only in the hitherto less well-respected fields of work.

Rosemary White has made a major contribution to our knowledge of nursing history by bringing the Poor Law Nurses into a picture hitherto dominated by the voluntary hospitals and their eminent nurse leaders. The story is illuminated and brought into focus by being presented in the context of the social changes of the period. She has not been content merely to record and the insights she offers into the value of this branch of nursing highlights the contribution made to modern nursing care by the long, patient service given by the Poor Law Nurses.

H. MARJORIE SIMPSON, OBE, BA, SRN, FRCN
formerly Principal Nursing Officer (Research)
Department of Health and Social Security

AUTHOR'S NOTE

The system of referencing that has been used is a modified form of the Harvard system. This was chosen in deference to the reader's convenience but it has to be admitted that it is not the most convenient system for use in a historical work. The titles of official papers are often very long and cumbersome and do not lend themselves to abbreviation. The full reference of any source is given once at the end of the relevant chapter. If the same source is quoted in subsequent chapters, the reference is curtailed. Full references are also included in the Bibliography at the end of the book.

A distinction has been made in the text between the infirmaries which were administered by the workhouse and the Infirmaries which were separately administered. In the former instance the word infirmary has been spelt with the 'i' in the lower case and in the latter instance the upper case (I) was used.

In order to distinguish more clearly between the voluntary hospitals and the Poor Law infirmaries, the former are described as hospitals and the latter as infirmaries or Infirmaries. This practice was pursued as far as possible but had to be suspended, in the interests of accuracy, when a quotation was used or when, as in the case of the Royal Leicester Infirmary, the name of the voluntary hospital was in contrast to it. In the early days of the twentieth century it became the practice of some people to call the large, independent Infirmaries 'Hospitals', especially as those institutions took in more acute cases. In these instances the character of the institution has been clarified in the text.

Acknowledgements. I have had a great deal of help and support in my researches and in the preparation of this text and it is with great pleasure that I acknowledge my gratitude to:

Geraldine White for setting me on the rails and giving me the momentum towards a new world; Jean McFarlane for keeping the wheels in motion; Alwyn Smith for his faith and support; Marjorie Simpson also for her support, in more ways than one; Helen Howarth for her practical research suggestions and introduction to the world of research nurses; Michael Rose for his supervision and guidance; my colleagues in the Department of Community Medicine and the Department of Nursing, University of Manchester, for their stimulation; all the librarians with whom I came into contact for their professional guidance and ready help; Gillian Roberts for preparing the typescript of this book; Margaret Thwaites for editing and correcting the text and for her helpful comments; my friends, the Poor Law Nurses for the wealth of material and the dedication which they handed on to me and my profession. Lastly I acknowledge the support of the Department of Health and Social Security who awarded my Research Fellowship and funded the research.

Rosemary White

ABBREVIATIONS USED IN THE TEXT

B of G	Board of Guardians
BNA	British Nurses Association, later Royal British Nurses Association
CMB	Central Midwives Board
CMO	Chief Medical Officer. In this text, of the Ministry of Health
Coll. of N	College of Nursing, later Royal College of Nursing
DPH	Diploma of Public Health
GBH	General Board of Health
GMC	General Medical Council
GNC	General Nursing Council
LBH	Local Board of Health
LCC	London County Council
LGB	Local Government Board, in this text frequently referred to as 'the Board'
MAB	Metropolitan Asylums Board
M & CW	Maternity and Child Welfare
MO	Medical Officer
MOH	Medical Officer of Health
PL	Poor Law
PLB	Poor Law Board
PLC	Poor Law Commission
PTS	Preliminary Training School
RAMC	Royal Army Medical Corps
RBNA	Royal British Nurses Association
RCN	Royal College of Nursing
Supt. MO	Superintendent Medical Officer
Supt. Nurse	Superintendent Nurse
SRN	State Registered Nurse
VAD	Voluntary Aid Detachment

INTRODUCTION

The National Health Service was born in 1948 and reorganised in 1975. Out of its birth came the establishment of a single, unified hospital nursing service which incorporated nurses from the Voluntary Hospitals, the Municipal Hospitals, the Poor Law Institutions, the County Asylums and privately run charity hospitals. In 1975 the local authority nurses who worked mainly in the community or domicilary areas were absorbed into NHS management to form a comprehensive nursing service with the hospital nurses.

These two major pieces of legislation brought about the most profound changes in the nursing profession in Great Britain. These changes affected the structure, organisation and education of nurses: they bit deeply into the profession's philosophies, objectives and image and changed, more or less overnight, the entire ethos of British nursing.

An upheaval such as this was effected not by the profession itself but by legislation which, in its turn, was brought about by social change.

The upheaval may have been sudden since it depended on the nomination of an appointed day, but the social changes which required the passing of the 1946 and 1974 Acts were the products of two major wars and many years of social development.

The design of the National Health Service in its 1948 form was, with hindsight, predictable. It was not a brand new concept nor, in fact, was it a complete design. There were many components which were omitted at the time. Some of these were introduced in the 1974 Act, such as the integration of the institutional and the community services; some other concepts such as the large Health Centres, though mentioned in the 1946 legislation, were introduced at other stages. Some 'developments', it could be argued, were retrogressive. An example of these might be cited as the separation of the social services from the health services. The point to be made is that our present position is rooted in the past. From the past have been generated the social attitudes that produce change. In order to understand our present situation with its acknowledged successes and deficiencies we can study the history of social change. It may even help us to foresee future changes.

The nursing profession is as much rooted in social history as is the National Health Service. It has been born from social change, it has been shaped by the social climate and it has developed and responded to changes in social policy. Too often it is said that nursing follows in the wake of medical advances. This statement is as open to challenge as is the theory of sex roles. It is a statement which derives from a superficial study of the profession; it depends more on the observation of the tasks performed by the nurse than on a study of the development of the profession.

There are many problems facing the nursing profession today: it is emerging as a profession which is at the same time trying to define its own functions and to discover its own role in the multidisciplinary health care professions. Many conventions, procedures, practices and attitudes are leftovers from bygone days and are now ana-chronistic. They were developed, in their days, from a pragmatic response to problems or conditions which prevailed at the time. The conditions may have changed but the rituals sometimes continue.

On the other hand, nursing has sometimes been accused of throwing out the baby with the bath water and it is as well to prevent this when possible.

It is hoped that a history of the nursing profession, or at least, of a very important part of British nursing, may help present-day nurses to be selective and give them a tool with which they could test professional values in rejecting the old and accepting the new.

These are days of rapid and numerous changes which sometimes tend to generate feelings of insecurity and aggression: individuals are working in multiprofessional teams, professions are giving up components of their work and taking on new ones; roles are changed, functions are changed, philosophies have to be reassessed, as do values and customs. It is in the knowledge and understanding of our roots that we can find security, a rationality and a base from which we shall feel freer and more able to move onward from the present. In this book I have tried to describe how the nursing profession has been shaped by social needs and social changes.

It may be asked why the little-known Poor Law Nurses were made the subjects of this study. Originally they were selected for methodological reasons since, it was felt, they might have been more co-ordinated and therefore more susceptible to developments and changes as a body. In contrast to them it was thought that the Voluntary Hospital nurses were fragmented between many separate hospitals and employing organisations. In the event, it was discovered that there was already a wealth of material about the Voluntary Hospital nurses who were very well documented but that there was no comprehensive history of the Poor Law Nurses, still less an interpretative history.*

It will be seen that the Poor Law Nurses formed a very substantial part of the nursing profession in Britain and that they nursed 75% of all hospitalised patients. In the 1920s there were twice as many Poor Law Nurses as there were Voluntary Hospital nurses. There was a loose organisation of these nurses in every section of nursing and in almost every parish in the country. Hodgkinson (1967) has described the Poor Law Medical Service as being the origin of the National Health Service and Ayers (1971) has described the Poor Law hospitals as our first State hospitals. If these statements are accepted it can fairly be claimed that the Poor Law Nurses were Britain's first National Nursing Service.

REFERENCES

Ayers, Gwendoline M. (1971), *England's First State Hospitals*. The Wellcome Institute of the History of Medicine. London.

Hodgkinson, Ruth (1967), *The Origins of the National Health Service: the Medical Services of the Poor Law, 1834–71*. The Wellcome Institute of the History of Medicine. London.

---

* The material used in the book has been taken from my thesis written in part fulfilment of the requirements for the degree of Master of Science (Public Health) at the University of Manchester, England, in 1975. The title of the thesis was *The Development of the Poor Law Nursing Service and the Social, Medical and Political Factors that Influenced it: 1848–1948*. The Study was undertaken as a scientific enquiry into the development of a single health profession within the NHS and the factors influencing this.

SETTING THE SCENE:
BEFORE 1848

The first general Poor Law Act was passed in 1601 during the reign of Elizabeth I. It was designed to help the poor by payments in kind and in actual cash. Relief could be given to the poor by periodic payments or donations as they continued to live at home (outdoor relief) or it could be given to them as inmates of the local poorhouses (indoor relief). It was not until after 1834 that the term workhouse was commonly used.

Before the third quarter of the nineteenth century, there was only a very primitive form of local government in England. The parish was the local unit and there were very few full-time or paid officials. Even the large cities were broken up into parishes which were independent of each other. The Poor Law was therefore administered by the parishes and was paid for out of parish rates. The parish elected officials to oversee the administration of the Poor Law and these were collectively known as the Board of Guardians. The Local Government Board was the central government department which administered the Act.

Medical care was always part of the relief given under the Poor Law and local physicians were appointed by the Guardians. The Guardians also appointed an Overseer (later called Relieving Officer) to supervise all relief, to select suitable candidates and to decide on the way in which it should be given. The aged, infirm, handicapped, orphans, widows and poor sick were traditionally accepted as being valid candidates for poor relief. The unemployed were viewed with greater care as it was felt that there was normally enough work available for them. If they were unable to find work, or if no one would give them work, the parish usually tried to find them work of a community nature in order that they should earn their parish relief: hence the phrase 'setting the poor to work'.

Before the Poor Law (Amendment) Act of 1834 each parish had its own poorhouse. These were usually small (often a cottage was used in the rural parishes) and some were quite homely. The sick were looked after by the other inmates but no special provision was made for them. The inmates were set to work to earn their keep and were also used in the poorhouses as domestic labour.

The administration of the Poor Law was pragmatic and the conditions for receipt of relief varied from parish to parish. It was not until the early part of the nineteenth century, when unemployment became a serious problem, that concern mounted and the varying rates of relief became a matter of public scandal. There was no general policy for the administration and control of relief and in 1832–3 a Royal Commission was set up to look into the matter. Two of the Commissioners were Nassau Senior and Edwin Chadwick. They were also the joint authors of the Report which was produced in 1833. The Poor Law (Amendment) Act of 1834 was the result.

This Act is frequently remembered for its harshness which helped to generate the fear and loathing of the Poor Law and everything to do with it. However, it was also the basis of all official social policy until the National Insurance, National Assistance and National Health Service Acts of 1946–8. It was, in fact, not so much the Act itself which was harsh but the Orders which were subsequently made and the manner in which they were implemented and interpreted. There was great reluctance on the part of the central government to interfere with local matters, especially where the use of local funds were concerned.

But in spite of its determination to leave responsibility within the local units, the Government was slowly drawn over the following years into a reluctant path of centralisation. The 1834 Poor Law Act was the first occasion when a central government body was established to determine policy and standards and to control the administration of the Poor Law: at this stage however, the Poor Law Commission had little power with which to enforce its authority and was very reluctant to use what power it had. It still had to work through the numerous local units. Later, more centralisation developed but it continued to suffer from the same constraints on its authority.

The New Poor Law introduced another novel development: it permitted the amalgamation of two or more parishes into a Union with a common workhouse. 'It shall be lawful for the said Commissioners by order under their Hands and Seal, to declare so many Parishes as they may think fit to be united for the Administration of the Laws for the Relief of the Poor and such Parishes shall thereupon be deemed a Union for such Purposes, and thereupon the Workhouse

or Workhouses of such Parishes shall be for their Common Use . . .'
(Bruce 1973).

This was the start of a development that increased over the ensuing years. It was also a means of effecting economies and alleviating the burden on the rates: if there was one overriding sentiment relative to the administration of the Poor Law of this period, it was the search for ways of keeping down the rates levy.

The Act sought to control the indiscriminate relief of poverty by limiting the giving of outdoor relief. In order to do this, it required that there should be a test of destitution or 'less eligibility' which made it necessary for the entire family of anyone seeking relief to be admitted to the workhouse. This test assumed that the conditions of the workhouse inmates would be 'less eligible than that of the independent labourer of the lower class'.

This test resulted in conditions of great hardship being established in workhouses because the standard of living of the independent albourer was already at a very precarious level.

The Report which preceded the Act envisaged that there should be separate accommodation in the workhouses for the elderly, the ill, children and pregnant women. There was a spate of new and larger workhouses after 1834 but segregation of these categories did not take place. Accommodation did not keep pace with the necessary influx of the poor brought about by the workhouse test since there was great poverty at the time and unemployment was widespread.

The receipt of poor relief automatically disenfranchised a person for the following year and effectively pauperised him. No one could receive relief if he had any resources at all, including an article of furniture. Relief was therefore reserved for the destitute.

The sick poor had either to seek paid medical care or find it through the avenues of the Poor Law. Local overseers had previously employed doctors to give medical attendance to the sick. Before the New Poor Law Act, this had been given either as out-relief or to the inmates of the workhouses. Under the 1834 Act the sick poor had to be admitted to the workhouses together with their families.

Employment of nurses in the workhouses was rare: if nursing of the inmates was required it was given by the other inmates who were set to nurse the sick as part of their duties.

The 'nurses' were an assorted selection and the quality of the nursing must have been equally assorted. The period was before the 'reform of nursing' and can only be assessed in that light. There were few refinements to life for the poor who lived in primitive circumstances; they had no running water, no drainage, heating was used for cooking rather than for comfort, personal hygiene was not common even amongst the upper classes still less amongst the poor; food for the rural poor depended upon what they could grow and rear and glean whilst food for the urban poor had to be bought with their meagre earnings and consisted largely of carbohydrates (bread and potatoes) with a sparse ration of vegetables and infrequent helpings of meat or fish. There was no alleviation of the principle of 'less eligibility' for the sick unless the workhouse doctor ordered extras, and the nurses had little equipment with which to work. Theirs was a job thrust on them, their duties were few and consisted of giving minimal personal attention, portering the meals, keeping a light burning through the night and administering the simple treatments ordered by the doctors. The doctors performed what dressings were thought necessary but the nurses applied the bandages. The pauper nurses were also responsible for the linen (the little that was used) and kept the wards clean. Without doubt there was considerable drunkenness in the country, not least amongst the poor within the workhouses; beer was issued daily, in the morning, and the pauper nurses in the Strand Workhouses were said by Rogers (undated) to be drunk before his daily visits. Little could be done to alleviate the sufferings of the sick because so little was known about illness, disease and suffering; there was a tendency to send the acutely ill to the local charity hospitals where the facilities were better since no specific facilities for the sick were provided by the workhouses. Nevertheless the facilities in the charity hospitals of this period were rudimentary and there was considerable neglect by modern standards

Visiting in these workhouses was discouraged and the buildings were frequently out of the way. The inmates, including the sick, were therefore isolated and much of their suffering could, with hindsight, be attributed to this factor.

If there was what Baly (1973) calls 'unmitigated callousness' towards the poor during the first 40 years of the 19th century this was because there was a callousness throughout life as judged by 20th century attitudes. Social sensitivities were only just beginning to be developed and psychology was a thing of the future. Certainly contemporaries complained of conditions in many workhouses, certainly there were workhouses that were badly run, certainly there was undue pain and suffering and a lack of sympathy for the sufferers. On the other hand, social attitudes in England were different from those obtaining today and were not as advanced in some ways as they were in parts of continental Europe. Much of the callousness can be attributed to the ignorance of the period and the social philosophy of the day. Indeed there were many workhouses where the conditions were not so bad and in some cities, such as Manchester and Liverpool, the Guardians were ahead of their times.

To argue thus is not to condone the conditions nor yet to infer that there was no room for improvement: it is necessary to give a perspective to the period and the conditions therein. As Abel-Smith (1970) has said: 'It is not unusual for reformers to overstate the evils they are hoping to correct.' It can also be understood from this that there were reformers intent on improving the situation.

The social scene in the United Kingdom was changing rapidly at this time. One of the most remarkable changes was the impressive increase in the population. In 1801 it was calculated by the first national census to be 8·9 millions; by 1851 the population was 17·9 millions (Stern 1962). Thus the population had doubled in a mere 50 years. Birth rates showed a slight decline but the death rates had also declined. Thus the age of the population began to increase slightly. Much of the increase in the population figures could be attributed to immigration, mostly from Ireland.

There was also a significant migration from the rural areas to the cities which became overcrowded as country people sought work in the new industries. An acute housing shortage followed and social conditions were dangerously impaired.

As a consequence of the growth of industrialisation and the development of the banking system the class structure of the country was changed. Whereas the landowners, whose wealth was tied up in their property, had previously enjoyed an unchallenged position of power there developed a situation where the industrialists, who employed the mass of people and who had easy access to cash, began to assume power. Similarly, there were members of the growing middle classes who had invested their money in property or the banks and were able to live off the proceeds, thus establishing a section of people with considerable leisure time. It was from this section that many philanthropists came.

The Victorian Age is distinguished by a moral earnestness which was manifested in acts of social reform and was a period of philanthropy such as has not been equalled since. These acts of reform were committed within the social framework of the day and the reformers did not seek for social revolution. Their philanthropy was a bridge between their religious consciences and their commercial dealings. They sought to instil into the poor good principles and a desire for independence, and to raise their moral standards.

Wealth had made the upper classes more concerned with respectability and materialism and they held that indiscriminate help for the poor resulted in the undermining of a person's character (Young and Ashton 1956). They believed that the less fortunate should be encouraged to help themselves. There was a belief that poverty was caused by improvidence which could be alleviated by discipline. The State had no place in the relief of the individual poor but should give some help through the voluntary organisations. Relatives and families should be encouraged to support their own; the poor should help the poor; the rich should help only as a last resort and then as a means of achieving moral uplift in the poor.

Within the working class there also developed subgroups. The craftsmen and small tradesmen separated into the upper section and the unskilled workers and labourers settled into the lower section.

Similarly, the poor became classified into the deserving poor or the sick poor and the able-bodied poor. There was a clear distinction between the poor and the destitute. Thus contemporary society was beginning to assume some complexity and the layers were increasing.

During this period there was an enormous increase in the numbers of Voluntary Hospitals. By 1825 there were 154 Voluntary Hospitals but the numbers continued to grow rapidly.

These hospitals were maintained by subscription and were very selective in their choice of patients. The sick were not normally admitted without an introduction from a subscriber and usually only cases with favourable prognoses were received since the doctors were reluctant to block their beds with long-stay patients. The consultants gave their time but gained great prestige from their Honorary Consultantships. They were able to develop lucrative private practices and used their hospital cases for teaching purposes. Patients with uncommon and interesting diseases were therefore preferred.

Medical students paid fees for their tuition and were responsible for most of the bedside care of the patients. The nurses were more properly ward maids and the Sisters (who were of a slightly superior level) supervised the nurses, gave the patients their medicines, applied poultices and saw to the feeding of the patients. Their social status was low and their conditions of service were variable and, compared with modern standards, abysmal.

The nurses and sisters were resident and were responsible directly to the doctors. Frequently, a close working relationship developed between the doctor and the sister but there was little involvement between one ward and another.

The Matrons were of a higher social level again and were said to be of an order equivalent to that of a housekeeper in private domestic service. They had little responsibility in nursing but looked after all the female staff and the domestic affairs of the hospital in conjunction with the Steward who was in overall control on a day to day basis.

There was no system of resident medical officers at the hospitals and the honorary consultants made only intermittent ward rounds.

The 19th century is said by Garrison (1929) 'to mark the beginnings of organised advancement of science', but scientific medicine could hardly be said to have started at this time. What there was of the new understanding of medicine was centred around London but this was still limited to physical diagnosis of a very crude nature and gross pathological anatomy.

REFERENCES

Abel-Smith, B. (1970), *A History of the Nursing Profession*. London, Heinemann. p. 5.

Baly, Monica E. (1973), *Nursing and Social Change*. London, Heinemann Medical Books. p. 41.

Bruce, M. (Ed.) (1973), *The Rise of the Welfare State*. London, World University Press. p. 51.

Garrison, F. H. (1929), *An Introduction to the History of Medicine*. London, W. B. Saunders and Co. Chapter XII.

Rogers, Dr Joseph, Medical Officer to the Strand Workhouse Infirmary.

Stern, W. M. (1962), *Britain – Yesterday and Today*. London, Longman.

Young, A. F. and Ashton, E. T. (1956), *British Social Work in the Nineteenth Century*. London, Routledge and Kegan Paul. Chapter 1.

2

THE SYSTEM AND THE STIRRINGS OF REFORM: 1848–1867

It has been said that in drafting the New Poor Law of 1834, Nassau Senior and Chadwick were looking over their shoulders into the past and failed to foresee the problems of the future. In many ways this was true. The pace of change was quickening and, in fact, did not allow the philosophy of the Act ever to be wholly implemented.

In 1851 the population of the country was 17·9 millions but by 1871 it had risen to over 22·7 millions. In that year also the birth rate was 35·4 but the death rate had dropped to 21·4 per thousand. The country's population had begun its upward shift in the age ranges and a change in the ratio of females to males.

The era of the rail commuters was established by the 1860s and the upper and middle classes regularly commuted into central London. This started the separation of work place from home, except for the working classes who still tended to cluster together in communities near their occupations. The importance of this trend with regard to the situation of the hospitals will be seen later as the working classes, too, began to move away from their work places. The financial crashes of 1846 and 1866 brought the rush of railway building to a halt and threw into the labour market a mass of unemployed people. Until this happened, the destruction of houses continued for the building of the railway networks and the housing conditions of the working classes continued to be overcrowded.

These 20 years marked one of the country's most prosperous periods. The early building of gas works gave gas to houses and lighting to the streets. Cotton and wool manufacturing expanded rapidly and exports flourished. Companies and organisations became bigger and more complex. To match this, labour became organised within Craft Unions which were soon affiliated into larger Trades Unions. As organisations grew larger, management posts increased and a new class of professional managers developed. At the same time there was a widening gulf between Master and Worker and relationships became strained particularly where there was a greater intervention by managerial levels. Concurrently there developed a widening gulf between the national officials of the Trades Unions and the local members: society also was becoming still more complex.

The new middle classes were searching for a place in this new society, they had to find their relationships between the upper and lower classes. Their increasing material possessions ('conspicuous consumption') and leisure time marked them out from the lower classes and they emphasised their repugnance for 'the vulgar forms of labour' (Ryder and Silver 1970). The skilled section of the working class was also distinguished and held themselves aloof from the labouring section.

In religion there was a continuation of revivalism but the growth of Christian Socialism was challenging the Church's acceptance of the social order and their attacks had the effect of slowly transforming the appreciation of sin from a theological basis to a social one. Between 1851 and a hundred years later, the numbers of church attenders were halved. In an attempt to take Christianity to the working classes the Salvation Army was constituted in 1865 but in many ways it seemed that the established churches were inimical to the poor and disinterested in the problems of the cities.

Education was organised philanthropically, mostly by Church and educational societies and there was about 75% literacy in the population by the end of the 20 years. Whilst the middle and upper classes could progress to their public and grammar schools there was no formal route available to the lower classes for a secondary education. In the new universities new ideas were being tested, new curricula adopted and the period saw the birth of the social sciences.

There was a growing realisation of the need for more accurate information and social data was becoming increasingly refined. A variety of case work societies sprang up on an *ad hoc* basis to meet local or specific needs such as the Jewish Poor Relief Society, Accommodation Societies (to provide alternative accommodation to the workhouses), and Improvement Societies dedicated to improving the environment of the poor. Many cities started public libraries and developed parks for their citizens; prosperous manufacturers began to build houses for their workers in the city centres near their factories.

The momentum in changing attitudes was still only building up and social reformers and Government responsibility still had to contend with the underlying Victorian philosophy of laissez-faire and self-help.

In 1847 the Poor Law Commission had been disbanded and the Poor Law Board set up under a Government minister. The new General Board of Health was established by the 1848 Public Health Act. The era of the Victorian Sanitary Movement had started. This new Public Health arose out of new policies: the slow acceptance by the Government that public health problems were too massive for local effort or the local rates and that Government intervention was necessary. It also arose out of a newly developed but still primitive administrative machinery in which the central government set standards, established an inspectorate for their administration, and a common fund for their implementation. Lastly, new medical knowledge was allowing better understanding of environmental problems and the means of their control. Preventive Medicine had been born.

The period under review was also concerned with industrial legislation: with growing democratisation there was a spread of party politics into local government and the wider franchise resulted in reforms in the factories as well as sanitary administration. Legislation covered the employment of young children, young persons and women, hours of work and schooling. Much of the industrial legislation covered the textile industry but also extended to other industries such as mining and chimney sweeping and by 1870 there was a basic legislative code.

The building of voluntary hospitals continued. Subscribers to these hospitals were privileged people with an almost automatic right of admission, a gift which they could bestow on their dependants. Belonging to the middle and upper classes themselves, they were not disposed to receive medical care anywhere else but in their homes. Hospitals were still regarded as death houses and their fatality rates were high. In the years before Lister the mortality rate for compound fractures was 70%, for amputations it was 50%, and a great toll was taken by septicaemia, pyaemia, gangrene, tetanus, erysipelas and secondary haemorrhage following infections (Seelig 1925). Infant mortality was appalling: in the early part of the century, before the move to re-impose breast feeding, the ratio of neonatal deaths was said by Marshall Hall to be 7:10 of live babies born. (After mothers were compelled by the British Lying-In Hospital to breast feed their babies, the mortality rate of babies born there dropped by 60%.)

The hospitals relied on subscriptions for their continuance and a rivalry developed between them in seeking out donations. Subscribers helped to establish their own social status by their charity and the size of their donations related to their social ambitions (McMenemy 1974). Thus the hospitals became an influential factor in social life since they encouraged the professional and social interests of the consultants and the social status of their benefactors. The professional status of medical practitioners was established and legitimised by the setting up of the General Medical Council under the Medical Act of 1858.

The Public Health Act established a new type of doctor, the non-treating doctor or medical administrator, as he later became known. This type of practitioner used his medical training as a theoretical background for the assessment of public works and environmental situations and was epitomised by John Simon, the Medical Officer of Health to the City of London.

Other discoveries and developments also marked these 20 years although all were restricted by the continuing ignorance of bacteria, which were not detected until the 1870s. One of the most significant advances that took place was the new use of anaesthetics in surgery.

Medicine during this period was more skilled in diagnosing but as yet lacked the means to cure. Since diagnosis had become more refined and was using labels such as 'bronchitis' instead of 'inflammation of the chest', medical research was the better able to look for causal factors and specific cures. Similarly, because of the greater specificity of diagnoses and the availability of the microscope, scientists like Pasteur could develop their work with improved direction, but therapeutic medicine had yet to be developed.

The cures were still lacking: as far as their patients were concerned, there was still little advantage in going to a doctor rather than to the practitioners of fringe medicine, and quackery abounded.

Urbanisation and overcrowding increased the susceptibility of the population to communicable diseases and the displacement of people whose houses had been indiscriminately destroyed for industrial and commercial building further exacerbated the position. In London in 1841 the population density was 26 people per acre, but in 1871 this had increased to 44 per acre (Sheppard 1971), and in the 50 years after 1853 Rosen (1972) has estimated that 28 500 people were made homeless. Common lodging houses proliferated without adequate controls or inspection and became centres of diseases and the spread of infection. Sewage and garbage disposal were rarely available and common dunghills and cesspools were usual. In 1849 John Simon reported: '. . . there are swarms of men and women who have yet to learn that human beings should dwell differently from cattle; swarms by whom delicacy and decency in their social relations are quite unconceived.' Later in the same report he wrote: 'Contemplating such cases I feel the deepest conviction that no sanitary system can be adequate to the requirements of the time or can cure those radical evils which infest the under-framework of society, unless the importance be distinctly recognised and the duty manfully undertaken of improving the social condition of the poor' (Bruce 1973).

In 1864 in a further report to the Privy Council, Simon gave an account of an investigation carried out by one of his medical inspectors on house accommodation of rural workers: 'To the insufficient quantity and miserable quality of the house accommodation generally had by our agricultural labourers [sic], almost every page of Dr Hunter's report bears testimony. And gradually for many years past the state of the labourers in these respects has been deteriorating. . . . Except in so far as they whom his labour enriches see fit to treat him with a kind of pitiful indulgence he is quite peculiarly helpless in the matter. Whether he shall find house-room in the land which he contributed to till, whether the house-room which he gets shall be human or swinish, whether he shall have the little space of garden that so vastly lessens the pressures of his poverty – all this does not depend on his willingness and ability to pay reasonable rent for the decent accommodation he requires, but depends on the use which others may see fit to make of their right to do as they will with their own' (Bruce 1973).

Simon's attitude towards poverty, squalor and public health was compassionate and objective at the same time. He did not appear to blame the conditions of the poor upon the poor but demonstrated that their lives were not in their own control. At the same time, his concern was also for the control of disease in the community, the whole of which must suffer if the social conditions of the poor could not be improved. There was no sentimentality here: rather was there a hard headed pragmatism. He did not give evidence of wanting to raise the standards of the poor for altruistic reasons but he was intent on improving their lot for the sake of society as a whole.

The Outdoor Relief Regulation Orders after the 1834 Poor Law Act were put into practice more easily in the south than in the north.

Under these Orders the gradual cessation of out-relief meant that applicants for relief had to be admitted to the workhouse. The south was less industrialised than the north and did not suffer the cyclical unemployment experienced by the industrial towns. It was also said that the character of the southerners was 'softer' or less independent than that of the northerners. The south was still predominantly agricultural and it may have been that the land workers were more used to a paternalistic social climate. Whatever the reasons, the southern poor were less resistant to the indignities of pauperisation and, over the years, became more and more ready to apply for parish relief (or at least less and less resistant). From 1844–6 there was a period of prosperity in the country and many of the unemployed found work; many of them had emigrated to the cities and left their old or infirm relatives behind. These were the people who mostly had to apply for relief and who were the constituent population of the workhouses. Similarly, whereas previously many of the sick poor had been able to obtain some kind of medical relief at home from doctors who were paid by the parish, officially now they had to be admitted to the workhouses before they could obtain medical assistance. The workhouses therefore became filled with the sick.

Unfortunately this development had not been anticipated by the Poor Law Board nor by the local Boards of Guardians who had built their 'Bastilles' after 1834. There were no facilities for the sick and infirm and no provision for their nursing care. By 1863 there were 50000 sick and elderly paupers in the country's workhouses. Workhouse doctors and district doctors were appointed as separate posts but in both cases the salary was poor. The standard of medicine was variable, sometimes dedicated and skilled and sometimes casual and unskilled. They were not empowered to take prophylactic action but were able only to treat. Payment for extra work done by the doctors could be withheld by the Guardians as there was no clear agreement on these fee-for-service cases; the patient had first to wait for authority to be given by the Relieving Officer or the medical officer had to treat and accept the chance that he might not be paid.

In the workhouses the doctor had professional authority although he was often subject to the final sanction of the Master, especially in the areas which might be said to be within the administrative authority of the latter. These areas were quite commonly those where the doctors could do more good (such as ordering extra or special diets) lacking, as he did at the time, better methods of treatment.

As the workhouses were quickly filled with the sick and the old it became impossible to admit the able-bodied in times of distress and out-relief had to continue. The cyclical unemployment in the north made the situation even more impossible as there were occasions when the Poor Law unions would be inundated with unemployed but able-bodied people. Out-relief had to continue therefore, albeit against the philosophy of the 1834 Act.

Before this the workhouses had been small and, frequently, cottages or modest houses had been used. After the Act larger institutions were erected from two or three common plans, designed by architects for their purpose of deterrence and discipline. Longmate (1974) quotes 'a critic' who describes the new buildings and their subsequent overcrowding thus: 'the space assigned to 300 persons by the Poor Law Commissioners would not accommodate 45 on the scale of the London Hospitals and not above 65 on the scale of the military hospitals'. The same observer goes on to say 'here is no infirmary, no provision for dangerous disease. The very dying must die jammed up in their allotted space by their less fortunate sufferers. . . . Thus measles, ophthalmia, erysipelas, small-pox, dysentery, scarlet and typhus fever and all the long train of infectious diseases, are to be indiscriminately scattered through these buildings and the virulence of infectious poison intensely heightened by the dense mass of living creatures, crammed into these murderous pesthouses, contrived by the Poor Law Commissioners.'

The Guardians sought to achieve the standard of less eligibility by keeping equipment and furniture to a bare minimum with a cheap wooden bed, a flock mattress contained by sacking and two or three blankets. Pillows were not regarded as being necessary and sheets were rarely used. Frequently, beds were shared and arranged bunk-style in tiers. There was seldom accommodation for clothes and personal possessions and so little space was available that inmates frequently had to clamber over the ends of their beds to reach the floor.

Many of the workhouses had a small sick-bay built to house the sick inmates, but as more and more sick poor were admitted for medical relief these became totally inadequate and more general wards were taken over. It was not long before the workhouses were filled with the sick and the aged infirm and additional accommodation had to be built for the comparatively few able-bodied paupers.

The Master was in charge of the workhouse, appointed by and

responsible to the Guardians. The Matron (usually, but not invariably, the Master's wife) was responsible for the female staff and the female paupers. In 1847 the Poor Law Commission published its 14th *Annual Report* in which it discussed the appointment and duties of the officers whom the Guardians were empowered to appoint. Included in this list were the Master, Matron and Nurse. The appointment of these officers had to be made by a majority of Guardians and had to be reported to the Commission. There were few qualifications required of the Matron – who was not regarded as a nurse in any way. She was required only to be 'fit' to hold the office and had to be able to keep accounts. The Matron was deputy to the Master and she was expected to supervise the children and women, the cleaning, all clothing, admissions to wards, allocation of labour to the inmates, the housekeeping of the female wards, to make evening rounds of the females' and children's wards, to ensure the moral conduct of the women and children and supervise the repair of all linen and clothing; she was responsible for the diet of the women 'particularly the parturient women' and had to help the Master in overall discipline and with the stores. These duties were continued by the Poor Law Board at its inception in the following year.

By the middle of the 19th century, 70% of all pauperism had its basis in sickness; a survey in 1861 showed that more than one-fifth of the adult population (14000) had been inmates for more than five years, 6000 were old and infirm and 5000 were suffering from mental troubles. By 1863 the London workhouses were handling about 50000 sick people annually (Longmate 1974). The workhouses had become the State Hospitals.

At the start of the period under discussion, the sick were subject to the 'less eligibility' test and were housed together with the other inmates. Women and children were segregated from the men, married couples were separated. What nursing there was, was done where the sick lay and the nurses (pauper inmates) had to travel from ward to ward to look after their patients. Slowly, as the sick ousted the able-bodied, they and the children were allowed a supplementary policy based more on the need for treatment than on the principle of deterrence. Hodgkinson (1967) explains this trend: 'Economic considerations provided the dominant influence but the prevailing social philosophy and growth of humanitarianism had this effect on the welfare of the sick poor.' It cost money to house the sick who would otherwise be wage earning or at least independent of parish relief: the more quickly they could be cured the more quickly they could regain their financial independence.

The workhouse test was gradually relaxed for cases of sickness, and medical relief might be given in certain cases if the head of the family was simultaneously earning wages. This was in contrast to the earlier practice as a result of which the entire family was pauperised and frequently made to enter the workhouse if one member required medical relief.

By 1853 nearly all medical officers had security of office and were responsible to the Poor Law Board. It was reported in *Hansard* that there were between 3000 and 4000 medical officers for a total of 835000 persons: the cost of medical treatment was rising but the doctors were mostly still required to pay for the medicines they prescribed. Members asked for an improved system of dispensing drugs but the Secretary of the Poor Law Board replied that he had discussed the proposals with the former president of the College of Surgeons and had been advised by the latter that 'the present system could hardly be bettered' (Parl. Debates 1853). In spite of the reformers there was still an overwhelming complacency and apathy in the House of Commons and within the Government.

In 1854 the cost of medical relief stood at £4000000 and a Select Committee was set up to enquire into the *Administration of Medical Relief*. The Poor Law Inspectors were ill-equipped for their duties and over-worked – they relied heavily on the Guardians and were easily overruled by them. When they were called to give evidence they discussed 'the improvements' to the system and reported that they did not see how the system could be bettered.

The Select Committee inquiries over the 1861–4 period had similar evidence given to it: 'the poor were never so well attended as they are at the present time' and the Report expressed the opinion that there were no grounds 'for materially interfering with the present system of poor relief'. It was ordered, however, that expensive medication such as cod liver oil and quinine should be provided at the expense of the Guardians (Parl. Papers Vol. IX).

The Select Committee of 1863 did have one important feature for the purposes of this discussion: one of the people who had given evidence was Miss Louisa Twining who spear-headed the movement for reform of workhouses and workhouse nursing. Louisa Twining had, in 1853, paid a visit to the Strand Workhouse to see an old blind woman. She had been deeply distressed at this woman's isolation from her previous companions and family and at her unhappiness in the workhouse and had subsequently embarked on regular visits to other workhouses 'for the purpose of reading to the inmates and giving comfort and instruction' (Twining 1880). She formed a group of public spirited ladies from the leisured class who continued to make visits to the workhouses in order to read to the inmates, give them instruction (mostly on religious subjects) and comfort. During their visits they collected observations of conditions in the workhouses and began a campaign to improve conditions. In 1858 the Workhouse Visiting Society was formed with this group as a nucleus. Louisa Twining continued her campaign for the improvement of the treatment of the sick poor into the 20th century. Her work for the improvement of the workhouses took two main aspects: she was concerned about the isolation of the workhouses and of their inmates and she was concerned about the poor quality of the Poor Law officers including the Masters, Matrons and nurses and their lack of training.

The isolation of the workhouses was in many cases both geographical and social. In many unions the workhouses had been built well outside the centres and it was difficult therefore for citizens to maintain any sort of contact with them. But the greatest isolation was from society and social concern. 'The workhouse would exist behind closed doors which hid from outsiders the grim reality of the paupers' monotonous routine.' Only those people directly concerned with the workhouse knew the dreariness of life within the walls of its environs and Louisa Twining was instrumental in opening up these closed doors to public scrutiny and judgement.

Her campaign against the inadequacies of the Poor Law officers is reminiscent of the modern movement for 'better training for the job'. Whether or not she was following the same trend evident in the sciences – that of replacing the gifted amateur with the full-time professional – it is difficult to say, but she publicly criticised the lack of proper training given to the Masters and the nurses. She compared the treatment given to criminals in prison with that afforded to the paupers: 'The prison offers a clean, comfortable lodging, food far superior to the usual fare of the criminal and to that of workhouses, kind and attentive officers of a grade above those provided for the non-criminal poor' (Twining 1858). And in the same article she writes: 'The evils of the employment of pauper nurses is

B

dwelt upon by all who have considered the subject of workhouse management. When we consider the persons to whom such extensive power and responsibility are entrusted, in the care of 50000 sick persons in the London workhouses alone, we can hardly wonder at what is told of the results of the system. The only way in which an employment of the inmates could be successfully carried out would be under the constant supervision of superior persons. . . .'

Before visiting inmates at the workhouses, Louisa Twining and her supporters had to obtain permission from the respective Masters. In a paper read to the National Association for the Promotion of Social Sciences in Birmingham in October 1857 she complained of the need to be accompanied by the Master during her visits to the sick and suggested that this was unnecessary. She had in fact been refused permission to visit and this refusal had been supported by the Poor Law Board, on the grounds that it was contrary to policy. The PLB subsequently reversed its decision provided that the visiting was done quietly and without fuss.

In 1866 she joined forces with other reformers including Dr Joseph Rogers, founder of the Workhouse Medical Officers Association, the Earl of Caernarvon, Earl Grosvenor, the Archbishop of York, John Storr (one of the Guardians of the Strand Workhouse) and Ernest Hart, a personal friend of Rogers, to form the Association for the Improvement of Workhouse Infirmaries. Farnall, one of the Poor Law Inspectors, gave the Association his support as did Villiers the then President of the Poor Law Board.

The two associations with which Louisa Twining was involved were supported in their campaign by the National Association for the Promotion of Social Sciences and the Epidemiological Society. In 1864 Timothy Daly, a pauper in the Holborn Workhouse, died and the press took up the campaign supported by *The Lancet* which set up a Commission to investigate the Poor Law infirmaries. This was followed by the Select Committee enquiry of the same year.

At this stage it is necessary to look at the developments which were taking place in general nursing in the voluntary hospitals under the influence of Florence Nightingale.

The life and work of Florence Nightingale have been fully documented by many historians, nurses and social scientists to whom she still remains an enigma. However, only a brief outline is intended here so that the scene can be set and her place in this account put into some perspective.

Florence Nightingale returned from the Crimea determined to do something to improve the quality of nursing. She had at her disposal a considerable fund of money collected for her by the nation as a mark of esteem and she decided to use this to start a nurse training school at St Thomas's Hospital. In her usual fashion, Florence Nightingale had carefully considered the scheme and her overall purpose of improving the quality of nursing. She therefore decided that the best use of her resources would be to set up a school designed to train nurses to teach other nurses. In July 1860 the Nightingale School of Nursing opened.

Until that time, nurses were of very low status; only the rare woman from the more gentle reaches of society ventured into nursing and when this occurred, it was either to supervise the work actually done by the lowly nurse in the fashion of the lady of the house supervising the work of one of her maids, or else she might undertake a nursing mission rather as the old fashioned knights had undertaken a crusade. In these cases, her conduct could be condoned on the grounds that it stemmed from religious quixotry. Nurses were invariably from the working classes and from the domestic servant section. If they had spent any time in domestic service they would have received a certain amount of training before becoming nurses, training which would have been very appropriate to their work since even as late as 1857 it was still that of a ward maid.

John South, senior surgeon at St Thomas's Hospital, wrote a very helpful account of the organisation of a ward. His pamphlet was originally written in reply to a letter in *The Times* on 13 April 1857 in which the writer (under a pseudonym) had criticised hospital nurses. South stoutly defended the nurses at his hospital and differentiated between the sisters and the nurses. He explained that only three sisters were older than 50 years and were treated by the surgeons and dressers 'as if they were old superior family servants'. He affirmed that 'a mutual respect' existed between the surgeon and the sister 'who has for many years presided over his ward'. He denied that the nurses were bullied or seduced (or at any rate fewer were than household servants) and claimed that the nurses were mostly both attentive and kind to the patients. He continued to say that the sister was in control of the ward and performed the same duties as a private nurse. She received directions from the surgeon or physician for the administration of medicine, diets, etc., reported anything untoward to the Apothecary or Matron and made a report on the patients to the physician or surgeon at each of his visits. She supervised the work of the nurses and 'regulated' the patients. The sister may have given special attention to one patient if he was very ill over 24 hours, 'in hope of being rewarded by the recovery of the patient and the approbation of her surgical superior'. She lived in a bedroom and sitting room adjacent to the ward but the greater part of the day was spent on duty.

The nurses cleaned the ward, made the beds, made and applied poultices, helped the bed patients, washed children, slept in a dormitory and worked from 6.00 a.m. to 8.00 p.m. if they were not kept up at night to help the night nurse. The night nurse's duties were similar but in addition she was responsible for giving medicines. Her hours of duty were 8.00 p.m. to 6.00 a.m. at which time she reported to the sister but did not seem to be free to leave the ward until 11.00 a.m. South also explained that whereas nurses used to be promoted to be sisters they no longer were as it had been found that their level was not suitable. The sisters were of a better intelligence, about thirty years old and had to serve a period of 'probation' as a supernumerary for a time depending on ability and on the occasion when the next sister's post fell vacant, usually between 12 to 18 months. Nurses, South said, were 'of the level of housemaids and required little teaching beyond poultice making, bed making and hygiene'.

He resented the criticism of nurses over the previous two years by admirers of Florence Nightingale's ideas and wrote that any further training for sisters was 'superfluous'. He maintained that Miss Nightingale's proposals for nurse training had 'not met with the approbation or support of the medical profession'. He displayed an interesting attitude of complacency, proprietorship and aloofness.

Throughout this period there is a confusion of terms and function between the 'sister' and the 'nurse'. South distinguishes between their relative stations and work but did not apparently understand Florence Nightingale's use of the term 'nurse' as being more appropriate to his 'sisters'. Florence Nightingale pressed for domestic staff to take away from her 'nurses' the domestic work.

Since there was this confusion in terminology it is not surprising that there was a lack of agreement in the training and standing of nurses. This confusion of terminology has persisted and has resulted in a confusion of role, status and function into the present day: there is some justification for an argument that patients in hospitals never (or very seldom) have been attended by trained nurses. They have received their care from untrained attendants, partially trained attendants or probationer and student nurses. The trained nurse has almost always been preoccupied by administrative or teaching duties. The possible exception to this is the staff nurse whose function has been to give more advanced care to the patients, deputise for the sister in her ward-administrative duties and supervise the trainee nurses. But the staff nurse's position was described by the Wood Committee of 1946 as being one of an extended trainee.

South's description of the sisters and nurses may be contrasted with the reputation and work of the pauper nurses. In some workhouses there were superintendent nurses, sometimes paid but frequently unpaid, sometimes with some training but often with no training at all or appointed as a lay person with the responsibility only to supervise the nurses rather than to practice any nursing. South's nurses were paid and answered to the sister: they did not any longer appear to have any prospects of promotion. The pauper nurses were not paid and were under the control of the Matron who was not a nurse. They too had no promotion prospects except only very rarely. South's sisters were trained and were clearly responsible for their wards; the pauper nurses for many years had to look after patients located in different parts of the workhouses and had no defined responsibility for the running of any single ward.

South's sisters were 'permanent' staff (he wrote that many had been in charge of their wards for over 15 years) and had a relationship of 'mutual respect' with their medical men. The pauper nurses were very much inclined to be itinerant and certainly did not have any comparable relationship with the Poor Law Medical Officers. On the other hand, the duties described by South for the Sisters were comparable with those set down by the PLB for the pauper nurses.

In 1848 the Poor Law Board took over from the Poor Law Commission and reiterated the duties of the nurses in the infirmaries. These were the same as had been promulgated in 1847: 'To attend upon the sick in the sick lying-in wards and to administer to them all medicines and medical applications, according to the direction of the medical officer. To inform the medical officer of any defects which may be observed in the arrangements of the sick in lying-in wards. To take care that a light is kept at night in the sick wards.'

The only qualification required of the nurse was that she should be able to read the written directions upon the medicines. Her remuneration was subject to the direction or approval of the Commissioners.

There are two inferences to be drawn from this quotation: that the nurse was paid and that the duties of the nurse as described in 1848 were more responsible than those of the nurses at St Thomas's Hospital in 1857 and were more nearly the duties South described for the ward sister.

The nurse discussed by the Poor Law Board is therefore the paid nurse employed by the Guardians who usually was responsible for supervising the work of the pauper nurses. She was herself subject to the supervision of the Matron who was not a nurse. In 1850 there were 248 paid nurses in England and Wales with a total salary bill of £3451; the average annual salary for the paid nurse was £14 and in addition she received board and lodging and certain other allowances commonly paid to the other officers. It is worth noting that she was classified as an 'officer' together with the Master, Matron, teacher, gatekeeper and one or two other employees. The Board in their Report do not explicitly distinguish between the paid nurse and pauper nurse but do so implicitly because after describing the nurses' terms of employment and duties they end the section by stipulating that the pauper nurses are to be given a diet according to the Guardians' discretion, but should receive 'no fermented or spiritous liquors on account of the performance of such work' except by order of the Medical Officer. This instruction does not appear to have been implemented by the Guardians of the Strand Workhouses where Rogers complained that his pauper nurses were invariably drunk before he made his daily rounds as they had their daily ration dispensed (with the other inmates) first thing in the morning.

The paid nurse (who can be called 'the nurse' and may be distinguished from the 'pauper nurse') received no formal training since none was available at that time, but she was qualified to the extent that she would possibly have received some experience in a hospital of one sort or another. It was not until later in the period covered by this chapter that any formal requirements were made for her qualifications or training, and in the early stages it is not known what previous experience she may have had or where she may have had it. The only firm basis for distinguishing her from the pauper nurses is that she was paid by the Guardians, was an employee (and therefore not a pauper) and, presumably, wished to be a nurse. Even this latter presumption should be taken in the light of the understanding that there was very little other employment available to women, who, for whatever reason, had to go out to work. She may have been a single woman who could not rely on her family for her maintenance or she may have been a widow. It is known that women from the working class commonly went out to work whereas women from the middle and upper classes did not take paid work.

The line that separated the officers of the workhouses from the inmates was very fine and it was not unknown for an officer to end his days as an inmate.

Some of the workhouses employed nurses, but nurses were also occasionally employed by the District Medical Officers. Most commonly the poor sick in the district were nursed by other poor women and very occasionally the Guardians would allow a small payment to be paid to a woman to 'nurse' a district patient. Hodgkinson and others have also shown that District Medical Officers would themselves employ a 'nurse' to care for a patient. Occasionally a Medical Officer who had the double function of Workhouse and District Medical Officer would send out a workhouse pauper to look after one of his district patients.

By 1848 there were very few able-bodied poor in the workhouses which by now were filled with the sick and aged. No policy had been framed for the care of these people and it was, in fact, not until 1867 that the President of the PLB (the Earl of Devon) officially recognised that the workhouses had become 'in many cases little more than hospitals or infirmaries' (Parl. Debates 1867). If this development was not recognised *de jure* until 1867 it had been recognised *de facto* some time previously and, whilst no central policy was available, many unions had turned their workhouses into infirmaries and built new annexes for the able-bodied. Others had built new infirmaries.

The work of indoor relief had therefore become predominantly that of sheltering the sick. If the Poor Law Board did not have a policy they did authorise the expenditure of money for these buildings and a group of medical officers was beginning to understand the need for better care of the sick inmates. As early as 1849 Dr Sieveking had called for the training of 'pauper' nurses in the workhouses and for the use of inmates as nurses in the district.

During the 1850s however there was comparatively little movement in achieving any system in the provision of nurses for the sick poor.

Discussion in Parliament centred around the cost of medical relief, the adequacy of relief, the medical officers, problems of local administration, the philosophy of help and self help, whether or not there was any need for some sort of medical inspectorate and the system of payment of medicines. There was no mention between 1848 and 1858 of the nurses.

However, Dr Sieveking had been supported in his call for training for the pauper nurses by the Epidemiological Society of which he was a member, and in 1856 they wrote to the PLB enclosing a scheme by which suitable female paupers should be 'systematically instructed in the preparation of sick room diet and in nursing the sick in the workhouse infirmary'. These pauper nurses, it was proposed, should have instruction in domestic duties followed by some training in the infirmary by the Medical Officer and the Workhouse Matrons. It was proposed that the Master of each workhouse providing this training should maintain a register of the 'nurses' that had been trained: there should be two levels of training; a first class certificate given to those women who had undertaken two months' training, could read and write, were of good moral character and were neat, obedient, enjoyed a good memory and had a thorough knowledge of sick room diet. A second class certificate should be awarded if the recipient had received one month's training and was of less ability than the 'first class nurse'. Both certificates would have a record of the numbers of confinements attended by the trainee.

It was further proposed that the Master should hire out the nurses for 'monthly nursing' or private cases and should book these in an Engagement Book. Needless to say the fees would be paid to the workhouse to defray the cost of the nurses' training and keep. When not 'engaged' it was proposed that the nurse should work in the infirmary or on the district.

The Board circulated its Inspectors for their reactions expressing its own opinion that such a scheme would be impracticable and that it would be inexpedient 'to establish authoritatively in the workhouses a general system of training for nurses'. They did feel that where a paid nurse was employed she could be used to supervise the pauper nurses, train them and enable them to 'become nurses in their own independent account'. They agreed to a register being maintained of those nurses so that 'recourse could be had of their services'. Before ending its letter, the Board wrote that they were aware of 'the evils resulting from the want of a sufficient number of trained and efficient nurses for the poor'.

The Board subsequently wrote to the Epidemiological Society advising them that they did not feel able to issue a General Order in this matter but that the Inspectors would discuss the proposals locally where they felt that the workhouses had the necessary facilities.

However, Dr H. W. Rumsey, a prominent medical practitioner associated with the Poor Law Medical Service, did not agree with the proposals. In the Supplementary Notes to his book of essays (Rumsey 1856) he criticised the Epidemiological Society and Dr Sieveking for a lack of understanding of the situation and of the type of woman to be found in the workhouses. He wrote that the necessary qualities required for nursing sick people were not likely to be found in the able-bodied pauper women (giving an average of 23 of these women in every union workhouse). He believed that 'it is also a great mistake to suppose that the very poor might be nursed only by those equally low in habits and depressed in circumstances with themselves'. He went on to ask 'how or by whom, these paupers are to be taught to nurse?' He believed that for training purposes the scope of observation was too narrow in the sick wards of the workhouses and that proper teachers were not available. Even if suitable women could be found amongst the paupers, he wanted them trained in the hospitals. He felt that 'a select few of the younger and more intelligent inmates might, perhaps, be advantageously employed as Assistants to thoroughly qualified and superior nurses, who might be appointed to the sick wards of every Workhouse'. He criticised Dr Sieveking's plan also on the grounds that it would not provide 'a sufficiently numerous *corps* of nurses'.

The use of this word 'corps' (which he emphasised) is interesting: could it be that, without any further expansion or explanation of the idea, he was thinking of the need for a cohesive body of nurses, a Nursing Service for the Poor Law? There seems some grounds for thinking this as he discussed the need for a multiplication of Institutions of 'Nursing Sisters' in every 'first class Town or sanitary district . . . as a centre of supply to the surrounding district'.

In fact, very little became of this scheme although several workhouses started to give their pauper nurses some sort of training.

At the same time, the Poor Law Board was having to contain the over-enthusiasm of some of its medical officers who were trying to use nurses more. The medical officers were feeling over-burdened with work and were unable to give their patients in the districts and the infirmaries adequate supervision. Some of the more progressive Guardians were beginning to understand that it might make better economic sense to employ 'trained' nurses to help their patients recover more quickly. There was therefore a tendency to employ nurses from time to time, especially during an epidemic. But every appointment had to be sanctioned by the PLB and in 1850 they wrote to the Guardians telling them that they were employing too many nurses; they complained that there were five paid nurses in Croydon compared with one only at each of Wandsworth and Clapham workhouses. In writing thus they were contradicting the advice given to the Guardians by the Medical Officers.

One other observation of these years is interesting: each discussion of the nurses' duties specifically mentioned her responsibility for the diet of the sick poor. Discussion about the work and payment of the Medical Officers and the cost of medical relief were also very much concerned with diet. In the light of the paucity of cures in medicine, and the lack of therapeutic medicine, it does seem that the Poor Law Medical Officers relied very heavily on nourishment and supplementary diets for their patients and that this duty of the nurse should be accepted as being of more importance than a superficial consideration might lead one to suspect today. In the training of nurses diet continued to be emphasised for many years after the development of scientific medicine and improved food supplies might have made it less critical.

At the same time Louisa Twining was also campaigning for better nursing for the sick poor and for better conditions in the workhouses. Besides discussing the 'evil of the employment of pauper nurses' she complained also of the circumstances of their employment. She wrote that the pauper nurses were not suitable people and that the patients were left, with minimal supervision, to their mercy. She claimed that the pauper nurses received no respect from the patients and had no authority: they relied therefore on bullying to gain their way. Later she claimed that there were, in the London workhouses, 70 paid nurses and 500 pauper nurses and assistants. Of these nurses, half were over the age of 50, a quarter over 60, many not less than 70 and some more than 80 years old (Longmate 1974).

The ten years 1858-67 saw a great development in the nursing world and this had repercussions on the Poor Law Institutions.

The Nightingale School of Nursing, started in 1860 at St Thomas's Hospital, was soon sending out its trained nurses to initiate training schemes in other hospitals. But their numbers were comparatively few and the demand was vast. Hospital nurses were trained in the field of acute medicine and did not choose to work in the Poor Law infirmaries where the incurably sick and infirm were sheltered. There was the notable stigma of pauperisation which clung to these institutions and detracted from the personal standing of those who chose to work in them. The medical officers lacked the professional and social status of the Voluntary Hospital consultants. Even the Government saw the post of President of the Poor Law Board as a secondary post and paid him a smaller salary.

In 1865 however, William Rathbone, a wealthy merchant in Liverpool, approached Florence Nightingale to ask for her help in setting up a nursing system in the infirmary in Liverpool. Rathbone had already demonstrated an interest in the poor sick and in nursing. He had been instrumental in developing a system of district nursing in his city and had instituted a nurse training school at the Royal Infirmary, Liverpool, from which it was agreed that half the number of trained nurses would be allocated to district work under the voluntary 'Lady Superintendent'. He and Florence Nightingale together persuaded the Guardians at Brownlow Hill Infirmary to set up on a trial basis for three years, the employment of trained nurses. Rathbone undertook to pay the cost of this experiment and Florence Nightingale sent Agnes Jones and a team of nurses there. The scheme involved only three wards in the infirmary but there were plans to take probationary nurses for training and to use the existing pauper nurses as assistant nurses.

Brownlow Hill Infirmary was one of the largest in the country with 1 300 patients and 60 pauper nurses and was better than most in structure and equipment. It was run by the Liverpool Select Vestry which had earned for itself a reputation for being energetic and efficient. It had an advanced organisation of medical coverage, as it was served by a full time medical officer with assistants and also had the part time consultant service of a small panel of honoraries from the Liverpool Royal Infirmary. The doctors were encouraged to ask for anything they required in the way of food and medicines for the paupers. There was also a head nurse who was employed to supervise the work of the pauper nurses, to carry out the instructions of the medical officer, to visit the wards regularly in order to ensure that the patients were being properly cared for. She was in charge of the patients' diets and medicines, had to see to admissions, maintain a record of admissions and discharges, take charge of new patients' clothing and possessions, and was responsible for the maintenance and cleanliness of linen, beds and wards. She was also expected to accompany the medical officers on their rounds. The pauper nurses were 'often of a low and even vicious type'; at night the old and infirm were locked up in their wards and left unvisited all night. Where the patients were not so old and infirm, it was found expedient to have a policeman patrol during the night.

The plans for this experiment are interesting for several reasons: the first and obvious point of interest is the innovation of a Nightingale team in a Poor Law infirmary. The nurses were to be under the control and direction of the 'Lady Superintendent', Agnes Jones, rather than under the authority of the Matron. Another point is that this was a scheme which involved the training of nurses on a formal and planned basis within a Poor Law infirmary. Yet another innovation was that the assistant nurses were to be paid and were not to be regarded as paupers (it was hoped that their self respect would be restored and that they might receive enough on-the-job instruction to be able to regain their independence by later continuing to find employment as 'nurses'). One of the most significant aspects of this scheme however was that all 'non-nursing duties' were to be removed from the nurses – all the nurses, including the assistant nurses – and a team of scourers, cooks, a house steward, housekeeper and storekeeper were selected from the inmates for this purpose. The experimental unit was to be comprised of male wards only with a total of 522 patients.

The term 'heroic' has usually been used to describe both Agnes Jones and her achievements at Brownlow Hill. The challenge that faced her was certainly daunting: there was a concurrent cotton famine which had thrown a large mass of people out of work and many of these had found their way into the infirmary where the wards were so overcrowded that three people slept in a bed. Discipline was lax, one of the officials did all he could to hamper her and the experiment to use the female paupers as assistant nurses proved a failure. They could not be left unsupervised for an instant and lost no opportunity to obtain supplies of intoxicants. Bickerton (1936) quotes a passage from one of Miss Jones's letters: 'I am almost distracted between sickness and anxiety and drunkenness. I have one head nurse in great danger, these ex-pauper women whom we are training were paid their wages on Friday and the next day five came in tipsy. . . . How little I can do!' In spite of all these problems, however, there is glowing praise of her achievements. Bickerton describes the results of her work as 'a revolution'.

In 1865 the PLB had appointed Dr Edward Smith as an Inspector and he had been asked, with Mr Farnall, the Metropolitan Inspector, to make a report first on the Metropolitan infirmaries and subsequently on the provincial infirmaries. His report on the Brownlow Hill Infirmary described the new system running parallel with the old system and compared the male wards with the female wards. He quoted the verdict that the Medical Officers could place more dependence on the nurses in the male wards whilst the female wards were kept cleaner and more trouble was taken to adorn them. The PLB *Annual Report* for 1866 reprinted letters received from the Master and from the visiting consultant physician. The Master's letter gave statistical evidence that the expectations regarding the recovery of the male patients had not been justified, but he suggested that this may have been because the trial period for the first year had not been long enough. (It may also have been because the figures for the previous year, used as a comparison, included a large number of malingerers whom Agnes Jones promptly discharged.) He described the change brought about in the demeanour of the male patients by the presence of the trained nurses, the improved discipline in the wards and the better care given to the male patients. Two hundred of the male patients had been discharged as malingerers, the efforts to employ the assistant nurses had been abandoned as a failure and he discussed the difficulties of finding suitable candidates to employ as probationer nurses. Of 40 employed, 21 had resigned and three were dismissed. There were therefore considerable problems in maintaining the training programme, much less extending it. He expressed the conviction however that 'the experience of the past year renders it certain that the Poor Law as now exists offers no impediment to the successful working out of the most complete scheme for the efficient nursing of the sick in the manner advocated by the best friends of hospital nursing'.

The Consultant's letter reported on the marked improvement in the standard of nursing, rehabilitation of the patients and implementation of the medical orders. It also praised the new demeanour of the patients, their increased comfort and order, and he earnestly desired after one year's experience of the system to see it introduced into 'all the parochial hospitals of the Kingdom'. He believed that the 'admirable results' would be enjoyed by all the inhabitants of Liverpool.

Agnes Jones lived only three years after her appointment before she contracted typhus and died. Before her death she had converted the vestry and shown that trained nurses in a Poor Law infirmary could bring comfort, hope, dignity and cheer to the patients. If the statistical evidence of the recovery and earlier discharge of the patients was lacking, this may have been attributable to the short trial period and the false basis used for the comparison, but it may also be attributable to the lack of therapeutic remedies available at the time. Agnes Jones did demonstrate a humanitarian and disciplined approach to nursing the sick poor and she did institute a formal nurse training scheme in a Poor Law infirmary. The scheme was extended to the whole of the infirmary and the training school was continued. Her example was accepted by her probationers who handed it on as they qualified and continued her work.

The year 1865 brought other changes in the work of medical relief. There had been a series of reports of the neglect of sick inmates in infirmaries which had prompted the Board to encourage its Inspectors to make more regular visits. They had however, emphasised at the same time that the onus of responsibility rested with the Guardians. They had authorised the Guardians to pay for some of the more expensive medicines and had appointed Dr Smith. The evidence given to the Select Committee 1861–4 had prompted questions in the House of Commons about 'the employment of trained and competent nurses in workhouses' (Parl. Debates 1865). Mr Villiers' reply had played down Louisa Twining's evidence and said that it had been 'overstated'. There were, he said, 43 paid nurses in the London workhouses and only 8 of the 39 workhouses in the metropolis had no paid nurses. He went on to say that there was some doubt about the competence of the paid nurses and there was a great deal of difficulty in deciding who were competent. After discussion with Miss Nightingale, however, he felt that there was every reason to suppose that well-qualified nurses could be obtained in sufficient numbers if only the Guardians were willing to engage them.

It was in this year that the PLB circulated all Guardians that the regulations laid down that anyone could visit any pauper in the workhouses, subject to the permission of the Master and the conditions laid down by the Guardians.

The PLB also circularised the Guardians advising the employment of paid nurses 'with the view of promoting a better system of nursing in the hospitals and sick wards of the workhouses throughout the country'. This circular gave rise to the employment of additional nurses in many workhouses. The *Annual Report* of 1865 commented on the risks undergone by the nurses in these infirmaries because of the dangers of exposure to infections: 'we regret to state that several of the nurses employed . . . have been attacked by the fever and some have died of it'. Regulations already provided for the employment of paid nurses and for assistants to them. The Report also set out the duties of the nurse, but after 18 years they remained the same as they had been in 1847. However, the Board reported that these duties were seen by them to be responsible and required a person of experience, respectability, diligence and decorum. The nurse could not discharge her duties in the infirmary alone and required 'the assistance of others of both sexes'. The nurses should be adequately remunerated and 'strictly' selected and the assistant should also be adequately paid. By these means, it was said, the Guardians would be able to hold these officers 'responsible for negligence or misconduct as in the case of the superior officers of the workhouse'. Employment of pauper nurses was discouraged and the Board asked Guardians to discontinue this practice. In their Circular the Board anticipated that there might be some difficulty in finding suitable applicants for these posts but felt that they would be forthcoming if 'fair and remunerative wages or salaries' were paid. Special accommodation should be provided for the nurse and the assistants, convenient to their patients.

It will be noted that no hours of work were laid down and in fact the nurse was still expected to look after her patient throughout the 24 hours of the day. It was not the usual practice to employ night nurses in the infirmaries, although John South had described the night nurses employed in St Thomas's Hospital at his time.

Brownlow Hill was not the only infirmary to establish a nursing system: Chorlton Infirmary in Lancashire also established one but in an entirely different way. There had been an epidemic during the year and the Guardians had experienced considerable difficulty in finding enough nurses to staff their new infirmary. They accepted the offer of two sisters from the Protestant All Saints' Convent in Manchester, to come as Superintendent Nurses and these two were put in complete charge of the nurses. Once again the nurses were removed from the control of the Master and Matron and placed under the control of trained nurses. Many of the nurses died of the fever but the sisters were able to reorganise the nursing.

During the 1860s reformers were gradually chipping away at the lethargy of the Government and the Guardians. These latter officials were ordinary lay citizens who had little understanding of the management of institutions and the administration of hospitals: the early workhouses sheltering the poor had become hospitals and their function had become more complex. The Guardians had little knowledge of sickness and no one to whom they could turn for advice. The Medical Officers made demands which placed a greater burden on the rates and there was no point of reference or central policy from which the Guardians could obtain guidance.

A London survey in 1861 (Longmate 1974) showed that more than one-fifth of the adult inmates (14 000) had been residents of the infirmaries for over five years; 6 000 were old and infirm, 5 000 were sufferers of mental diseases. In 1863 the London infirmaries were handling about 50 000 sick people annually and the commonest disease was tuberculosis. There were no special arrangements made for children many of whom suffered from ophthalmia, an infectious disease of the eyes.

The workhouse visitors were slowly helping to improve the wards in small ways: they introduced pictures into the wards and prevailed upon the Guardians to supply armchairs and lockers. The visitors brought in sewing and books and helped to provide means of occupation and distraction for the inmates. The early nurses and Matrons were unsympathetic and a whole new generation of nurses had to enter the workhouses before the visitors had any degree of support. The new nurses were still few and far between and one visitor was able to write 'In an immensely large proportion of houses the sick are attended by male and female paupers who are placed in such office having had the smallest instruction or experience and who often have the reverse of friendly feelings towards their helpless patients. As payment they usually receive allowances of beer or gin, which aid their too common propensity to intoxication.'

As there were so few trained nurses available, the reformers concentrated on getting one or two into each infirmary to supervise the work of the pauper nurses. Frances Power Cobbe and Louisa Twining led the movement for classification of the sick and separation of the groups, and were instrumental in raising public interest which was triggered by Timothy Daly's death.

Timothy Daly was an Irish labourer and his name has been perpetuated in social history for no other reason but that he died in the Holborn Workhouse in December 1864. His death occurred at a crucial moment because it was revealed at the inquest that he had died from gross neglect. *The Times* which had been supporting the reformers' campaign printed the inquest proceedings in full. A couple of months later (in February 1865) a second pauper, whose name was Gibson, died in the St Giles workhouse. His death fanned the flames. Florence Nightingale (who was currently co-operating with William Rathbone in his nursing ventures in Liverpool) was quickly in touch with Charles Villiers, the then President of the Poor Law Board and subsequently with H. B. Farnall, the Poor Law Metropolitan Inspector. Together they drew up and circulated a 'Form of Enquiry' to every London Infirmary. In the next few weeks the PLB issued their 1865 circular to the Guardians. This circular, advising the employment of paid nurses, was permissive and had only a limited effect.

Concurrently, *The Lancet* set up a commission of enquiry consisting of three doctors who visited every London workhouse infirmary. The journal published their reports week by week and disclosed unbelievable environmental and management situations – unbelievable in fact to the readers of the day as well as to the readers of the 20th century! They drew a picture of overcrowding, bad ventilation, insanitary conditions, lack of nursing and an absence of appliances.

In 1866 the Association for the Improvement of the Infirmaries of the London Workhouses met and agreed a plan of reform which included a demand for trained nurses, resident medical officers and the supply of medicines from the rates. In fact, they were demanding an implicit acknowledgement by the Government that the Poor Law infirmaries were hospitals.

Florence Nightingale was also busy on an administrative design. Whereas Louisa Twining was calling for the separation of the various categories of the sick and the provision of trained nurses, Florence Nightingale recognised that none of these could be achieved without a restructuring of the machinery. She drew up her ABC of reform for the Metropolitan area and presented it to the Prime Minister, Lord Palmerston. This ABC included the classification of workhouse inmates and separation of the sick, insane and children into proper institutions; she also asked for the separation of the sick poor from the able-bodied poor in terms of the administration of relief with its concomitant pauperisation. Secondly she wanted a single, central administration for the Metropolitan area to replace the many different unions. Thirdly she wanted a consolidated levy of rates to be raised for the financing of medical relief. She claimed that local rates and appointments were insufficient for the scope of the problem and encouraged only a piecemeal approach (Woodham-Smith 1950).

The *Annual Report* of the PLB for 1866 referred to the deaths of Daly and Gibson and mentioned that these led to official enquiries as to the treatment they had received. These enquiries and their results caused the Board serious concern. They received deputations from the Association for the Improvement of Workhouses and noted the reports and recommendations of *The Lancet* commission. They reported that as a result of all this they had asked Dr Smith and Mr Farnall to make an official report on the Metropolitan workhouse infirmaries. These reports had been published in June of that year and were subsequently followed by their reports on the provincial workhouses. Several nurses working in London workhouses also gave evidence of scandalous conditions, notably Nurse Matilda Beeton and Nurse Jane Bateman (Parl. Papers 1866). This evidence showed that there was a lack of equipment such as waterproof sheets, towels and bed linen. They complained of maggots in the flock beds, inadequate invalid diets, deficient laundry services, uncared for and verminous patients.

The concerted efforts of all these people appeared to be about to bear fruit and it was confidently hoped that Mr Villiers would introduce fresh legislation. Unfortunately, there was a change of government at the critical period and the moment was lost.

The new President of the Poor Law Board was Mr Gathorne Hardy. Florence Nightingale approached him with her plan for reform and attached to it a scheme for the institution of a nurse training system in approved Poor Law infirmaries. Gathorne Hardy, however, preferred to use his own ideas and declined her invitation to a discussion, although in the end the legislation which he introduced did seem to go some way towards meeting Florence Nightingale's proposals.

Hardy had available the evidence to the Select Committee, *The Lancet Report* and the several reports of his Inspectors. In her evidence to the Select Committee, Louisa Twining had strongly encouraged the use of properly trained and selected paid nurses. She made the point that the infirmaries were now the hospitals of the poor and that they should be run as such. She considered that it was not economical to continue to use peripatetic pauper nurses (who were neither suitable nor trained) to care for the patients. There would therefore be no stable nursing staff to be taught or who, once taught the rudiments, would remain and carry out the orders of the Medical Officers. The Medical Officers were therefore severely handicapped in their treatment of the sick, their time was wasted and the poor sick remained as patients for longer than was needed thus causing the ratepayers additional expense. She proposed a Parliamentary Grant which should be used for the provision of one paid nurse in each Workhouse. Her arguments appear to have been on an economic basis although there is no doubt that she was motivated by humanitarian emotions.

The information derived from the Form of Enquiry sent out by Florence Nightingale in 1865 was illuminating: in the Metropolitan infirmaries 11 had pauper nurses only, 21 had paid but untrained nursing supervisors, and 6 had trained and paid nurses. These last were paid between £20 to £30 yearly. All nurses were selected by the Master and Matron with some assistance from the Medical Officers. About half the nurses were on duty or available for a 24-hour day. Until 1863 none of the provincial infirmaries employed trained nurses. After the 1865 circular, issued by the PLB, more unions had employed trained nurses. Frequently one nurse only was employed as a superintendent to overlook the work of untrained or pauper nurses.

Hardy's Metropolitan Poor Law Act, passed in 1867, proved to be a milestone in the development of medical relief. It provided for the classification of the sick and for separate accommodation to be provided for each category; it combined unions and parishes into larger districts each of which would have one or more asylums (the word is used in its traditional sense, i.e. 'a shelter' or 'a hospital') as the PLB might direct. Each district was to have a Board of Managers constituted as an incorporated body with powers to buy, own and sell property for the purposes of operating the asylums; the managers were to be partly elected and partly appointed; the PLB was empowered to direct the managers of a district to provide an asylum of a specified style and size and could also direct them to allocate a workhouse for use as a district asylum. The PLB was empowered to pay the managers for the use of those workhouses which they might have allocated as district asylums or for the improvement of them. A clause was also inserted allowing the PLB to lay down the method of admission of patients to these. The managers were to have authority to appoint and employ paid officers but the number of posts, duties and salaries were to be regulated by the PLB.

The Act also gave permission for the sick and insane asylums to be used for medical or nursing instruction but this was quickly withdrawn.

The PLB was to have power to direct unions or parishes to set up outdoor dispensaries where the District Medical Officer could attend to the sick poor on an outpatient basis. The unions were to be responsible for all medicines, appliances and requisites prescribed for the sick poor attending these dispensaries.

In order to achieve all this a Common Poor Fund was to be set up, raised by contributions from the unions and parishes of the Metropolis.

The Act set up a separate authority, the Metropolitan Asylums Board, to administer 'auxiliary asylums' to accommodate the group of 'harmless chronics' as the lunatics and insane inmates had been categorised by the Lunacy Commission. The MAB was also charged with the responsibility of receiving poor people suffering from infectious diseases and smallpox. The MAB was to become a potent factor in the development of hospitals for special cases, a comprehensive medical and nursing system, ambulance services, bacteriological and antitoxin laboratories and hospitals, special schools and convalescence homes for children.

Although the 1867 Act did not change the route for admission of patients to Poor Law establishments it did, as has been noted, give the Poor Law Board power to lay down the method of entry. Admission to infirmaries was still through the Relieving Officer and still involved pauperisation of the patient. There was a widespread feeling that this was no longer appropriate as 70% of all paupers were in receipt of medical relief. However this policy was not changed for several years.

The Act gave the PLB much greater authority and powers of direction over the new managers and Guardians in the metropolis.

This was the start of a medical policy for the sick poor and an advance in the trend, started by the 1834 Act, towards centralisation. At the same time, the 1867 Reform Act had extended the franchise to working men in the towns and their votes made a considerable difference in the political considerations of the Boards of Guardians and the new managers. These Guardians became known as the 'new generation of Guardian' who felt quite differently from their predecessors about the administration of relief. The policy of deterrence was beginning to crumble.

Although the start of a policy on medical relief had been formulated by Gathorne Hardy's Act and although there were powers to train nurses in the asylums, he had not gone on to formulate any policy for this training, nor had he established any policy for the systematic employment of trained nurses. This still had to evolve in a rather haphazard fashion. Enoch Powell is remembered as saying (in 1962) that if there were hospitals, the nurses would appear. He was not the first to think this; Gathorne Hardy, if he gave the matter any thought at all, must have believed it in 1867. He established a substantial system of hospitals but omitted to create any infrastructure upon which the hospital system and the care of the patients could rest.

REFERENCES

Bickerton, T. H. (1936), *A Medical History of Liverpool*. London, John Murray.

Bruce, M. (1973), citing the First Annual Report of the Medical Officer of Health to the City of London. p. 78.

Hodgkinson, Ruth (1967). Chapter 2.

Longmate, Norman (1974), *The Workhouse*. London, Temple Smith, pp. 90, 197, 201.

McMenemy, W. H. (1974), 'The Hospital Movement of the 18th Century and its Development.' In Poynter, F. N. L. (ed.), *The Evolution of Hospitals in Britain*. London, Pitman Medical Books.

Parliamentary Debates. 1853 Vol. cxxix 134 f. 1865 Vol. 178 1533 f. 1867 Vol. 190 315 f.

Parliamentary Papers. 1861–4 Vol IX. Select Committee on Poor Relief. 1866 Vol. LXI, 4951, 523, 556. Mismanagement of the Sick Poor.

Rumsey, A. W. (1856), *Essays in State Medicine*. London, John Churchill.

Twining, Louisa (1858), 'Workhouses and Women's Work'. in *Chucrh of England Monthly Review*. London, Longman.

——— (1880) 'Workhouse Visiting and Management'. London.

Woodham-Smith, Cecil (1950). Chapter XX.

3

AN OVER-VIEW OF SOCIAL CHANGE: 1867–1919

Flora Thompson (1944) says in her book *Lark Rise to Candleford*, 'All times are times of transition; but the eighteen-eighties were so in a special sense for the world was at the beginning of a new era, the era of machinery and scientific discovery. Values and conditions of life were changing everywhere. Even to simple country people the change was apparent. The railways had brought distant parts of the country nearer; newspapers were coming into every home; machinery was superseding hand labour, even in the farms to some extent; food bought at shops, much of it from distant countries, was replacing the home-made and home grown. . . .' She contrasts the comparative affluence of the country folk in *Lark Rise to Candleford* during the 1840s when many of them were able to achieve a freehold ownership of their cottages and had enough income to allow them to set something aside for their old age, with the hardships of the subsequent 'beseiged generation' during the 1880s and describes the dream of one of the women that she might receive a weekly income of one pound per week for the maintenance of the family; instead her husband earned 10/– a week and this wage, together with the food they grew for themselves, kept the family of four. Beer was twopence a pint, the rent was one or two shillings a week (where it was not a tied cottage), the pigling which they raised and eventually killed for their supply of meat and bacon cost between 10/– and 15/– and they bought their bread which 'was a heavy item'.

Between 1871 and 1921 the population in England and Wales rose from 22·7 millions to 37·9 millions, the birth rate dropped from 35·4 per 1000 to 13·5 per 1000. The trend towards an older population was confirmed: in 1851 the age group 15 to 64 showed a return of 598 per 1000 but in 1911 it was 639 per 1000, and for the age group over 64 the respective figures were 47 per 1000 and 53 per 1000 (Stern 1962).

With the rise in population the density of population also continued to increase in the major cities: in 1871, in London, there were 389 people per square mile and in 1911 there were 618.

The trend towards living away from the city centres continued and by the 1880s working class suburbs were being built; the Government intervened with the railway companies and made them establish workmen's rail fares. The easing of travel conditions encouraged free movement from one area to another, of people, goods and ideas. National newspapers were taken in even the poorest homes; markets were widened and commercial life benefited. Britain established strong shipping organisations and became dominant in ship-building during the latter part of the 19th century. But the expansion of shipping brought with it greater competition from overseas industry. Road transport was mostly horse drawn until the turn of the 20th century and in 1901 the first petrol engined motor cycle was introduced into Britain; motor cars came into Britain at about the same period and motor taxis were introduced to London in 1909. The first motor bus ran in London in 1899 and a regular motor bus service was introduced in London in 1905.

In 1863 the first 'tube' railway, the Metropolitan Railway Company, was inaugurated, and in 1905 the Bakerloo and Piccadilly lines were opened.

Socially speaking, probably one of the most important transport innovations of the period was the bicycle which came in at the start of this period, in the late 1860s, and quickly proliferated. This cheap form of transport enabled the poorer people to move about more freely and to learn about their neighbouring communities. It brought the urban people to the countryside to enjoy the rural attractions and absorb a rural way of life and it allowed the country folk to visit their neighbouring towns. This easier and relatively free means of travel brought the communities together, broke down barriers and spread ideas, particularly in the working classes. Comparisons could be drawn, new ideas, jobs and ways of life could be adopted and the sharp distinction between rural and urban workers slowly blurred.

During the 1870s a decline started in Britain's industrial supremacy: it had been amongst the first to be industrialised and its machinery and ideas had become outmoded. Whilst other countries, particularly Germany and America, were developing they had improved on Britain's technology and had overtaken it with newer ideas. The British had for years enjoyed a supremacy and had become complacent. In the early days of the Industrial Revolution, the craftsman who pioneered an invention became the manufacturer, but this combination had been overtaken by a separation of the roles and the inventors were more inclined to be removed from the manu-facturing process whilst the manufacturers had become remote from developmental work, specialising in production and marketing areas.

Trades Unions were becoming more organised and powerful. In 1868 the Trades Union Congress was founded representing only the skilled workers. By about 1880 unskilled workers were also organised and represented in the TUC, and the first group to strike were the women match workers in 1888.

The unions however lacked both political power and representa-tion in Parliament until, in 1893, the Independent Labour Party was established, devoted to the promotion of the workers' cause.

By 1884 28·5% of all voters were from the working class (Ryder and Silver 1970) and the political parties were more concerned with designing policies that would attract their votes; the sharp social class distinctions had become blurred by the prosperous middle classes and further sections of the middle class were becoming apparent. The institution of inspectors by legislation had separated the 'inspectorial' level of government and local government officers: the Poor Law Inspectors, the Factory Inspectors, the Inspectors of Nuisances. These were not policy makers nor did they belong to the administrative or clerical levels. These posts were instruments of control and were of an intermediate level, a level made necessary by increasing Government intervention in local affairs and an increas-ing, if reluctant, acceptance of responsibility for influencing the direction of changes. If legislation had to be used to control public health, travel and factory conditions, inspectors had to be employed to supervise the use of public money and ensure the implementation of regulations.

Similarly, in commerce and industry the structure of organisations became more complex as their spheres of influence grew and became national. The direct relationship between master and worker was, perforce, interrupted by the growth of the managerial level. As the organisation grew larger so did the distance between the master and the worker. For the first time it was no longer possible for the worker in these organisations to take his complaints directly to the master and industrial disputes became more serious. The managerial levels proliferated and found their places in the middle classes. The middle class had become more numerous and its boundaries much less distinct.

Within the working class, divisions were also evident. This pheno-menon was not only recognised but underwitten by the Trades Unions. The recognition within the working classes of the poor and not so poor had long been a recognised feature. There was an equi-valent recognition of the 'respectable poor' and the 'unrespectable poor' (or 'rough poor') as there was a widely held distinction be-tween the 'deserving poor' and the 'undeserving poor', this latter distinction being implicitly incorporated into the social legislation of the country.

In religion the falling off in church attendance continued. A religious Census in 1857 and census of church attendances in Sheffield in 1881 showed that they had roughly halved in that city during the 30 years. Immigrants to the towns and cities during the last half of the 18th century lost the constraints of their native com-munities and their church-going lapsed, whilst working class people who were born in the towns had never developed the habit. By the end of the century, the strictness of Victorian moral ethics was begin-ning to wane and a more relaxed attitude became apparent. This may have loosened the rigid observance of the Sabbath but did not do away with it entirely. The conflict between science and the church continued; between the theory of evolution and the early chapters of Genesis there remained an uncomfortable gap. The intellectuals became more and more anticlerical, antireligious and materialistic. This controversy struck at the heart of British society and disturbed many families. By its attack on religious dogma, on which the patri-archal society rested, the social structure of Victorian order was it-self undermined. An agnostic and materialistic philosophy grew and there developed a more hedonistic way of life.

The new 'laxity' in life, coupled with growing industrialisation, gave working class women opportunities for earning their own living which they had not previously enjoyed. By the end of the 19th century they were able more easily to earn their own living in in-dustrial occupations and were no longer tied to their homes. In the middle classes there was the choice between material possessions or large families and large families became less common. This trend spread into the working classes by the early 20th century. Smaller families gave women greater leisure time and as they were less tied to their homes their social status was enhanced. The relaxation of family discipline and of the patriarchal ethos allowed greater free-dom to the children. Earlier marriages became more common, sex was indulged in for its own sake and women began to enjoy their position in society more. There were fewer household servants, particularly with the onset of the 1914–18 war, and household amenities and gadgets began to proliferate, making the housewife's ties even lighter.

The war brought even greater emancipation to women by extending their opportunities for employment. Jobs were available on the buses, in the munitions factories, in service and administrative occupations and in nursing. The country began to accept a general employment of women and even the middle and upper class women, who had for so long been restricted and frustrated in their employment openings, found that it was patriotic to take paid employment.

The information brought out by increasing social investigations showed more and more the plight of the poor. Reformers were slowly making their impact on both public opinion and Government action. During the 1870s, hit by competition from foreign manufacturers, profits dropped for the first time in a hundred years and many middle class people began to feel the pinch. Business men who could not be labelled 'undeserving' began to feel threatened and could begin to appreciate that their incomes depended on extraneous circumstances apart from their own industry and providence. The existing trend towards greater social liberalism was therefore given an additional impetus by economic factors. There was more interest in the causes of poverty, there was the start of a definition of poverty *per se* and a growing appreciation of the distinction between primary and secondary poverty. The 1870s saw a renewed discussion on housing and living conditions which resulted in the 1890 Housing of the Working Classes Act. During the 1880s Charles Booth started his survey of *The Life and Labour of the People of London* (completed in 1903) and his preliminary report demonstrated that 35% of the working classes had been 'at all time more or less in want'. His findings in London were supported by Seebohm Rowntree who investigated poverty in York in 1899. Booth showed that the causes of poverty were multiple, not only laziness and improvidence. He demonstrated that low wages and old age were the two most important factors of poverty and these were not subject to control by the poor.

The individualistic philosophy of the first half of the 19th century was slowly giving way to a more collectivist way of thinking and a feeling that the State had a responsibility for the weaker sections of the population. The weaker sections were still considered to be the poor of the working class and it was not until the 1914–18 war that it was found necessary to give support to other classes. The momentum of changing attitudes had become powerful by the 1890s but collectivism and State responsibility still had to compete with the underlying Victorian philosophy of individual responsibility. In 1869 the Charity Organisation Society was born and during its long and influential life it maintained the old attitudes towards the poor: self help or no help at all.

During much of this period the British Government was pursuing an expansionist and militaristic foreign policy. The period was marked by minor wars and the British Army was kept very much in action, not always successfully; Florence Nightingale kept up a persistent campaign to improve conditions for the British Tommy and slowly achieved an improvement not only in his status and physical conditions but in terms of human dignity.

Unlike most of her contemporaries, Miss Nightingale felt passionately about human dignity: her contemporaries evidently did not, and the treatment of the British soldier (and the poor) was evidence of an attitude felt by the middle and upper classes for the poor classes. The upper classes were trained from childhood to accept a responsibility for their retainers and workers; this responsibility was often exercised in a kindly and sensitive manner. Where there was no overt contractual or feudal responsibility, the poor were usually regarded as a rabble, in a collective sense; they were seldom seen as individuals. So long as no contractual responsibility was felt, and so long as the poor could be viewed as a rabble, it was easier to deny any personal responsibility and to avoid any suspicion that human feelings were involved. The rising middle classes adopted, for the most part, the same attitude although they had not been brought up to feel the same responsibilities. Their treatment of their servants was often less kindly therefore and their intermediate situation in the social hierarchy probably made their own relationships with their servants less secure.

The numerous military activities called for a large number of recruits and both the Government and the nation were alarmed at the numbers who had to be rejected because of poor health. This finding was reinforced by industrialists who had discovered that it was difficult to maintain adequate labour forces for the same health reasons. The nation was therefore alerted to a deteriorating supply of manpower at a time when its security and prosperity depended on these human resources.

There was an abundance of domestic legislation, much of it of a social nature: broadening the field of education and making it compulsory, extending the franchise, giving workers compensation for industrial injuries, trying to ease the chronic housing shortage, and an unsuccessful attempt by Joseph Chamberlain to introduce an old age pensions scheme.

The women's suffrage movement was very active over this period seeking the enfranchisement of women on the same terms as men. The movement consisted generally of the militant suffragists who were aggressive in their tactics, and the other faction who sought to achieve their goal through constitutional means. In 1907 the Qualification of Women Act permitted women to sit upon County and Borough Councils. The women's suffrage movement was closely parallel to the movement which grew up during this period to register nurses and to give nurses control of their own profession. The protagonists of the movement were often active in the struggle for the registration of nurses and the antagonists of the movement, such as Florence Nightingale, were also often against this.

In 1908 the first Old Age Pension Act was passed by the Asquith government and gave a pension of 5/– a week to the old people over 70 years, other than those receiving Poor Law relief or those whose income exceeded £25 a year.

The *Majority* and *Minority Reports of the Royal Commission on the Poor Law* were published in 1909, and brought to the notice of the public one of the authors of the *Minority Report*, Beatrice Webb. Both reports advocated workhouse reform but their views and attitudes differed significantly. Although the Government remained uncommitted to the views of either side, the *Minority Report*, in the end, gained the day (see chapter 8).

In 1911 the National Insurance Act introduced a new concept into social welfare, that of the insurance principle. Contingencies would be covered by premiums paid by certain workers on a weekly basis. The contingencies catered for by this Act were sickness (and the need for medical treatment) and unemployment. This Act covered all men over 16 years earning less than £160 per year, but did not cover their dependants. The Act set up a new medical system throughout the country for the inspection and control of claims.

All this social legislation was a demonstration of the growth of liberalism and altruism. It was a tacit acceptance of the end of the laissez-faire political theory and the demise of the self-help social theory. By introducing this legislation, both Government and country accepted responsibility for the welfare of the individual. This was a fundamental change in attitude which was not finally completed until 1948 but which was the start of the breakdown of the Poor Law administration (since the new Acts were centrally administered and by-passed the Poor Law authorities). It was the start of a central policy of social insurance: the beginning of the end of parish relief.

REFERENCES

Ryder, J. & Silver, H. (1970). p. 74.

Stern, W. M. (1962). Chapter 2.

Thompson, Flora (1944), *Lark Rise to Candleford*. London, Oxford University Press. p. 57.

4
THE REFORM OF NURSING AND THE GROWTH OF SCIENTIFIC MEDICINE: 1867–1895

By 1867 there was an outflow of Nightingale nurses to the country's main voluntary hospitals. When the progress of social liberalism is compared with the rate at which the reform in nursing swept the country, the speed of the latter is remarkable. In 1861 the first probationers were accepted for training at St Mary's Hospital in London under the matron, Mrs Wright. In 1862 a training school for midwives was started at King's College Hospital, London; the Bristol Training Institution was started; the Liverpool Nursing School was set up at the Royal Infirmary, and trained sisters were appointed over the wards at Great Ormond Street Hospital for Children in London. In 1865 the Leicester Nursing Institution and the Manchester Sick Poor and Private Institution were started. Burdett (1893) writes that by this date 'enthusiasm on the subject of nursing was spreading rapidly'.

In 1867 the Middlesex Hospital built a new nurses' home for 60 nurses to accommodate its increased nursing staff, and the new nursing system had spread to Hampshire, Norwich, Lincoln and Tottenham.

In 1868 the Middlesex Hospital received the first of its new probationer nurses. In 1870 the Edinburgh Royal Infirmary converted to the Nightingale system. In 1874 the London Hospital reorganised its nurse-training and training schools were started at the Queen Charlotte Hospital and the Westminster Hospital. The same year saw the inauguration of the famous National and Metropolitan Nursing Association in Bloomsbury Square under the superintendence of Florence Lees. In 1877 St Bartholomew's Hospital was enlarged and accommodation set aside for an increased nursing staff. In 1879 a new matron, Miss Burt, was appointed to take over the nursing at Guy's Hospital 'where the nursing was falling somewhat behind the times' and by the 1880s most of the voluntary hospitals in the country were employing trained nurses; many of them had their own training schools.

There is a somewhat conflicting account of nurse training given by Florence Lees (1874) who was a disciple of Florence Nightingale and Lady Superintendent of the National Association for Providing Trained Nurses for the Sick Poor (later the Metropolitan and National Nursing Association). The Association asked Miss Lees to investigate and report on the training of nurses in the London Hospitals and on district nursing generally. Parts of her reports on district nursing were published at the time but her reports on nurse training in London were not published until 1974. She visited the major voluntary hospitals in London and gave a detailed account of their general and nursing organisation and training. She found that there was no 'systematic training' at Guy's Hospital (where the period of training was three months), King's College Hospital, Charing Cross Hospital, the London Hospital, St Mary's Hospital, nor University College Hospital (three months' training). At the Middlesex Hospital the training content was copied from the Nightingale Training School and there were 15 to 20 probationers (310 beds) who were certificated if they satisfied the Medical Committee. The Royal Free Hospital also used the Nightingale scheme and their probationers had lectures from the House Surgeon and the Lady Superintendent: their training was for one year after which they received a certificate on successfully passing an examination. Unlike many of the other hospitals, a hospital register for nurses and their progress records were maintained. Miss Lees gave no details of the training at St Bartholomew's Hospital. At St George's Hospital the probationers trained for two years but received no certificate nor did they have any systematic instruction but only occasional tuition from the Head Nurse. At St Thomas's Hospital the probationers received instruction from the Medical Instructor and Home Sister. At the Westminster Hospital the training was given by the Lady Superintendent of the training school; it was reported to have been very sketchy, and lasted for one year. Most of the hospitals trained nurses only for their own use but two or three also trained for the Nursing Associations.

These reports also gave a fascinating insight into the daily work of the nurses who did much of the ward cleaning (except at St Thomas's, St George's, the Royal Free and the Middlesex). The conditions at all of these hospitals were very sparse and many seemed no better than the infirmaries as they were reported by the *British Medical Journal* in 1894–6. The Westminster Hospital, for instance, had no hot water system, there was one wheeled bath per six wards and the beds were similar to those found in the Poor Law infirmaries. One of the head nurses complained to Florence Lees that 'there was nothing worth nursing, only chronic cases'. There was a meagre supply of lockers and chairs; basins and bowls were made of tin, sometimes the patients provided their own towels, butter, tea and other extras. Occasionally the nurses were reported as not being allowed by the doctors to take temperatures, pulses and respirations, not being in evidence on the wards and barred from 'clinical wards'. In some of the hospitals the walls were unplastered brick, similar to the infirmaries. At Guy's Hospital there was a new block of wards which had recently been completed but the nurses were not permitted by the doctors to enter these. The Medical Superintendent engaged and discharged all nurses. King's College and Charing Cross Hospitals were staffed by nurses from St John's Home, an Anglican nursing order. Miss Lees did not find the discipline very good at these two hospitals.

At the London Hospital the sisters were subject to the House Committee and House Governor. At the Middlesex there was a Lady Superintendent who was responsible for all the nurses to the Weekly Board and Medical Committee but this responsibility was not clearly defined because the Resident Medical Officer had to authorise off-duty and report 'those who do not fulfill their duties'.

The nurses at the Royal Free Hospital were reported as being responsible for registering and recording temperatures, pulses and respirations (as were the nurses at St Thomas's) and were described as looking clean and respectable.

The sisters at St Bartholomew's Hospital were responsible to the House Committee, and although there was a Matron she did not seem to have much to do with the nursing. The nurses there did all the cleaning, including the scrubbing. At St George's, which generally met with more approbation on the part of Florence Lees, there was a Lady Superintendent who was responsible for the nurses. There were no lockers for the patients and no food could be brought into the wards by the patients' friends: 'One almost missed the smell of stale oranges, sugar, marmalade and other odours peculiar to the locker of English hospitals'.

There was a Matron at St Mary's who had responsibility for the sisters and nurses but, it was reported, the sisters and nurses were not permitted by the Secretary to take temperatures, pulse beats and respiration rates. At this hospital, there were only three tin basins for each ward (the earthenware basin positioned on the ward's centre table was for the use of the doctors only), there were no lavatories (wash-basins) on the wards and, in common with all the other hospitals, chamber utensils, bedpans and urinals were kept under the beds or on the bedside chair when there was one. These were emptied variously but usually twice a day. They did not normally have covers.

The Matron at St Thomas's reported to the Treasurer and had complete control over the nurses. Florence Lees complained about some aspects of the training (one year) since the ward teaching was, she found, 'variable' in value; there was scarcely any training in invalid cookery and the renowned nurses' diaries (of which so much has been written and which were so dear to Miss Nightingale) were irregularly maintained.

The nurses at University College Hospital were Sisters from All Saints' Convent, Margaret Street. They were trained probationers for three, six or twelve months. There were hot pipes in the wards of this hospital and also water closets. She found the nursing here to be preferable and more orderly than at the Middlesex Hospital whose nurses came from St John's House.

On the whole Miss Lees found that the patients looked clean but 'not comfortable'.

The reform of nursing was supposed to have embodied more than a planned system of training for a defined (if variable) period of time. Florence Nightingale was insistent that probationers should be carefully selected for the right physical, spiritual and moral qualities. She required an adequate level of intelligence and a suitable home background. In order to find these products she turned to the upper and middle classes from which she took her 'lady probationers' and to whom she gave a shortened training of one year. She felt that these were to be preferred, not because they were ladies, but because they were educated. When she accepted probationers from the lower social classes she demanded a longer training of two years during which she felt able to develop their character and skills appropriately. These candidates were the more plebian 'nurse probationers'.

In addition to this rigorous selection and training, she also demanded that nurses should be under the control of 'one female trained head' who should be the Matron and be 'responsible for everything [regarding internal management and discipline] being carried out'.

a

This involved the removal of authority for the nurses from the doctors and gave rise to considerable opposition which has continued to the present day.

Miss Nightingale's ideas were that nurses should be intelligent and skilled assistants to the doctors but that they should have an additional and indigenous function, that of caring for the patient and achieving for him those conditions which would be most favourable for his ultimate recovery or greatest comfort, both mental and physical. From her writings it is clear that in using the term 'assistant' she did not mean to imply any subservience although she did recognise the doctor's complete clinical responsibility. Her work in the Crimea demonstrated that she was inclined to view this clinical responsibility strictly and excluded from it such aspects as the general diet, the patient's environment and comfort, his welfare and overall care. All the same, she was very ambivalent about the nurse:doctor relationship.

It will come as no surprise therefore that there was considerable opposition from many medical men. Their authority over the nurses and their control over the patients were being attacked and undermined. Matrons were installed wherever the new nurses were employed and by the 1880s every hospital, irrespective of its size, had its Matron or Lady Superintendent. But their absolute authority for the nurses is something that was never absolutely won. This conflict persisted and during the years that followed there was always a strong and vocal faction of doctors who opposed any move made by nurses to improve their status, education and training and to attain complete control over their own profession. Florence Nightingale's Matrons went out to their mission fields in the voluntary hospitals with considerable zeal but relatively little political sense. There were therefore frequent clashes not only with the doctors but also with the administrators. Whether or not a more sophisticated and political approach might have proved more successful, it is difficult to say. Certainly professional politicians have found their skills taxed fully in later negotiations with the medical profession.

One of the clashes between the new style matrons and the doctors occurred at Guy's Hospital in 1880 when Miss Burt reorganised the nursing without the advice of, nor any consultation with, the medical staff. Plotkin (1961) wrote that the fact that the hospital was so tardy in reorganising its nursing system was symptomatic of the 'conservative attitude of a significant part of the medical world with regard to nursing by "educated ladies" '. The medical staff at Guy's criticised the new system very quickly and defended the old nurses in the same terms as did John South. They maintained that they were the best judges of the quality of nursing. One of the doctors, Dr Gull, maintained that the new nurses represented 'a new element' that came between them (the doctors) and their patients. The nurses were supported, in a situation which became more and more complex, by the Treasurer and Board of Governors and ultimately the senior physician and senior surgeon resigned. *The Lancet* joined issue and made strong representations in support of the principle that the sick 'must be under direct medical control'. But the two senior doctors were replaced and the issue died.

In contrast to this opposition it must be said that many doctors were more than willing to allow control of the wards to rest with the nurses so that they could devote their time and energies to the clinical conditions of their patients without worrying about the cleanliness of the wards and the efficient administration of their prescribed treatments. They readily accepted that they had to rely on the skilled observation and discretion of the nurses who were in constant attendance on the patients (in contrast to the doctors' intermittent visits) and felt therefore that any improvement in the nurses' training was beneficial.

The conflict between the doctors and the matrons could be seen also as a conflict between one profession which had only recently secured a professional status and was still struggling for a social status and a second group working closely parallel with the doctors, who were showing signs of looking for a professional identity. Many of the nurses in authority were from an equivalent social background in a society where the man still expected to dominate. The struggle was therefore complicated by issues of sex and power. The doctors did not wish to see their newly won power in the hospitals being eroded by another group. The 'Crisis at Guy's' demonstrated this clearly, and Burdett, writing about that story in 1893, said 'It is scarcely worthwhile to refer to this old scandal save to point out how necessary it is that the doctors should be recognised as the chief person to whom the nurse is answerable.'

During this period there was a considerable expansion in the establishment of hospitals. Not only were more voluntary hospitals established but cottage hospitals proliferated in the rural areas. According to Burdett (1896), the idea of these charity hospitals was originated by Albert Napper who founded the Cranleigh Cottage (or Village) Hospital in 1859. The idea was quickly taken up by doctors and by 1896 there were some 300 in the country. There was always some reserve felt about these smaller establishments with up to 100 beds (Burdett did not feel that they should have more than 25 beds), but the country doctors enjoyed their amenities and felt that their use allowed 'medical practitioners to achieve skill equal to leading surgeons of today'. He was evidently a great protagonist of the idea and was of the opinion that 'there is no operation, however difficult or complicated, which the staff have not proved their ability to successfully perform'. The cottage hospitals helped to raise the status of the country doctor and brought the services of 'good nurses' to the agricultural districts.

Whether or not the 'good nurses' provided by the cottage hospitals were capable of providing a standard of nursing comparable with that of the trained nurses turned out by the voluntary hospitals is open to question.

These cottage hospitals were supported by the Poor Law authorities who were empowered to pay a retaining fee to ensure the availability of beds or, alternatively, to send in Poor Law patients on payment of the fee.

The number of beds provided by the voluntary hospitals increased. Not only were there more hospitals being built but more beds were being provided by the hospitals. The ratio of free beds per 1000 population varied considerably from town to town. In London there were just over 7 beds per 1000 population, Manchester had 2·83, Birmingham 2·58, Portsmouth 0·64, Edinburgh 3·80, Dublin 6·39. The provision of free (or 'charity') beds in the United Kingdom, however, never reached the generous proportions provided by the continental countries where Paris had a ratio of 9·83, Rome 18·26, St Petersburg 9·08 and Madrid 4·0 (Burdett 1893).

The voluntary hospitals were, by the end of the 19th century, beginning to find that expenses were increasingly heavy. The recently instituted Hospital Saturday Fund, one of the more popular provident societies, had been a new means of attracting funds to their exchequers but had also helped to increase the numbers of their patients. There was still a status discrimination between the voluntary hospital patients and those others who had to take their medical care from the Poor Law infirmaries, the 'riff raff', as Burdett uncompromisingly labelled them. The hospitals remained self-governing; there was no system of Government inspection, control nor licensing and standards varied very widely from the plutocratic London hospitals to the small, poor, provincial ones.

Poor management, made more remarkable as the size of the hospitals increased, often dissipated or abused the funds that were available. Money was derived from donations, partial payments by patients and from the fees paid by probationer nurses for their training. It was estimated that about 0·69% of the total income of the great London hospitals (0·70% in the provinces) came from these fees.

Throughout the period, there was constant complaint in official reports and contemporary histories of the inadequacy of records, medical, administrative and financial. There is evidence to show that there was frequently a discrepancy between the hospitals' income and expenditure. In 25 years between 1865 and 1890, costs had gone up by 25%. Contemporary writers agreed that this rise was caused by a variety of reasons including an improvement in the environmental standard, better food, an improvement in the nursing (this represents the change-over from the 'old type' to the 'new type' of nurse), better hygiene and sanitation, aseptic techniques and more and improved dressings. The new aseptic techniques demanded a considerable increase in the amounts of dressings used but, on the other hand, had been instrumental in reducing the surgical mortality rate from between 25%–40% to a low of about 4% during the same period.

The cost of nursing had also been increased by improvement, in this case the reform of nursing, during the last quarter of the 19th century. Many authorities in the health field repeatedly insisted that good nursing demanded good quality women: these good quality women would not be forthcoming in the numbers they required unless the conditions for nurses were sufficiently good to attract them. The need for nurses had never been so great and the awareness of that need had never been so acute. The great philanthropic and humanitarian wave, boosted by economic and military needs, demanded better health care. The cost of nursing a patient had consequently quadrupled in the 30 years between 1860 and 1890. This was considered to be due to the cost of new nurses' homes (each nurse was expecting and getting her own bedroom), new sitting rooms for off duty hours, shorter hours, longer holidays with pay, better food, higher salaries, pensions, cost of training and the equipping of libraries for the training schools. The higher cost of nursing is said to have been offset by better care for the patients, greater efficiency, a reduction in the death rate, and the modern treatment of disease. It is difficult to understand in precise terms what these benefits mean. It has always been next to impossible to cost the benefits of nursing, similarly it is difficult to establish the efficiency of a nurse. The patients did, evidently, have better attention from the new nurses who, unlike their predecessors, received training in the care of patients: there was certainly a greater turnover of patients and the historians of the day speak of the new trend in discharging patients before a final recovery. Convalescent homes were being provided towards this end as the pressure on beds in hospitals grew. Medical treatment was implemented more reliably and efficiently and therefore the better nursing was contributing to the reduction of the death rate. Much of the reduction must however lie with improvement in medical treatment and surgical techniques, deriving in turn from new scientific knowledge. However, the antiseptic techniques and the administration of the new medicines did rely largely on the nurses to carry them out even if the doctors had to initiate them.

'Nursing has come to be regarded as a recognised calling for which a special apprenticeship must be served.' So wrote Burdett (1893) who gave a considerable amount of space in his books to an account of the nursing systems of the world. His attitude towards nurses appears today to have been patriarchal, kindly, appreciative and condescending. Nowhere in his many volumes did he ever acknowledge nurses as the equals in status of the doctors nor of his own colleagues, the administrators.

By the end of the century, in the large hospitals, the Matron was taking the place of the lay Lady Superintendent. Sometimes, as at the Manchester Royal Infirmary, the Matron actually took over that title. There was a developing nursing hierarchy: the Matron was supported by one or more assistant matrons, a home sister and sisters and staff nurses. The increasing complexity of the country's organisations was mirrored in nursing; the gap between the nurse and the Matron widened and the direct contact between the two levels, so dear to Florence Nightingale, had already been interrupted. The patients, who in the previous period had been expected to help with much of the domestic work, were then expected to contribute to their recovery by lying docilely in bed. Domestic staff proliferated in order to relieve the patient but also because the nurses were no longer expected to perform 'non-nursing' duties. (This expression has never been adequately defined but at least nurses were not by then equated with ward maids as they were by John South.) The hospitals were becoming more expensive and their organisation more complex. The growth of urban populations made increasing demands on the hospitals but as the population of the cities became suburbanised, the hospitals became further and further removed from their patients' domiciles.

The attachment of the medical schools to the hospitals helped to provide them with the pick of the graduating doctors, provided a career structure for the better doctors and maintained an academic or clinical challenge for the senior doctors as they were able to pick the most interesting cases for admission. Students did much of the dressers' work, thus providing free labour (as did the probationer nurses), the consultants gave their time freely, so it was only the few full time doctors and the trained nurses whose salaries had to be paid.

In order to augment their incomes, the hospitals began to take paying patients. This was a boon to the consultants as treatment and operations increased in sophistication. It was also the beginning of a reverse democratisation, as far as the patients were concerned, as the moneyed classes had up till then preferred to be cared for at home.

With the advance of scientific and medical knowledge, there was a fairly rapid shift in the philosophy and goals of medical treatment from alleviation of suffering to cure. Medicine became more scientific, the pharmacopoeia extended, drugs were becoming more complex and costs were rising rapidly. There was some discussion about the payment of consultants but the feeling of the day was that this would reduce the status of the consultants to that of the Poor Law medical officers and put them under an obligation to the hospital.

The duties of the Matron remained largely domestic: she was responsible for all the female staffs of the establishment to the house committee or the management committee, she made routine inspections of all the domestic offices, wards and departments, was responsible for the nurses' duties and the patients' discipline. She supervised and checked all stores, issued supplies, supervised the cooking, controlled the hiring, firing and payment of the female staff. She was also responsible for linen and bedding and had to teach or supervise the teaching of the probationer nurses; she kept the pass books for the tradesmen, controlled and issued the wines and spirits to the patients (nurses were no longer allowed spiritous or fermented drinks) and kept the patients' valuables. In the larger hospitals, where the staff was in excess of about 100, she had an assistant matron for these housekeeping duties and concentrated her own energies on the patients and nurses and in liaising with the hospital Visitors and the Ladies' Committee. Her hours were usually 9.00 a.m. to 5.00 p.m. but she had to give some lectures to the nurses in the evenings and was expected to make night rounds of the wards. According to the size and status of the hospital, her salary varied between £50 and £250 per year with board and lodging.

The ward sisters of similar hospitals worked from 8.00 a.m. to 10.00 p.m. with about three hours off duty in the evening. They received a salary in the range of £30 to £60 per year, also with board and lodging. Their duties were to receive and carry out the orders of the doctors and to train the probationers in their wards, to make the rounds with the resident doctors or the visiting consultants, to draw up a daily diet sheet, make daily bed returns and reports for the Matron. They were also responsible for receiving the new patients, serving dinners, doing the medicine round and supervising the order of the ward.

The staff nurses were responsible for doing the actual treatment for about 15 patients; they worked a split day from 7.00 a.m. to 9.00 p.m. and had two hours off duty during that time. Their pay was between £20 and £30 per year.

By the 1890s, training lasted from one to three years: St Thomas's Hospital gave a one year training, the London Hospital two years and the training at St Bartholomew's Hospital was increased from two to three years in 1882, mostly in order to increase the numbers of nurses available to the hospital. This innovation was quickly followed by most hospitals who were all short of 'pairs of hands'.

Probationers did minor dressings, applied fomentations and poultices, gave injections, applied leeches, gave enemata to male and female patients but catheterised only the females. They treated pressure areas, helped the patients to manage their surgical appliances, gave bed care to helpless patients, put on bandages, made bandages and dressings, padded splints, attended to operations, did a small amount of sick cookery, kept observations on patients and recorded temperature, pulse and respiration.

By the start of this period, the advance of science was organised and scientific surgery was created. Before the end of the period the bacterial theory of disease was dominant, the social sciences had become established and were slowly gaining influence, not only in therapeutic medicine but also in medical and general attitudes.

Anaesthetics were very quickly adopted in surgery and allowed more extensive and adventurous operations to be made. Hector (1970) claims that the advent of anaesthetics allowed women to attend operations and so extended the area of work of the nurse. Certainly anaesthetics took the brutality away from surgical operations and refined surgery to an art. As operations became more extensive, so the postoperative nursing needs of the patient became more complex and demanding.

No amount of surgical adventurousness could have been successful without the advent of Lister's aseptic principles. It was these as much as any other theory that developed the nurses' technical skills during the period.

As greater specialisation in medicine and surgery developed, so did greater specialisation in nursing grow. Florence Nightingale insisted on her probationers rotating around the different wards in order to gain wider experience, but the ward sisters remained more permanently on their wards and developed an expertise in the fields covered by the consultants who had beds there. The system of bed allocation therefore was greatly influential in the growth of nursing specialisation.

In the pre-bacterial era, medicine concentrated on public health and sanitary measures, but once Koch had described bacteria in the 1870s, the bacterial paradigm quickly spread and enhanced the measures for control of infection: there was a recovery in the importance of medicine (as contrasted with public health and surgery) and a greater emphasis on medical research.

X-rays, discovered in 1895, transformed diagnostic techniques and became an important therapeutic agent. Electrocardiography was demonstrated in 1903 and electroencephalography in 1929. Biochemistry quickly developed and by the latter part of this period was becoming a dominant factor in medicine. The pharmacopoeia available to doctors was transformed. A better understanding of nutrition was possible and in 1906 vitamins were discovered. This paved the way to a large-scale reduction in rickets and a spectacular improvement in diet and therefore general health. Thus the bacterial paradigm was upset within 30 years of its institution.

Chemotherapy reversed the method of treating diseases symptomatically. Treatment by specific drugs for specific diseases became possible. The understanding of bacterial contagion gave rise to the development of inoculations. Smallpox vaccinations had been available through the Poor Law Medical Services since 1840, and in 1841 an Amendment Act made it clear that the acceptance of vaccination did not disenfranchise the recipient. In 1867 the Vaccination Act completed the comprehensive and compulsory service and was reinforced by a further Act in 1871 at the time of the country's worst epidemic which extracted a toll of 44000 deaths. Under the 1867 Act it was obligatory for the parent of every child born in England to take that child to a public vaccinator and to return that child for inspection and ascertainment of the result. 'It is hereby declared that the vaccination of any person in a union or parish . . . shall not be considered to be parochial relief, alms, or charitable allowance to such person or his parent and no such person or his parent shall by reason thereof be deprived of any right or privilege or be subject to any disability or disqualification' (Bruce 1973). Other inoculations against rabies, diphtheria, typhoid fever, cholera and plague were developed.

In 1890 the viruses were discovered; a further development of the understanding of toxins and antitoxins gave rise to the facility of serum diagnosis and, also in the 1890s, came the demonstration of the part played in epidemics by vectors in the transmission of contagion, particularly the responsibility of human carriers and animal carriers of parasitic diseases.

The whole of medicine was transformed: it was appreciated by then that the cause of disease was not the same thing as the disease process; that a wider set of issues had to be considered such as constitutional factors, geographical, economic and social conditions, many of which had previously been ignored. Public health received a boost and there was a resurgence of interest and activity based on a sounder understanding of preventative principles. It also became clearer than ever that public health had to be the responsibility of government; it was outside the scope of private medical practice. Virchow pointed out the importance of statistics in relating medical problems to social conditions, and in 1900 Grotjahn introduced the concept of 'social medicine'. The publication of Farr's vital statistics in 1885 was an important step in this process and gave valuable information to the public health movement.

In 1886 qualification of medical practitioners by examination was instituted and in 1888 the Diploma in Public Health was instituted. There was an increasing involvement by medical men in social organisations, statistical returns, factory health measures and Poor Law administration.

REFERENCES

Bruce, M. (1973), citing the Vaccination Act 1867. p. 87.

Burdett, Sir Henry (1893), *Hospitals and Asylums of the World*, Vol III. London, J. and A. Churchill. pp. 250, 251, 308.

—— (1896), *Cottage Hospitals*. London, The Scientific Press. p. 2.

Sir Henry Burdett (1847–1920) one-time secretary of the Queen's Hospital, Birmingham (now the Birmingham Accident Hospital) is best known for his early and active association with the Royal National Pension Fund for Nurses and his extensive studies and documentation of international institutions for the care of the sick. He also published *The Nursing Mirror*, *The Hospital* and *Burdett's Hospital Annual*.

Hector, Winifred (1970), *Mrs Bedford Fenwick*. London Rcn Research Series.

Lees, Florence (1874), 'One Hundred Years Ago', *Queen's Nursing Journal*, June–November 1974.

Plotkin, S. A. (1961), 'The Crisis at Guy's', *Guy's Hospital Gazette* 1961. Vol. 75.

5

A GROWING NEED FOR
TRAINED NURSES: 1867–1895

If there had been an acceleration of criticism and concern about Poor Law medical relief, workhouse conditions and nursing in the public field during the period between 1848 and 1867, this did not diminish with the 1867 Metropolitan Poor Act. Concern was felt for the state of the infirmaries in the provinces, there was public discontent and disquiet about the quality and activities (or lack of activity) of the officials, anxiety about nursing and a considerable amount of agitation in the press.

The Poor Law Board was stirred to action by repeated requests in Parliament for a further enquiry into the administration of medical relief but there remained a hard core of antipathy to any extra burden on the rates and any increase in central control. The problem of the rates was widely argued: if one union improved its amenities it suffered from an influx of poor from neighbouring unions. The cities, especially Liverpool, felt the burden as migrants flooded in. The Acts of Settlement were gradually being relaxed and the vast thronging of people into the cities was in any case making them unworkable. Liverpool, as a port, suffered from a constant tide of migrants. Irish immigrants flowed through the city in search of work in England: English emigrants flowed through the city on their way out to the colonies. All were poor and many became ill during their stay in the city. The burden was immense. The cry was for a common fund to share the problem.

In the years after 1867 there was a further amalgamation of unions into districts. These Sick Asylum Districts, particularly in the metropolis, were an innovation made expedient in the search for a rationalisation of the economics of medical relief. Each district had a central sick asylum which would help to economise in capital expenditure. In 1867 the President of the PLB, the Earl of Devon, had accepted that the workhouses were then little more than infirmaries or state hospitals. In the dawning of appreciation that the infirmaries were not suitable for their recently recognised functions it was seen that new buildings were necessary. A central hospital would clearly be more economical of capital, maintenance and staffing resources. In the unions which had not been included in the new district organisation, new infirmaries would be built. The larger districts, it was anticipated, would alleviate problems stemming from the Acts of Settlement as the single, central sick asylum would have a wider catchment area and fewer sick poor would have to be removed to their settlement parishes.

In an effort to raise and standardise conditions the PLB circulated a letter, dated 13 June 1868, addressed to the Boards of Guardians and setting out specifications for ward fittings, etc. They stipulated that sick wards should be more carefully furnished than ordinary wards. The list of fittings (see Appendix I) may be compared with the description of ward fittings given by Florence Lees (1874) for the London Voluntary Hospitals in 1874. It should be remembered that the PLB was setting a standard for all Poor Law infirmaries throughout the country but that the hospitals, visited and reported upon by Miss Lees, represented the best of all the Voluntary Hospitals. A comparison between the specifications by the PLB and the reported actuality of the Voluntary Hospitals will show that the former were at least as good as the latter and were often of a higher standard. The number of 'arm and other chairs' recommended for the infirmaries exceeded, on the whole, the numbers of chairs reported for the Voluntary Hospitals, there was no mention of bench cushions by Miss Lees. Some of the basins in the Voluntary Hospitals (e.g. the Royal Free Hospital) were reputed to have been pottery but many were said to have been made of tin; wash hand basins and towels were deficient in the hospitals and not all had bedside lockers.

As far as the Poor Law infirmaries are concerned, it should be remembered that the specifications marked a minimum standard: there was no regulation to prevent higher standards. Indeed by the following year it seems that the new generation of Guardians had outdone themselves in their reformatory zeal (at least in some areas if not all) and the PLB felt itself obliged to write in its 1869 *Annual Report* 'The extreme parsimony displayed by boards of guardians of the older school has in some of the larger unions given way to a desire to conduct all the duties devolving upon the guardians upon a somewhat grand and liberal scale. The Guardians of a Lancashire union for instance, who have built one of the best infirmaries in the Kingdom and conduct it with a numerous staff of trained sisters a few years ago, connected the workhouse with the main offices, distant about three miles by a telegraph line, and lately they were found to be erecting a greenhouse to supply the infirmary with flowers.

'In many cases the Poor Law Board are now compelled to intervene in order to check the outlay which the guardians would be willing to incur on the more ornamental parts of the various structures which they propose to erect.'

But it would be unwise to generalise too much from these extracts as in 1867 questions were asked in the House of Commons about adverse reports of infirmaries at Clifton and Bedminster and the appointment of a notorious character, Mr Catch, to the post of Master of the Lambeth workhouse. The contrasts serve only to show that there was a wide range of standards in the country and that the PLB was still very nervous of too generous expenditure by some unions. There is also some evidence that the PLB sought to highlight the better aspects of the Poor Law in its annual report: this is not an unusual tactic, nor need it be reprehensible. By demonstrating (even if only to reprove) the more ambitious or imaginative practices of some unions, it was possible to show that conditions were not always as bad as liberal critics made out and, on the other hand, to show to the conservative critics that the Board was exercising control and moderation. In their Report of the following year (1869) the PLB commented that the expenditure on salaries and rations of officers had risen and explained that a large portion of this was due to the appointment of paid nurses, 'a great improvement in poor law administration'.

There was considerable criticism not only of the administration of the Poor Law but increasingly of the policies, financing and philosophy of the law. In 1869 during the May debate in the House of Commons (Parl. Debates 1869) a member told the House that there should be a central fund to finance the Poor Law; it was unrealistic, he argued, to expect local authorities to finance education (the Poor Law authorities were responsible for educating the children of the workhouses), medical relief, provision for old people and to take a long term view of the prevention of ill-health. He felt that 32% of the poor patients were suffering from preventable maladies and he complained that medical relief was the most neglected section of the Poor Law. At the same time he applauded the start of a recently introduced dispensary system where the poor could attend casually for outpatient care.

Many members felt that to spend more on the Poor Law would only lead to an increase in pauperism and undermine the independence of the poor. Sir Michael Hicks Beach was of the opinion that there was a danger of the demands leading to a social revolution: the workhouses had become hospitals for all the sick poor in the country and they were so overcrowded that there was no longer room for the able-bodied poor who consequently had to be given outdoor relief. He did not complain about giving the poor medical care in the workhouses but felt that conditions should not be too comfortable, even for them. There was a repeated call for proper classification and separate accommodation: the principle had been accepted for the metropolis and it should be accepted for the provinces.

Another member wondered if the 1834 principles were still acceptable under the current conditions: poverty could not be abolished simply by making relief difficult to obtain with no distinction between the idle and the deserving poor. According to Dr Southwood Smith of the London Fever Hospital, 'a large proportion of the subjects of fever' were agricultural labourers and 'provincial mechanics' who had been driven onto the roads to look for work. They had succumbed to illness because of sleeping out, lack of clothing and hunger.

The Secretary of the PLB, Mr Goschen, in reply, explained that since 1864 there had been a stirring of the public conscience and a resultant demand for better care of the sick poor. The increased expenditure was not because there were more paupers but because the public had demanded that more should be spent on the sick in the workhouses; improvements had been demanded and a higher standard of treatment was being established. The country had to decide what it wanted: better treatment for the poor and higher rates, or lower rates and a lower standard of care for the poor. As for giving a pension to the aged poor at the expense of the State, he felt that this was Communism.

Public discussion was in fact focusing around a central fund for poor relief, gratuitous medical care for specific sections of the population (without penalty) and pensions for the old, either non-contributory from the State, or on an insurance basis via the friendly and insurance societies who were already providing a service to the poor for some illnesses and funeral grants. In 1869 the PLB had proposals for experimenting with a grant to Birmingham, Leeds and Liverpool for sick relief. The Metropolitan Poor Act had provided a Common

Poor Fund which was able to help with the agglomeration of poor into the more generous London unions. Local administration was poor on the whole and the system of rates collection was faulty. There was a tendency to economise on the rates by paying low salaries to local officials. This rather naturally gave rise to a poorer calibre of official, some of whom were clearly incompetent.

The reports made to the PLB by Dr Smith (House of Commons Sessional Papers 1867) and the Board's Inspectors on the provincial workhouses gave clear evidence of neglect by officers and lack of supervision by the Guardians. There was a shortage of accommodation and serious overcrowding. This problem of medical relief was becoming embarrassing; 70% of all pauperism was caused by the need of the poor to obtain medical care. The poor could not receive medical care without being pauperised. If one member of the family was pauperised the whole family was also involved. If the family sought poor relief (for whatever reason) it had first to sell up its home since it was a requirement that the family should be without resources before relief could be granted and even a dresser or a chair could be classified as a 'resource'. If the family were homeless its momentary need for medical relief became a permanent need for poor relief and the total problem escalated unmercifully.

The philosophy of the 1834 Act was wholly against outdoor relief. Many unions took a less rigid line and interpreted 'resources' more liberally; many unions did not require the whole family to be pauperised for the needs of one member and were liberal with outdoor and medical relief without requiring the family to be separated. Nevertheless to many people it appeared that medical relief should be available separately from the rest of the Poor Law. If this were to be so then how better to finance it than from a central State fund? This would remove the burden from the rates, lighten the burden on the more hospitable unions, provide for central control and therefore a more universal standard; to many people it was also becoming clear that infirmaries were developing into complex organisations with increasingly large budgets and which needed more expert management than the unions and Boards of Guardians could provide. Expert professional management was required together with a more technically qualified staff than the existing Steward or Master and staff could provide.

Although the country was not yet ready for these developments the PLB felt obliged to acknowledge the movement of opinion in its

Annual Report of 1869 and discussed the extension of gratuitous medical relief beyond the pauper class. It was characteristically ambivalent in its conclusions but admitted that 'the economic and social advantages could over balance the disadvantages'.

As far as prevention of ill health was concerned, the PL Medical Officers were not empowered to undertake prophylactic measures. Many of the poorer patients in fact were kept at home and there was a growing realisation that the lack of adequate nursing there could be as uneconomical as lack of adequate nursing in the infirmaries. Fulham Union reported that they sent out nurses from their infirmary to look after cases at home if it was felt that by so doing they might prevent a deterioration in the patient and a consequential admission to their infirmary. Similarly the Holborn Union reported that fewer cases might be admitted to their infirmary if social conditions were better and if efficient nursing were available at home. The Stepney Union had actually gone so far as to employ nurses to do home nursing.

At the time of the 1867 Act and until 1871, Public Health was largely outside the control of the PLB and there was a lack of co-ordination in such areas as infectious diseases. In 1871 the Poor Law Board was disbanded and the Local Government Board set up, taking under its control both the Poor Law administration and the Public Health organisation: these were run parallel to each other under different medical officers. After this event the Poor Law was very much overshadowed by Public Health and the Annual Report of the new LGB gave scant information on the former whilst the Annual Report of the Public Health section was elevated to the status of a Parliamentary Paper.

Epidemics of relapsing fever and smallpox hastened the development of the infectious diseases hospitals in the metropolis. During the 1870–1 epidemic of smallpox, the worst the country had ever known, several temporary smallpox hospitals were opened to cope with the quantities of patients but there was an acute shortage of nurses to attend to them. Such was the shortage that nurses from religious orders were asked to help out. The dearth of nurses was exacerbated by the small wage offered them by the Poor Law authorities and the Metropolitan Asylums Board felt bound to increase this. Mothers of afflicted children were asked to enter the hospitals to nurse their children but themselves fell prey to the infection. This epidemic was of particular interest statistically because, for the first time, the mortality rate for small children was lower than that of adults and older children, showing the benefits of the Public Health campaign for smallpox vaccination of children and new-born infants. Of all cases admitted to the MAB hospitals only 6% were children under five years and about 16% of the fatalities were of this group. These figures can be compared with those of the latter half of the 18th century where 80%–90% of all deaths were children under five years (Ayers 1971).

In the MAB hospitals the Medical Superintendent was confirmed as having overall responsibility. The House Steward was responsible for all administrative matters and male staff and the Matron for all nursing staff. The newly appointed management committees assumed personal responsibility for their hospitals and the Medical Superintendent, Steward and Matron governed the hospital on a day to day basis as a triumvirate. It soon became necessary to have resident medical officers. Whilst previously there had been a dichotomy of some sort between the workhouse medical officer and the District medical officer (although some doctors held joint appointments) this dichotomy had by now become a complete divorce. Where paupers were admitted to the MAB hospitals there was no cross-charge made to the unions for their maintenance.

By the 1880s the MAB smallpox hospitals were taking in non-pauper cases for the local authorities and increasingly the infectious diseases hospitals were accepting patients with only a certificate from their medical practitioners. Thus the situation slowly developed where admission to the MAB hospitals was on the grounds of 'need of treatment' rather than on the traditional grounds of 'lack of means'.

By the early 1880s there was a demand for a complete removal of all pauperisation for the MAB patient and this was accomplished by the 1891 Public Health (London) Act.

The freeing of the MAB hospitals from pauper connotations was advanced by the reduction of the rate of mortality for the infectious diseases, specifically smallpox. The long established fear of admission to any hospital and the association of hospitals with an almost certain death slowly gave way. The success of the hospitals was recognised and people began to understand that hospitalisation was necessary for the successful treatment of their fevers. More people were willing to enter hospitals and patients of the more privileged classes accepted admission.

Whilst the special hospitals developed under the MAB, the Poor Law infirmaries remained under the aegis of the PLB and later the Local Government Board. Here too there was progress but probably not as remarkable as that of the fever hospitals. The prestige gained by the MAB hospitals was not reflected to the PL infirmaries. General diseases did not claim the active attention of the public or the Government as did epidemics of smallpox. At that period the infectious diseases were the killer diseases and gained easy attention. Then too, the fever hospitals were organised throughout the metropolis by a single administration and policy. The general infirmaries were still under the authority of several administrations and different unions and lacked co-ordination. In addition to this they continued to suffer from the disadvantage of their close association with the Poor Law. It was still the paupers and the aged who formed the bulk of their population. The infirmaries were bound to accept any sick poor, whatever the diagnosis and however poor the prognosis; whereas the voluntary hospitals could pick and choose their cases and could discharge their patients before a complete recovery, the infirmaries could not be selective and could not make early discharges except in the few instances where the social conditions of their patients' homes were appropriate. Their wards were therefore filled with the chronic sick, the old or senile and the dying.

The new infirmaries built after the 1867 Act sought to employ paid nurses. But the supply of trained nurses was inadequate and the reports of the Local Government Board repeatedly stressed this fact. The LGB published the figures for nurses in 1860 and 1870 and during all this period there was an increase of only 108 throughout the country. In 1860 there had been 246 and in 1870 there were 354. (Their salary bill had risen from £4520 to £7280.) Taken in terms of a percentage increase however, this represents an improvement of something like 54% in staff. Dr Smith's report on the provincial infirmaries in 1867 indicated that there was a general feeling that paid nurses should be employed in the establishments where there were over 100 inmates. In the smaller workhouses it was felt that the Matron should be able to care for the sick or at least supervise their care by the pauper nurses. Most of the inmates were elderly and needed little actual nursing it was believed, and the pauper nurses were probably as adequate as the paid nurses. However, Dr Smith thought that even in these small workhouses there was usually someone who was sick or lying-in and therefore there should be a trained nurse.

He also advocated the promotion of suitable pauper nurses after some retraining as this would boost their self-respect and give them independence. These 'promoted paupers' could act as assistants to the trained nurses. He reported the use of male nurses for male patients but disagreed with the practice as he felt that men did not have the quality for nursing as did women. He urged that nurses should have their duties restricted to the care of the sick and kindred responsibilities such as looking after the linen and medical equipment. He felt there might be difficulties between the senior nurse and Matron if their areas of responsibility were not clearly understood. Either the nurse should have certain wards allocated to her and be subjected to the ultimate responsibility of the Matron or the nurse should be entirely responsible as a Superintendent Nurse.

So far only Liverpool and Chorlton had appointed Superintendent Nurses in place of Matrons and he felt that there had been insufficient time to prove the system. In the large workhouses several nurses were employed under Superintendent Nurses and here Dr Smith felt the system worked well and efficiently.

Dr Smith also discussed the organisation and displacement of the wards. He had observed the way in which sick patients and sick wards were scattered about the workhouse. In some cases, where there were separate buildings or wings for men and women, there was a considerable walk outdoors to get from one ward to another. He argued that this scatter was inconvenient and wasteful of the nurses' time. It would be more convenient, he felt, if the wards were brought together. It would also be a more economical use of a nurse who, he thought, should be able to care for 30 patients.

He had no firm recommendations however for any administrative lines of communication. It was generally assumed that the nurse of the workhouse would be responsible to the Matron for administration and to the medical officer for treatment of the patient. The Board of Guardians was responsible for the appointment of the paid nurse, sometimes with the help and advice of the medical officer, and sometimes without.

There was always a problem of judging the ability and efficiency of the nurse. The so-called trained nurse might have received her training from any hospital which could be a perfectly adequate centre for training nurses or a thoroughly inadequate one. Many of the trained nurses were trained by experience alone and at all times it was difficult to verify a nurse's protestations of training. It was not unknown for a doctor to issue a nurse with a certificate of training on his own authority.

In 1870 the new infirmary at Highate was taken over by the Central London Sick Asylum District and staffed by nurses trained at St Thomas's Hospital following the pattern of the successful experiment at Liverpool. The new Matron there established a plan to affiliate a training school for nurses with the Nightingale School but unfortunately died before the plans could be brought to fruition. Louisa Twining wrote that the nursing at Highgate reached 'as high a state of excellence as we need ever look for or expect in similar institutions'. Later the nursing at the Hampstead Infirmary was taken over by the British Nursing Association whose nurses were trained at the Royal Free Hospital.

After 1869 more night nurses were appointed to the Metropolitan infirmaries. The authorities, however, had considerable difficulties in recruiting enough trained nurses. Few Poor Law institutions were authorised to run their own training schools and the Voluntary Hospitals were not producing enough trained nurses to satisfy the growing demand. Furthermore, the conditions of work within the infirmaries and the nurses' subordination to the Matron did not attract the Voluntary Hospital nurses who were used to working in establishments with fewer bureaucratic trappings, with better nursing equipment and under the authority of other trained nurses.

Under Section 29 of the Metropolitan Poor Law Act 1867, certain asylums, which had to be specified by the LGB, could be used for training nurses. This was a facility which Florence Nightingale had managed to persude Hardy to add to his Bill. In May 1873 regulations were issued by the LGB authorising the managers of the Central London Sick Asylum District to receive single women or widows between 25 and 35 years of age to be termed 'Probationary Nurse'. The persons so received had to undertake, except in the case of ill-health or special circumstances, to remain as probationers for a period of one year and were to be employed under the control of the Medical Officer and the Matron as assistant nurses. The same regulation was also issued to Poplar and Stepney. In 1875 the LGB hoped that all new infirmaries, as they were opened, would adopt this procedure of 'training and supplying its own nurses'. In the previous year, 1874, the LGB had authorised the reduction of the lower age limit to 18 in order to increase the number of candidates.

Over the next few years conditions for nurses in the infirmaries slowly improved, particularly in the metropolis. Better living accommodation was provided for them away from the wards and the new buildings had purpose-built accommodation for them. More night nurses were appointed and there was a small upward trend in their salaries: in 1860 the wage for nurses under the Poor Law had been about £8 to £10 per year, but by 1870 it was between £20 and £30 per year. A ward sister received in the region of £50 and a Matron about £100.

Facilities for training nurses were not available to the provincial infirmaries and many regretted this. In 1869 the senior officials of all the Warwickshire unions met together and sent a resolution to the PLB 'to take steps for securing the Boards of Guardians the power to train nurses, or to contribute to some approved institution for the training of efficient nurses, with the power to employ nurses from any such institutions for nursing the sick poor'. In noting this resolution, *The Lancet* commented on the awakening of a sense of duty in the public and Guardians. And in 1873 William Rathbone made an offer to Manchester to have trained at his own expense a Lady Superintendent and six or eight nurses for the Manchester Workhouse Infirmary.

During the years 1871 to 1913 it is possible to trace the growth of nursing posts through the country in tables published by the LGB in its Annual Reports (see Appendix 2). These tables were designed to show the numbers of officers who had left their posts for various reasons but the total number of officers under each title was given each year. It is interesting to note that none of the dispensaries set up by the MAB and the Poor Law authorities employed nurses. Medical officers, dispensers and clerks were available at each dispensary but it apparently never occurred to anyone to use a nurse.

By 1878 there was a notable increase in the numbers of nurses through the country but the medical officers were not yet satisfied with their own lot and wrote to the LGB asking that:

Medical relief should be under central control rather than under the local authorities.

Payment to medical officers should reflect the amount of time spent on their duties.

The supply and dispensing of medicines should not have to be made by the medical officers.

Medical relief should be distinct from the workhouses.

Medical officers should be free to prescribe 'medical comforts', without the need for authorisation of the Relieving Officer.

Paid nurses should be available to treat the poor at home.

In its reply to the doctors, the LGB infuriated them by quoting the finding of the 1866 Select Committee Report which had concluded that the administration of the Poor Law did not need substantial change. The Board also replied that there was nothing to stop the Guardians from supplying the paid nurses for domiciliary work except the shortage of nurses.

By 1879 there was a trend towards the establishment of Infirmaries under distinct management from that of the workhouses. Leeds and Holborn were the initiators of this. But it was also becoming clear that the training of nurses in the new Infirmaries would not supply the ever-increasing demand and the Association for Promoting Trained Nursing in Workhouse Infirmaries and Sick Asylums was formed. HRH Princess Mary Duchess of Teck accepted the Presidency, the Secretary was Louisa Twining. Although the President of the LGB felt able to say that he had succeeded in abolishing pauper help almost entirely in the new Infirmaries this was not strictly true: the pauper nurses had simply been regraded in many cases and were given different titles and they were still functioning in the provinces. Even in 1881 the LGB had to admit that 'it is now our general practice to require that persons appointed to the office of nurse should have received previous training in some public institution. Considerable difficulty however is experienced in obtaining nurses for Poor Law establishments, notwithstanding that the salaries and emoluments offered are by no means inadequate'.

By 1885 the Association for Promoting Trained Nursing in Workhouses was successfully training nurses on its own initiative. The Association (known also as the Workhouse Nursing Association) paid for the nurses' training and uniform and afterwards 'placed' them in workhouses. They realised however that relatively little could be achieved without the leadership and support of a good Matron. They urged the LGB to ensure that these posts should be given to 'educated and refined women' who had received some acceptable training. They deplored the standard of women usually appointed by the Guardians. The LGB acknowledged the approaches of the Association: 'the importance of placing the nursing staff in these institutions under the care of trained and skilled matrons has been urged by us on the managers, and appointments in conformity with these suggestions have recently been made'.

In 1892 the LGB in a fit of cheerful optimism, reported that 'the character of the arrangements for the nursing of the sick poor in workhouses continues to improve generally throughout the country, both as regards the number of nurses employed and their qualifications for the office'. This improvement was particularly noticeable in the metropolis and the larger cities.

In 1892 the Board issued a General Order to all Boards of Guardians authorising the appointment of district nurses and prescribing regulations for these appointments. In their letter to the Guardians, which was circulated with the General Order, the LGB wrote that it was felt to be generally better to nurse the sick in infirmaries but where circumstances were such that the sick had to be nursed at home, a nurse could be provided. She should have suitable qualifications, be an officer under the control of the Guardians and appointed by them. The nurses were to be styled District Nurses and their conditions of appointment were similar to those of the infirmary nurse.

In stipulating a 'suitable training' the Board defined it as a minimum of one year's training at a training school for nurses, if possible with previous home nursing experience. A good moral character was necessary and 'special personal qualifications'.

Fairly precise instructions were given about the nurse's duties which should be prescribed by the Guardians: punctuality of attendance, obedience to the doctor's orders, maintenance of records on a prescribed form. The nurse was not to be allowed to undertake midwifery cases. The Guardians were also instructed to ensure the doctor's understanding of the nurse's duties. Types of work were to be determined by the Guardians: night duty should be exceptional; the nurse was to be especially responsible for the personal cleanliness of the patient, the patient's room and furniture. She should not bath the patient without prior medical orders; she was to lay out the dead, produce records for the Guardians at every meeting and for the medical officer as required.

The Guardians were also advised to protect the nurse from infection and from spreading infection, she was not to be permitted to receive gifts nor to dispense them; she should report patients who needed relief to the Relieving Officer who could order her to attend to cases if he thought it necessary. The Medical Officer could also order her to attend cases, give her written instructions for treatments and the prevention of the spread of infection. The nurses had to attend meetings of the Boards of Guardians if so required and to perform such other duties in relation to her offices as the Guardians might direct. She was to be provided by the Guardians with a uniform, bag and 'nursing kit'.

Whilst many unions did in fact employ their own district nurses, particularly in London, others preferred to use the nurses supplied by the several Nursing Associations and the Queen's Institute which had been set up in 1889 by the Queen's Jubilee Fund.

The Queen's Nurses, as they became known, received a six months' training and those nurses who worked in the rural areas also received a three months' maternity training. In later years the various institutes affiliated and expanded into Scotland. There were therefore a variety of organisations supplying district nursing facilities.

REFERENCES

Ayers, Gwendoline M. (1971), *England's First State Hospitals, 1867–1930*. London, Wellcome Institute of the History of Medicine. p. 54.

House of Commons Sessional Papers, 1867, Vol. LX, 325 f. *Report of Dr Edward Smith on 48 Provincial Workhouses*.

The Lancet 1869, Vol. i, 134, cited by Hodgkinson, Ruth (1967).

Lees, Florence (1874), 'One Hundred Years Ago', *Queen's Nursing Journal*, June–November 1974.

Parliamentary Debates 1869, Vol. 196, 471.

6
THE NURSES AND THEIR MASTERS: 1895–1902

The years 1894 to 1896 saw a marked change in the attitude of the Local Government Board towards the administration of poor relief. In 1894 Booth had shown that at least a third of those coming to the age of 70 had to accept poor relief. Many of these folk lived in dread of the workhouse unless they had children to support them once old age had made them give up work. Booth was able to demonstrate the relationship of old age to poverty and provoked public concern about the treatment of old people, particularly in the Poor Law institutions.

In 1896 the President of the Local Government Board suggested that 'worthy poor' old people should be given outdoor relief in order that they might be helped to keep up their homes and avoid the necessity of entering the workhouse. He also called for improvements in their conditions within the workhouses and asked for greater freedom for the inmates.

The previous year, 1895, the *Royal Commission on the Aged Poor* had advised special wards in the workhouses for the aged and in that same year the LGB sent out a Circular Letter to all Boards of Guardians setting out points connected with workhouse administration. The Board accepted that the character of the inmates and the type of relief given had both altered considerably since 1834 and that, as a result, workhouses were being used predominantly for the sick and the aged.

The letter set out the duties and responsibilities of the medical officer, emphasised the need to use bed cards for all patients on which would be recorded the history and treatment of each case and on which the medical officer should write all his prescriptions. The card should be consulted by the nurses and should be preserved for subsequent reference if required.

The letter continued: 'The office of nurse is one of very serious responsibility and labour and requires to be filled by a person of experience in the treatment of the sick, of great respectability of character and of diligent and decorous habits. Such persons cannot discharge the duties of the office singly, but must have the assistance of others of both sexes; and there is scarcely less need of the same qualities in the persons who are to be the assistants than of those required for the chief officer. Hence it is necessary that the nurses should be adequately remunerated and that they should be appointed after a strict investigation of their qualifications for the office.' The letter continued by emphasising the responsibility on the part of the 'paid assistants; it deprecated the practice of using pauper inmates as 'assistant nurses' and urged the Guardians 'as far as possible [to] discontinue the practice of appointing pauper inmates of the workhouse to act as assistant nurses in the infirmary on sick wards'.

In discussing this letter, the 25th *Annual Report* of 1895–6 acknowledged the earlier difficulties experienced by the Guardians in finding nurses, but insisted that 'whatever may have been the case in the past, in view of the general advance that has taken place in recent years in the provision for training nurses no such difficulty should now arise'. The LGB drew to the notice of the Guardians the letter of April 1892 from Dr Downes, their Medical Inspector, referring to the general question of nursing arrangements in workhouses. The Guardians, said the Board, 'should be satisfied that the nursing staff by day and by night is in numbers fully equal to the proper nursing of the sick', but gave no further guidance. Thus, those Guardians who had previously been satisfied with their staffing arrangements would presumably feel that they were adequately covered. Once again the Board sat on the fence with regard to the use of pauper nurses: 'The Board are not prepared to lay it down as a rule that in no cases should pauper inmates act as attendants in such wards', but on the other hand, 'their services should only be used with the approval of the medical officer.'

The policy of *The Lancet* in the previous years (and mirrored by a majority of doctors) had been to resist the emphasis placed by the reformers on 'educated women' trained with a 'scientific education' (Sub-Committee of Reference 1875). In an editorial, *The Lancet* (20 December 1879) had said that nurses should be properly trained women of the lower class, and Stocks (1960) in her discussion of the problems wrote 'But *The Lancet* had always been hostile critics of the Nightingale thesis, inspired doubtless by the selfconscious reluctance of substandard members of the medical profession to collaborate with social and intellectual equals.' Put another way, it was the more forward-looking element of the doctors who encouraged, or who did not oppose, the progress of nursing and further training, or more careful selection of nurses. In fact, it is an interesting *a priori* observation that reformers of the higher social classes were more concerned to advance nursing as a profession than were those of the intermediate social classes. The Board's neglect to insist, at this stage, on the abolition of pauper nurses and their leaving the matter in the hands of the Guardians (who were predominantly tradesmen) and the doctors must be regarded as a retrograde step.

The 25th *Annual Report* continued by reiterating that infirmaries which were part of workhouse institutions must remain subject to the authority of the Master and Matron: 'It seems to the Board important that this should be understood as their experience shows that the improvement that is taking place in the character of workhouse nursing from the employment of trained nurses, occasionally leads to objections being raised to the legitimate exercise of the authority of the Master and Matron in the arrangements connected with the sick wards. The Board considers that so long as these establishments are constituted as at present, the nurses should be responsible to the medical officer for the treatment of the patients, but should clearly understand that in other matters they must defer to the authority of the Master and the Matron.'

The Board advised those unions where 'the present nursing arrangements have not been brought to the standard of modern requirements' to give this matter 'their most careful consideration'. It is quite clear that many unions had developed their 'nursing arrangements' well but there were still many unions where the bulk of the nursing was done by unqualified or pauper nurses. In 1894 the *British Medical Journal* had reported 'cruel and shocking defects in the treatment of the sick poor', and there were still large numbers of infirmaries or workhouses where no night nurses were employed. The situation still obtained where defects and mismanagement were not noticed or else not reported by the inspectors who were insufficiently qualified for the work, were over-worked and often misled by the Guardians. The two medical inspectors could not hope to monitor all the infirmaries and workhouses adequately. In most areas the nurses (paid, trained or unpaid and untrained) were still under the authority of the Matron who was still not necessarily a nurse.

It will be noticed that the Board still referred to 'nursing arrangements'. They had the same approach to these as they might have had for the Ladies' Visiting Committees or the gardeners: it was purely a local arrangement; local to the sick wards and local to the unions. Whereas they saw the corps of medical officers as a national body (even if they resisted a national system) they never saw the nurses as anything else but local employees. The nurses made no impact on the LGB. If they made any impact on the unions it was only in terms of being a budgetary item or of affecting the through-put of the workhouses and infirmaries. There was therefore no need to consider any organisation for nurses beyond the consideration of having one, two or three grades in post. The concern of the LGB was merely to provide adequate care for the sick poor and to avoid scandals.

The 1895 Circular refers to the Board's letter of 1865 which was itself a re-affirmation of a letter written in 1847. They made no refer-ence to the contemporary nature of medical and surgical treatments, to the swell of scientific medicine, to the development of technical diagnosis and therapy, to the extended pharmacopoeia. They saw no reason to discuss the need for adequate training for nurses, they did not see fit to require any special level of intelligence and there was never any mention of general educational requirements. They did not understand any reason to try to provide a level of nursing suitable to the new level of doctor (nor did the doctors consider this point) and they never considered that the patient had needs beyond those of physical comfort, or how those needs might be detected and alleviated.

Dr Downes' letter of 1892, which the Board enclosed with its circular to the Guardians, had not previously been printed although some fleeting reference had been made to it. In his memorandum, Downes had said that paupers were not suitable for employment on nursing duties and the saving of a paid nurse's salary could be can-celled by the wasteful habits of the pauper nurse. He suggested a paid nurse: patient ratio of from 1 : 15 to 1 : 10 including night nurses and allowing for off-duty for nurses. He encouraged the use of domestic staff who could suitably be recruited from paupers or would-be paupers. He felt that in the larger establishments nurses should be under the control of a trained and experienced Superin-tendent Nurse or head nurse, subject to the direction of the MO in all medical matters and to the Master and Matron in matters of discipline. On the other hand, in institutions that were administered separately, the Matron should be a trained nurse and have over-all control of the nursing staff. He emphasised the need for night nurses and the need for day nurses to be able to rest at night in accommodation away from the ward. He felt that the use of trained nurses could be argued on grounds of economy:

Debit	*Credit*
Salaries	Saving in waste
Uniforms	Efficiency
Rations	Saving in wear of appliances
Quarters	Detection of malingering
	Earlier discharge of patients
	Increased sick accommodation
	Training a supply of probationers

In addition to this balance sheet he felt that 'attention to warmth and ventilation of wards and administration of medicines, stimulants or food, the application of poultices, management of the natural wants of the feeble and paralytic and care for those in pain or dying are all duties which should be confided to none but responsible nurses'. He went on, 'The diminution of suffering consequent on skilled nursing is a gain which cannot be expressed.'

This memorandum formed the basis of all nursing policy until 1913. In 1897 and in 1913 the LGB issued Orders regulating nursing in infirmaries and took as its guiding principles these ideas set down by Dr Downes in 1892.

The Guardians had, in the past, given the reason for not employing suitable nurses as being the difficulty of obtaining them. This excuse the Board dismissed peremptorily, 'whatever may have been the case in the past, in view of the general advance that has taken place in recent years in the provision for training nurses, no such difficulty should now arise'. Abel-Smith has estimated that in 1901 there were 63 500 female nurses and 5700 male nurses in the country. In 1895 there was a total of 5449 nurses working for the LGB, a ratio of nearly 1:14 of all nurses. The Poor Law infirmaries and workhouses in 1913 had approximately double the number of beds and just over half the number of nurses of the voluntary hospitals. The numbers of trained nurses employed in the Poor Law institutions was therefore still very meagre. What was the comparison in employment conditions between the two competing types of health institutions?

The Poor Law nurses were less well paid until the early part of the

20th century. They worked longer hours than did the voluntary hospital nurses. Both had paid holidays but the Poor Law nurses had a contributory superannuation scheme. This was however, not so much of an attraction as might now be assumed. The retirement age of 60 was too old and nurses could not generally continue to work on the wards after their early 50s: their health broke under the duress of the working hours. Poor Law nurses were often therefore compelled to leave nursing before qualifying for their pension. The voluntary hospitals did not, on the whole, have any superannuation schemes until 1887 and these were not transferable from one hospital to another until after that date. The Poor Law institutions were mostly still workhouse buildings erected during the previous sixty years for pauper (but not sick) accommodation and although they were adapted, their standards varied considerably. Where there were new infirmaries these were superior. The voluntary hospital nurses worked in hospitals built over roughly the same period but which had been designed as hospitals. The Poor Law infirmaries were not suitably equipped for serious operations nor for emergency work and these cases were usually transferred to the voluntary hospitals.

The Poor Law infirmaries had basic surgical equipment only. The voluntary hospitals had to supply their consultants with the equipment they desired. It is fairly certain therefore that this would have been more modern, experimental and exciting as well as being more plentiful.

The Poor Law infirmaries were not associated with medical schools nor teaching of any kind and the professioanl stimulus of the workhouse nurses was negligible. The voluntary hospitals were frequently associated with the medical schools, most of them ran their own nurse-training schemes and the professional contacts of the nurses were wide. The status difference between the two types of hospital was also marked: the voluntary hospital nurses were accorded a status by the outside world which still reflected the Nightingale preference for 'Ladies'. Their patients were usually not paupers but came from the more elevated levels (the respectable poor and, increasingly, the middle and upper classes who came as private patients) and the nurses were able to associate with medical students, doctors and consultants.

Added to this there was the reward factor: the voluntary hospital nurses were still regarded as the angels of mercy and the 'Ladies with the Lamps' as had been their predecessors of the Crimean War. The paupers had had little reason to view their early nurses with anything but lingering suspicion and fear. The infirmaries were still associated with the old workhouses even if they were physically separated. The voluntary hospitals with their selected cases were, more and more, looked upon as houses of cure and therefore hope. But the Poor Law institutions could not compete with this (except for the MAB establishments) and people entering them went in devoid of hope, as a last recourse, with the inevitability of death facing them.

It was therefore small wonder that the Poor Law institutions found difficulty in attracting suitable nurses. But the LGB had not analysed this situation and had not recognised the problems. They did not understand, in spite of repeated warnings from the reformers, that suitable nurses, nurses of some sensitivity and 'gentle upbringing' had to have a suitable environment and reasonable conditions in which to function. Failing these, they would usually either give up and leave or resign themselves and degenerate to the level of their environment. Most people are not of the Nightingale stuff and will not continue to fight. Sadly, this is a lesson that has never been learned by succeeding authorities.

Between the years 1894 and 1896 the *British Medical Journal* carried out a survey of some 50 provincial infirmaries and published each survey as it was made. Of the 50 infirmaries, four, at Withington, Blackburn, Reading and Mill Hill (Liverpool), were said to be 'where the nursing and the arrangements are such as are found in general hospitals'. Withington Infirmary, cited as being as good as some of the large voluntary hospitals, was the infirmary for the Chorlton Union on the outskirts of Manchester. It was said to have 700 beds built within several pavilion blocks each with three floors. Each ward had from 30 to 36 beds and one or two separate, single-bedded rooms for special cases. Classification of cases, 'made on the best lines', was between male and female cases, medical, surgical and chest cases (kept in a ward with a 'suitable temperature'). Imbeciles were kept separately, as were the epilepsy cases, and the children were housed in a separate pavilion. Lock cases (venereal diseases) were also separated and the infectious diseases were in a separate block with its own laundry and stores and an outside staircase to enable staff to come and go without the risk of cross infection from the various floors. Diets were cooked in the workhouse kitchen and served in jacketed tins but special diets were prepared in the ward kitchens. The sanitary appliances were most modern with the closets and bathrooms separated from the wards by lobbies; there were no slop sinks so the bedpans had to be emptied into the closets but the urinals were fitted with a system to provide a flowing stream of water to keep them fresh. (Unfortunately at the moment of the survey someone had omitted to flush the system so the urinal was described as being 'not quite fresh'!) The nursing service at Withington was described as having one trained charge nurse to each pavilion with two probationers on each floor and three in the children's wards. There was one night nurse for each pavilion (shortly to be increased to two night nurses) and all ward cleaning was done by the workhouse inmates. The Infirmary (described by the *BMJ* as a hospital) was a training school for PL nurses and had a trained Matron in charge of the hospital nursing. There was a separate nurses' home with a home sister and there was also a resident medical officer.

If Withington Infirmary represented the best of those institutions that were surveyed, Bath Infirmary was distinguished as the worst of the sample. Here there were 'no appliances for sick nursing', cold water was supplied to the bathrooms but every drop of hot water had to be carried from the boiler house across the courtyard. Closets opened directly on to the wards. There was an estimated 60 patients confined to their beds, with one trained nurse and two uncertificated assistants; there was no night nurse and the bed-fast had to rely on pauper help. The mattresses were of the usual chaff or flock and there were no cupboards. The heating was said to be inadequate.

In its analysis the *BMJ* (1896) excluded the four separate Infirmaries leaving a sample of 46 of which 25 employed trained nurses by day and ten employed trained nurses by night. With a total of 4483 beds there were 48 nurses, i.e. 1:93·9 patients by day. There were 24 separate Infirmaries for the sick, 17 of the sample had no fixed baths, 12 had no piped water and 5 had only cold water laid on. Fifteen had no isolation wards. The report said that 'the weakest spot in the working of the Poor Laws is the nursing of the sick paupers and the careful tending of the infirm'. It also showed that there was still a tendency to leave the sick scattered about the workhouses rather than to ward them together as had been suggested by Dr Edward Smith in 1867.

D

The Report suggested that more infirmaries should be used to train probationers and commented on interference by the Workhouse Matron with the nurses. It ascribed the difficulty in recruiting Poor Law nurses to the fact that they were subservient to these Matrons. It recommended an upgrading of the nurse to a level with the school-mistress and said 'When we take into consideration the vast amount of sick nursing that is carried on under the control of the LGB . . . all these establishments represent an amount of practice second to none in any other public body. If this varied nursing were organised as a subsection of the medical department (of the LGB) the material could be utilised for training the nurses to work under the Poor Law, and the nurse, being given the position that is her due, the supply would be in readiness to meet the demand'.

The aged and the infirm were still being left to the other inmates for nursing; there was still evidence of blackmail by the able-bodied paupers of the infirm and the 'offensive' (incontinent) patients were isolated from the other inmates and denied skilled nursing.

Sick quarters were inadequate and had often previously been condemned by the LGB Inspectors. Classification would have to be improved if the 'administration of poor relief is to be brought into harmony with the existing social needs'.

In comparing Smith's report with the *BMJ* report there seemed little improvement except that some progress had been made in concentrating the sick into sick wards. The aged and infirm had been left in the general wards of the workhouses. In 1867 there were few paid nurses and in 1896 there were some trained nurses; in 1867 there were mostly pauper nurses whereas in 1896 there were paid assistants. There were still hardly any night nurses nor night assistants in 1896. The earlier report gave no indication of the nurse: patient ratio but considered 1:30 would be adequate; it did not specify the grade nor quality of nurse. The *BMJ* report gave a ratio of 1:93·9 by day and said the ratio at night was so dreadful as to be unmentionable. Both reports were very preoccupied by ventilation but Smith's report also gave in greater detail the inadequacy of furnishings and furniture. During the 30 years between the two reports, however, there had been a considerable advance in the general standard of living and in society's expectations, so it is reasonable to presume that the *BMJ* commissioners had taken these new values with them when they surveyed the infirmaries and had made their criticisms against those norms. If this were true, it could be said that the workhouse infirmaries were maintaining their normative gap.

The *BMJ* Report and its preceding surveys brought about a modest hue and cry from local and national papers and from the general public who had read them. Questions were asked in the House of Commons (Parl. Debates 1894) about the qualifications of the LGB Inspectors which the *Journal* had questioned: 'The appointment of Inspector should be given to those men and women who have by training and experience the qualities necessary for the work.' How was it that the conditions revealed by the Commissioners had not previously been reported? How could the situation be allowed to continue unreported where there were no trained nurses at night? What was the LGB proposing to do about the shocking defects in the treatment of the sick poor? Mr Shaw Le Fevre the then President of the LGB, said he was proposing to hold an inquiry.

In 1897 the LGB issued a General Circular followed by a General Order to Boards of Guardians prohibiting the use of paupers for any nursing duties; any pauper used as an attendant must have the authority of the medical officer and work under supervision.

The circular also laid down that a Superintendent Nurse should be employed to control any establishment of three or more nurses or assistant nurses. The Superintendent Nurse was to be under the medical direction of the Medical Officer and subject to administrative control from the Master or Matron. In contrast, in the separate Infirmaries, the Matron should be a trained nurse and have overall control of nursing staff.

The circular stipulated that the Superintendent Nurse must have had a three years' training in a training school for nurses but, where there were already three nurses on the staff, one of them could be promoted so long as she fulfilled the training criterion. All persons appointed as nurses or assistant nurses had to be suitably experienced except for those who were appointed as assistant nurses for training; training was to be permitted only where there was a Superintendent Nurse and a resident medical officer. Infirmaries or Schools (who had their own school nurses) administered separately from workhouses, were exempted from this order.

The *BMJ* gave prominence to this Order under the headline, 'At last! The Death Blow to Pauper Nursing'. It acclaimed the Order (an immediate reaction which was somewhat modified later) and took considerable credit to itself, claiming that the Order was a result of its Report. 'This order will do something though not all that is needed, towards improving the position of the nurses in the workhouses and workhouse infirmaries throughout the kingdom.' However, it was not long before the *Journal* began to be bothered about the sentence in the Order: 'Whilst the Board are not prepared to lay it down as a rule that in no case should pauper inmates act as attendants in sick wards, as clearly distinguished from nurses, they consider that their services should only be used with the approval of the medical officer and under the closest supervision at all times of paid officers.'

The *BMJ* wondered if the 'attendants' were to nurse the patients or to act as domestics on the wards and cited the parallel Irish Order, Article 3, as being more specific in using distinguishing phrases such as 'the nurse', 'the other nurse', 'the assistant nurses' and 'the attendants'. This criticism may have been valid as the Board had not previously used the term 'attendant' in its letters and had more consistently used the expression 'assistant' or 'assistant nurse'. On the other hand, the nurses in Poor Law institutions were still used largely for domestic duties in spite of Downes' suggestion that 'scrubbers' should relieve them of heavy domestic chores. Taking into consideration all the previous circulars, letters and reports issued by the LGB however, it is likely that the term 'assistant' was used synonymously with 'attendant' and also, generally speaking, with 'assistant nurse'.

There was evidently still confusion and discord between the trained nurses and the Matrons of the workhouses. The Board commented on the separation of administration in the infirmaries where the Superintendent Nurses held complete authority over the nurses 'with very beneficial results'. In the cases where the building formed part of the workhouse 'the Master and Matron necessarily remain the chief officers of the whole establishment and primarily responsible for its administration and discipline. It seems to the Board important that this should be understood, as their experience shows that the improvement that is taking place in the character of the workhouse nursing from the employment of trained nurses occasionally leads to objections being raised to the legitimate exercise of the authority of the Master and Matron in the arrangements connected with the sick wards'. The trained nurses were rebelling at the authority of the Matron over them. The Matron was not usually a woman of any quality, she had no training and she was of the level that might well end up as an inmate of the workhouse. It would be unfair to suppose that she would always necessarily oppose the goals of the trained nurse but she represented the old order and the trained nurses represented the new. There is ample evidence to show that, judged by their contemporary standards, the Matrons were frequently insensitive, sometimes callous and even brutal. They were not educated, nor were they trained. The nurses were trained and had a status of sorts, some of it reflected from the voluntary hospital nurses: indeed some of them were trained in the voluntary hospitals and were therefore of a higher social class than the Matron. They might therefore have held the Matron in some contempt and she must have seen them as a threat. If the nurses worked well with the doctors, they would have had his backing. Even if this were not the case, the nurses could have had more of a relationship with the patients than did the Matron. The Matron received her authority officially but the nurses won their authority through their personal qualities, their profession and their work. The Matron therefore derived her authority through fear whereas the nurses gained personal authority. It is hardly surprising if the nurses, with all the discipline that was instilled into them, resented their subjection to the Matron. Indeed, it would be surprising if they had not. It is easy to imagine everyday situations where there would be clashes between the nurses and the Matron, between a professional group and a non-professional superior. The doctors had successfully won their struggle against the supremacy of the Master: the nurses were struggling against the supremacy of the Matron.

The point of contention in the Workhouse infirmaries was that the head nurse had control over the nurses only so long as they were on the wards: at all other times, including the allocation of time off (what little there was) and her conduct whilst off duty, the nurse was under the authority of the untrained Matron. In addition, the Matron had control of the domestic arrangements on the ward, the kitchens, the stores and the laundry. There were Matrons who cooperated well with the nurses but there were also those who did not. They were responsible for keeping good order, maintaining the inmates and the workhouse generally on a minimum budget and accounting to their Board of Guardians for their actions. The Guardians were not always of the most philanthropic nature and were often self-seeking, bigoted and petty. These points are well illustrated by the correspondence between the Guardians of the

Strand Union, Dr Joseph Rogers and the PLB during 1866–7. The enquiry (*Mismanagement of the Sick Poor*, 1866) into the conduct of Dr Rogers and the Union provided evidence from one of the nurses of the conduct of the Matron and the chasm that existed between them.

The reports from the LGB Inspectors after the issue of the 1897 Order, showed that there was a general decrease in the numbers of paupers used for nursing duties but a continuing difficulty in finding suitably trained nurses, especially in the rural workhouses. Conditions for nurses continued to improve very slowly and more separate nurses' homes were built (in some cases the homes were so distant that the nurses complained of the need to journey between them and the Infirmaries). The Inspectors also complained of continuing lack of attention to the comfort of the nurses, their general well-being and over-long hours. There was mounting concern at the varying quality of training for nurses, the lack of any common standard that could be expected from a trained nurse and the difficulties experienced by Guardians in selecting them. The Inspectors felt that the Guardians were frequently too ignorant of nursing to be capable of any discrimination at all. Many new Superintendent Nurses were being appointed but the *BMJ*'s fears about attendants were justified because the Inspectors complained of some difficulty in differentiating between the duties of attendants and those of the nurses.

The 28th *Annual Report* of the LGB for the year 1898–9 euphemistically recorded the continuing growth of nursing in the Poor Law institutions and acknowledged the need to improve conditions for nurses in order to compete with the voluntary hospitals. It also optimistically recorded a lack of friction between the trained nurses and superintendents and the Masters and Matrons. Here again there is evidence of wishful thinking as this situation was not confirmed in the 1902 Departmental Committee set up to enquire into the *Nursing of the Sick Poor in Workhouses*.

Before this however, the 1902 Midwives Act had been passed and the Central Midwives Board had been set up as a statutory body charged with the training of midwives, the authorisation of midwifery training schools and the registration of midwives. Whilst the Act was a milestone in nursing history, the implementation of the Act might be said to have had at least as far reaching consequences. In the first place, the Central Midwives Board was composed of members who might be described today as belonging to the 'Establishment' or who had voluntary hospital and upper class values. Their common ground was the determination to make midwifery into a respectable and reputable profession judged by voluntary hospital norms. This way of thinking automatically meant a rejection of all things relating to the Poor Law, including the Poor Law training schools and Poor Law infirmaries. There was a period of grace allowed to hospitals in which to become registered for midwifery training and during which existing midwives could themselves register. The bulk of all midwifery cases was conducted in the Poor Law infirmaries; most of these applied for registration which was critical to them as they needed to be able to train their own staff in order to continue with their midwifery work. However the CMB was inordinately slow in effecting these registrations and both the LGB and the infirmaries became first anxious and then enraged by the apparent prejudice against Poor Law establishments. The *Poor Law Officers' Journal* (29 June, 1906) complained against the CMB 'in refusing practically to recognise Poor Law hospitals as Training Schools in Midwifery'. The President of the LGB was asked about the refusal of the CMB to recognise some of the large PL infirmaries as Training Schools for midwives and in 1907 at the annual conference of Poor Law Officers it was claimed that the Midwives Act had led to numbers of women giving up midwifery. Dr J. M. Rhodes, an eminent PL doctor in the Didsbury and Chorlton Union complained of the attitude of the CMB who had refused to recognise 'first class Poor Law Institutions for midwifery training'. There was not a single Poor Law representative on the CMB. A resolution was vociferously passed at the Conference asking the LGB to take steps to secure the licensing of competent Poor Law Hospitals.

In the following months, Miss Wilson, the Secretary of the CMB, published a letter defending her organisation and giving a list of 15 infirmaries licensed for midwifery training. A response was received in the *Poor Law Officers' Journal*, the following week comparing the 15 infirmaries thus licensed with the total of 600 Poor Law infirmaries and promising that the matter was to be raised shortly with the Privy Council. The controversy was further heightened by the insistence of the CMB on an inspection of every infirmary before it could be licensed. This inspection, by a body which was not responsible to any Government department (which provoked Lord Crewe of the Privy Council to term it an 'irresponsible body') of infirmaries which were already inspected by Government Inspectors, was felt to be totally unacceptable by the Poor Law Authorities and, after he had received a deputation, Lord Crewe had gone on record as saying that such inspections by the CMB could not be agreed by the Privy Council. He also admitted that at the time of passing the Act it had not been foreseen that there would be any such difference of opinion between the LGB and the CMB.

The inference was that if the infirmaries were not registered by the CMB they could not be considered to be competent. Dr Rhodes subsequently complained of a dual standard being applied by the CMB: one standard for the voluntary hospitals and another for the Poor Law institutions. He personally knew of an ex-tenement building that had been licensed quite unsuitably whereas some of the largest Poor Law infirmaries had been kept waiting. The White-chapel Infirmary had been licensed only the previous week after five years' delay. Indeed the infirmaries at Ashton, Rochdale, Bradford and Dewsbury had not yet been licensed and one of the large infirmaries had been told by the CMB to send their pupil midwives for training at a small voluntary hospital. Later in the same year (1907) it was reported in the *Manchester Evening News* that the LGB felt strongly in sympathy with Dr Rhodes' proposal that the Board should itself license Poor Law infirmaries for midwifery training; the article continued, 'the LGB are bound to protect the institutions under their charge'.

It is evident that there was the feeling, amongst the PL officials, that any matter relating to the Poor Law was almost certain automatically to provoke abuse and controversy in spite of their very real efforts and good will. In fact, the CMB had licensed approximately equal numbers of voluntary hospitals and Poor Law infirmaries but there were nearly twice as many Poor Law institutions as there were voluntary hospitals. The controversey continued through 1908 (when a *Departmental Committee* was appointed *to Consider the Working of the Midwives Act*) to 1910 (when the Committee reported) and the CMB, under pressure from the Government, indicated its wish to use appropriate PL midwifery departments for training. The controversy subsided but left deep scars on the LGB and the Poor Law Officers. They were left with a determination that nothing similar should be allowed to occur in the future.

REFERENCES

The British Medical Journal. Withington, 1894, Vol. II, 1380 f. Bath, 1894, Vol. II, p. 26. Analysis 1896, Vol. II, 857 f.

Departmental Committee, Nursing the Sick Poor in Workhouses, 1902. Cd. 1366, Vol. xxxviii.

LGB *Annual Report* 1895.

The Lancet, 20 December 1879.

Mismanagement of the Sick Poor, Parliamentary Papers 1866, Vol. LXI.

Parliamentary Debates 1894, Vol. 24, 358.

Poor Law Officers' Journal, 29 June 1906, 622–3.

Report of the Sub-committee of Reference and Enquiry on District Nursing in London (1875), cited by Stocks, M. (1960), *A Hundred Years of District Nursing.* London, George Allen and Unwin. Ch. 4.

7
NURSING THE SICK POOR: 1902

In 1902 the *Departmental Committee on Nursing the Sick Poor in Work-houses* had reported. The Committee had examined four aspects: the difficulties in obtaining an adequate supply of properly qualified nurses and assistant nurses and how far these difficulties could be alleviated; what requirements, if any, should be made as to the qualifications and training of probationers; what amendment, if any, was desirable in the Regulations as to the qualifications of Superintendent Nurses; and lastly, whether any, and if so what, provisions should be made for defining more strictly the respective duties of the Master and Matron of the workhouse and of the Superintendent Nurse.

It will be remembered that Poor Law training schools for nurses had to be authorised by the LGB and that the necessary qualifications for these training schools were that there should be a resident medical officer and a Superintendent Nurse, who, herself, should have had three years' training in an approved training school. The nurses produced from these approved training schools were the certificated nurses, the élite of the Poor Law nursing service, and were eligible for promotion in the burgeoning nursing hierarchy. They were also acceptable for private nursing and by the Voluntary Hospitals. In 1904-5 at the *Select Committee on the Registration of Nurses*, an eminent nurse, Miss Hughes, was asked if Poor Law Infirmaries would be acceptable as training schools for registered nurses: 'Would you allow Poor Law Infirmaries or would nurses have to be trained in hospitals?'

'I think Poor Law Infirmaries must be considered. They have responsible work and they teach special nursing that is left out altogether in the large general hospitals. There is no time in the large general hospitals for chronics and the convalescent cases, whereas in Poor Law Hospitals they get much less surgical nursing as a rule, but their nurses receive excellent instruction in the medical, chronic and a large bulk of cases.'

'If you had a register, would you allow a certificate of three years' training in Poor Law Infirmaries as well as hospitals to qualify?'

'Certainly.'

Miss Forest, a Matron from Bournemouth gave evidence: 'Have you any knowledge as to nurses in Poor Law Infirmaries?'

'They are very good.'

'Do you know what their training is?'

'No, I believe it to be excellent. I prefer taking nurses from Poor Law Infirmaries – a certain number of them.'

The 1902 Departmental Committee found that there were 1974 Probationers in Poor Law institutions (1049 in the metropolis and 925 in the provinces) recognised by the LGB as training schools for certificated nurses. Between 31 % and 32 % left before the completion of their training. In addition, there were 400 probationers in non-approved training schools which recruited them for a period of one, two or three years' training but could not give a certificate. These nurses were recognised as qualified nurses but were not eligible for promotion. In all therefore, totalling both the certificated and the qualified nurses, a sum of 700–800 'properly qualified nurses' was turned out by the Poor Law authorities each year. It was felt that the same number of recruits were required each year in order to achieve an 'economic balance'. About 55 % of Poor Law nurses left the service after training but an accurate figure was not available as many took the numerous openings available to them in other areas of nursing (district nursing, public health nursing, the Army Nursing Service, the Colonial Nursing Service, emigration to the Colonies, private nursing, school nursing and the general hospitals) but returned to the Poor Law institutions later. It was felt that there was very little difficulty in obtaining enough probationers as the Poor Law training was popular and training in the general hospitals could be expensive. Henry Bonham Carter, a member of the Council of the Workhouse Infirmary Nursing Association, felt that there was the need for a better selection of candidates as a fair proportion had difficulty in passing the written examination. On the other hand, Miss Wilson, the Honorary Treasurer of the same Association and who had been actively connected with it since 1879, felt that there had been a diminishing supply of probationers over the past seven years owing to the growing demand for nurses. (In clarification, she meant that the supply of trained nurses in the Poor Law Infirmaries was short of the demand.) She gave the opinion that this was due to the work of the Association which had succeeded in convincing the workhouse authorities that they needed qualified nurses in their

Infirmaries. Such was the demand by 1902 that the Association could no longer supply sufficient nurses. The Association concentrated its missionary efforts on the small, usually rural, workhouses which were not popular with trained nurses.

Dr Hawkyard, the medical officer of a small workhouse in Hounslet, Yorkshire, said that they could obtain probationers but when the young women found that the training would not lead to a certificate they left. They also experienced great difficulty in obtaining trained nurses for their small Infirmary. He felt that these difficulties would be removed if they could perform operations but their establishment was not even licensed to give anaesthetics. He called the nursing in workhouse infirmaries 'most repulsive work' involving only chronic and 'dirty cases'. He also felt that the nursing certificates given by the Poor Law Infirmaries were without standing as the examining body was not recognised.

Charles Leach, President of the Poor Law Officers Association, felt that nurses should be able to take their training between more than one infirmary in order to obtain better or wider experience.

Miss Gibson, formerly matron of the Brownlow Hill Infirmary (separately administered) and subsequently Matron of the Birmingham Infirmary (also a 'separate' establishment) was one of the most influential members of the Poor Law service and gave her evidence with great authority. She made a considerable impression on the Committee who evidently also felt that her ideas were too 'advanced' to be included in their report. She felt that no Infirmary with fewer than 400 beds ought to train nurses. She said that there was a need for a standard curriculum for all Poor Law nurse training schools, that there should be regulations about the size of the Infirmary and other conditions before they were approved. At the same time she baulked at the idea that nursing could be taught at a university and felt that it was not 'an educational subject'. Asked about the supply of nurses to the smaller infirmaries, if her limitation of training schools were to be implemented, she firmly said that there should be a national Nursing Service, centrally administered, with the nurses employed and trained by the Local Government Board and allocated to the Guardians. She compared her suggestions to the Army Nursing Service in which the nurses had a recognised status, were employed by the Army and drafted to units as they were required.

This opinion was supported by Miss Wates, a representative of the Matrons' Council of Great Britain (including Matrons of all types of hospitals and infirmaries) who said that her Council was firmly of the opinion that there should be a Nursing Department in the LGB with trained nurses in charge of it, inspection by nurses of PL nursing and advice by nurses to the President of the LGB for all nursing matters. She said that there were more than enough applicants for training but not always of the right calibre. These applicants were similar to those who might apply for training to the Voluntary Hospital – daughters of clergymen, doctors, tradesmen. None of her trainees ('Not one of them') stayed after training because of the lack of prospects for promotion.

Miss Marquardt, Matron of the Camberwell Infirmary, said it was easy enough to obtain probationers but not so easy to obtain trained nurses: 'If we do get them they do more harm than good, both in tone and training.'

Another witness said 'In regard to obtaining trained nurses in country workhouses and retaining them I should say that generally speaking it is because the supply of trained nurses is not equal to the demand, and because many partially trained but unqualified nurses with testimonials from doctors and others take appointments at low wages.'

Mr Davy, a Poor Law Inspector, said generally there was a shortage of female labour. Women were migrating into the towns from the country areas and the small workhouses were actually having to employ female labour because of the dearth of able-bodied inmates. He felt that the position of the nurse was exaggerated by the press and various voluntary associations and that this had given the nurses 'an undue sense of their relative importance [so that they] upset the workhouse Masters and Matrons, Boards of Guardians and medical officers'. He said, 'I have known medical officers who were positively jealous of the appointment of a Superintendent Nurse, thinking that it would interfere with their administration in some way or other.'

In an Appendix to the Report there is an extract from *The Times* dated 22 December 1897 sent in by Miss C. S. Wilkie, Lady Superintendent of the Halifax Workhouse Infirmary, together with a paper which she had read to the Central Poor Law Conference in London in February of the same year. Miss Wilkie described in her paper a scheme for a Central Poor Law Nursing Department with a nursing inspectorate, training schools for nurses, central recruitment, standard conditions of examination and service. The examinations were to be controlled by the central department and a minimum age of entry was to be established. Recruits were to be selected locally. She envisaged a four years' training, the first and second years to be served with full board and keep but with no salary. Scholarships however, would have been available via capitation grants to each training school. Practical examinations would have been held locally by the central nursing inspectors and certificates would have been granted at the successful completion of the first two years of training. The third and fourth years, she felt, would be a form of internship for the further development of the nurse. She urged that there was a growing need for a common standard of training; the smaller workhouse infirmary could be grouped with a larger one and probationers would be circulated through different wards during training. She felt that the whole cost of Poor Law nursing should be borne by the central department; she wanted to raise the level of the Poor Law nursing service, improve the status of the nurses and 'raise the whole tone of the profession'. She felt that most Inspectors did not give enough consideration to nursing and she reiterated the difficulties experienced by nurses in workhouse infirmaries.

The Times wrote that 'There is reason to believe that the body [LGB] has not sufficiently realised the difficulty in the way of securing competent nurses for workhouse infirmaries under present conditions, but the question arises whether the Central Poor Law Authority would not now be forced to establish some system of its own for the training of nurses for Poor Law services as it already does for the Army and Navy, and at the same time to reorganise the whole system as regards the status of the nurses when they have been trained.'

The Lancet (11 December 1897) also voiced a similar opinion: 'There is no doubt that the time has now come when the central authority shall take up the matter . . . so as to constitute a separate and more attractive service of its own on the lines as has been recently done in the Army and Navy.'

Louisa Twining, by 1902 an elderly, retired person living in Kent, also sent a letter to the Committee saying that all the matters mentioned in her letter to the President of the PLB in 1866 were still as desirable as when she first mentioned them. One of the points she made was that there should be a far larger number of women inspec-tors who should be trained nurses.

In their report, relating to the first aspect of their terms of refer-ence, the Committee wrote that they had found that probationer nurses were increasingly being used instead of assistant nurses, that the probationers had superseded the pauper nurses abolished in 1897 and were near to superseding the assistant nurses. Assistant nurses with the requisite training were difficult to find and, in any case, cost more to employ; it was felt that the probationer nurses treated the patients with greater sympathy and care than had the earlier grades of nurses. They reported therefore that the probationer nurses were preferable (i.e. better motivated and cheaper) to the 'ordinary paid nurses'. They also felt that probationers were a useful pool of reserve nursing labour in the event of another national emergency such as another epidemic or war. They felt that it would be wise to increase the numbers of probationer nurses and felt that as far as the larger infirmaries were concerned there would be no difficulties in this but that in the smaller infirmaries there could be some problem. They recommended increased facilities for training and an improvement in the image of the Poor Law nursing service. They commented on the lack of definition by the LGB of the work of the assistant nurses and of their necessary experience and qualifica-tions demanded by the 1897 order. They recommended that this grade should be phased out. They discussed the problem of the nurse:patient ratio and did not feel able to give any guidance. Witnesses had variously advised 1:10–11 for sick or bed-ridden patients and 1:15–16 for 'merely' old or infirm. Returns from the West Country showed an overall ratio of 1:15 and from the North West 1:12–13.

The Committee expressed their conclusion that the reasons for the recent shortage of nurses were a drain of 900 nurses to the Army Medical Service (to serve in the Boer War), the recent smallpox epidemic, the lack of appeal by the Poor Law nursing service and the constant turnover of nurses which tended to give the service a bad reputation. In 1901 the total new appointments had been 1387 nurses, of whom 628 were ex-Poor Law nurses returning; it was possible to feel therefore that this criticism was not justified; the total turnover was about 20% but the general hospitals had a similar pattern. 'The nursing profession includes a large number of women of a migrating nature.' They also reported that conditions of service under the Poor Law had not kept up with the 'increase in the social and professional status of Nurses in general'.

This part of the Report recommended increased status for the Poor Law nurses with more paid servants or a better class of paupers to do the domestic work.

In looking at this section of the enquiry and the minutes of the evidence it is interesting to note the early, strong stirrings of professionalisation demonstrated by the Poor Law nurses. Miss Gibson was a powerful figure with well considered ideas. She was in complete control of a large force of nurses, all the female staff and the domestic administration of one of the largest hospitals or infirmaries in the United Kingdom. She showed a strong sensitivity for the responsibilities of the nurses and the needs of her patients. She was also one of the band of people who urged the needs of the aged and chronic sick who 'require both constant and thorough nursing and constant supervision to keep them in a state in which they ought to be kept'. Nursing the chronic sick, she said against current opinion, 'is one of the highest and best proofs of a good nurse'. Although a Poor Law Infirmary, hers was a general hospital in the real sense, much more so than any of the voluntary hospitals: it took in all kinds of cases, including acute surgical, acute medical, terminal, chronic, infirm, paediatric and the specialist cases. The voluntary hospitals did not deserve the description of 'general' hospitals as their patients did not include any of the long-term conditions nor the infectious diseases. Miss Gibson had a long and influential career in the Poor Law and did much for the Poor Law nursing service.

The other infirmary matrons offered a similar pattern of thought in their evidence: they wanted a cohesive nursing service, they wanted nurses to be responsible for nursing, they wanted a nursing inspectorate and they were seeking a standard, accepted and worthwhile training. Their demeanour commanded respect and it was given to them, but they were not able to carry over the respect given to them personally to the commonality of their nurses. They asked for better training, better salaries, better conditions of service, already granted to nurses in the Army Nursing Service. But they found that nursing sick soldiers in time of war was more rewarding in status than nursing the same men in peace time when they were unemployed, disabled and poor. The public awarded their nurses a status and whilst in times of distress this was emotionally seen to be all things that were good and devoted, in times of peace it was reduced in their sentiments and seen in relation to the charge on their rates.

There was also evidence that the doctors were divided on the rising professionalism of the nurse. Some felt a loss of authority, some feared the increasing demands made by nurses for their patients, some were afraid of the growing power of the Superintendents and Infirmary Matrons, some wanted better training and a standard curriculum for the nurses and others wanted improved career prospects for the Poor Law trained nurses.

There was also evidence of a transfer of values from the voluntary hospitals to the Poor Law nurses. Henry Bonham Carter talked about training in character and moral standards in Nightingale terms. Asked about an associated training scheme between two or more Infirmaries, Miss Wilson quoted Nightingale's scheme in which the probationers did one year at St Thomas's and two years, under its supervision, in another hospital or infirmary. There was the boast, inherent in much of the evidence, that many of the large, independent Infirmaries were doing more and more operations and taking in acute general cases, the complaint that the work in the small infirmaries was boring and monotonous because there were no 'interesting cases' but only the chronic and infirm patients. Very few of the certificated nurses went to work in the workhouse infirmaries for this same reason, and Miss Kett reported that those who did frequently complained of professional isolation, 'rusting', insufficient experience and a lack of advancement in their career and professional knowledge. There was a growing demand for the better educated woman for nurse training and a need for her to be 'educated in the niceties of social life'. On several occasions there were complaints about the 'tone' of nurses, probationers or nursing in a general sense. Complaints were made about the requirement of the authorities that so much domestic work should be done by the probationer nurses; there was a frequent demand for more and a better class of paid domestic workers or pauper workers.

Most of the witnesses spoke of the need to establish a regular Poor Law nursing service: no one spoke against it. Miss Wilson, who gave the impression at first of being very nervous but who later displayed wide understanding and thoughtfulness and a real grasp of the Poor Law nursing service, spoke at length of the need for one: 'I may also say that if a Poor Law nursing service could be created it would be the greatest boon possible', and, 'I think that if a servic of Poor Law nurses was created it would attract a slightly different type of woman. . . .

'I had it in my mind that it could be approximated to the Army Nursing Service with certain conditions and certain encouragements which would attract a better class of woman.' She said that the idea had been first mooted around 1896 but the Government had said it would be too expensive.

The Hon Sydney Holland, Chairman of both the London Hospital and the Poplar Hospital (Infirmary) and honorary official of the Tilbury Cottage Hospital, Council member of the Queen's Jubilee Institute of Nurses and a member of the Board of Queen Alexandra's Imperial Army Nursing Service, also made the point that the Poor Law nursing service would have to become competitive as there were so many other, more attractive nursing services which were better paid and afforded the nurse better status. He made the point, not mentioned by other witnesses, that nurses should not be subservient nor subordinate to the medical officers but should be entirely responsible for nursing and answer only to the Board of Guardians. This very much followed the established practice of the voluntary hospitals where the Matron was responsible to the Board of Governors: 'If you will excuse my saying so, doctors do not necessarily know anything about nursing.'

Sydney Holland also called for a Common Poor Law fund for nursing: he suggested that the LGB should provide certain training schools, train nurses centrally at these schools and then 'they should be scattered about to these small infirmaries'. He wanted a Matron-in-Chief to be appointed to inspect nursing and the workplaces of the nurses. He felt that the LGB should be firmer with the Guardians: 'you must nurse your paupers properly' . . . if it needed an Act of Parliament, then get one. A charming, breezy, shrewd character!

One of the eminent Poor Law Medical Officers also called for a Poor Law Nursing Service. Dr Raw of the West Derby Union (Liverpool) who became a considerable spokesman on medical matters in the country, felt that once a Poor Law nurse was trained, there was no further place for her in the Poor Law except in rare instances. He wanted a Central Service which could draft her to the workhouse infirmaries.

But the Committee seemed to be more concerned about the problem of foisting nurses on to the Guardians, with the possibility of the Guardians' refusing a nurse drafted by a Central Service and with the traditional need to leave as much responsibility as possible with local officials. In spite of growing collectivism, the development of large national organisations such as the Trades Unions, industrial corporations, the national press and the railways, there was still a persisting reaction against centralisation, especially in Government matters. The local authorities had to be left to raise and spend their own monies and to be responsible for their own local services. Therefore the Committee made no recommendation on this matter and the opportunity was lost.

It is useless to speculate on what would have happened if the Committee had decided otherwise and had established a national Poor Law Nursing Service, but the imagination cannot help but wonder how different it would have been if they had. The organisation of hospital services through the impending wars of 1914–18 and 1939–45 would have been different, the growth of hospital services between the first and second wars would have been different and there would have been a very different situation in which to build the National Health Service in 1948. How would a national nursing service have affected nursing as a profession? What would have been the effect on voluntary hospitals who were even then going more deeply into financial difficulties? How would it have affected the later municipalisation of the Poor Law Hospitals? And when, in 1948, the two streams of hospitals were joined, what would have been the balance of power between, on the one hand, a fragmented and unco-ordinated group of voluntary hospital nurses and, on the other hand, a cohesive, national nursing service?

Returning to the second aspect of the Committee's remit, they investigated the qualifications and training of probationers.

Miss Wilson complained of a lack of any common standard of training, she felt that there should not be any untrained nurses at all except for the probationers (she wanted the class of assistant nurse to be abolished); she thought that there should be a stipulation of a minimum number of beds before an infirmary was approved as a training school (not less than 250 beds) and that a nurse : patient ratio should be established for training schools. She did not mention, in this context, any ratio which she might have had in mind but elsewhere in her evidence she had discussed a ratio of 1 : 30 as being reasonable for nurses. She also stipulated that the final examination might be conducted by an outside body rather than by the authorities of the training school. She did not feel that the existing regulation which required a resident medical officer to be in post before an infirmary could be approved was necessary; apart from her concern that there should be enough beds to provide experience for the probationer, she felt the quality of the Superintendent Nurse to be of paramount importance.

Miss Kett, the Secretary of the Northern Workhouse Nursing Association, described how that Association recruited girls, supported them during their training and then 'placed' them in infirmaries. The Guardians applied to the Association for nurses. The Association had been formed in 1891 by William Rathbone to find, train and supply nurses for the smaller workhouse infirmaries. The Association used, for training purposes, the large Infirmaries such as Brownlow Hill, West Derby, Paisley, Birmingham, Leeds, Sheffield and Bolton. The Association made the range of 24–35 years their age limits for would-be nurses. They had more applications than they could afford to train and they had more requests for nurses than they could meet. There were considerable complaints from 'their nurses' about the long hours of work, lack of domestic help, poor accommodation and bad employment policy on the part of the Guardians. Miss Kett did not agree that nurses should be on duty day and night; she firmly believed that nurses should have off-duty spells and three weeks' annual holiday and one month for the Superintendent. She agreed with Miss Wilson that the resident Medical Officer was not an important factor for the approval of the training school but she recommended a proper course of lectures and both theoretical and practical training. She felt a three year training to be necessary for a Superintendent Nurse and a two year training for a trained nurse.

Both Miss Wilson and Miss Kett were well-informed and authoritative figures who were familiar with the subject and enjoyed an enlightened, well-balanced grasp of the whole range of factors relating to Poor Law nursing.

An interesting contrast to these two women was the Secretary of the Meath Workhouse Nursing Association which recruited attendants from rural areas for supply to workhouses in the London area, specifically to look after the aged and infirm. The Meath Association had originally given their recruits a few weeks' training but found that the attendants' duties and responsibilities had grown and they later had to increase their period of training to one year, then two years and at the time of the enquiry it was three years. The Meath

Association gave no certificate to their recruits who had no standing as nurses: they remained attendants and were frequently placed under the authority of untrained nurses. Miss Lee, the Secretary, asked for these attendants to be given a recognised status by the LGB but volunteered the acknowledgement that if the attendants were given 'a proper training' they would no longer be satisfied to remain as attendants nor to work in the workhouses. She also admitted that her recruits had to come from rural women who did not have sufficient understanding about certificated nurse training to prefer that. She felt that there should be two grades of nurses: the trained nurses and the workhouse nurses. Her approach could be described by to-day's standards as reprehensible since there was the element of a confidence trick being played on the recruits but, on the other hand, measuring her approach by the attitudes of the day, the recruits were taken and given a training which could not otherwise have been available to them, maintained and placed in posts where their services were badly needed. Evidently her estimation of the level of intelligence enjoyed by the recruits was relatively low although Miss Lee did give evidence that the attendants often complained of poor conditions of work and monotony.

One of the other witnesses who discussed nurse training at some length and with great interest was the Chairman of the Poor Law Nursing Board in Yorkshire, Mr Tillotson. He was also Chairman of the Halifax Board of Guardians and his character came through in his evidence very clearly. He gave the impression of being a gruff, thoughtful stereotype of a Yorkshireman; kind, practical, paternalistic. He was involved in other charities besides the Poor Law and seemed very taken up with nursing. He seemed to be the sort of character that tried to have something done about any need he recognised. The patients from the Halifax workhouse infirmaries had recently been transferred to a new Infirmary, which was separately administered, and throughout this section of his evidence there was some confusion about which of the infirmaries he was discussing.

He reported that there was already a training scheme for nurses, many of whom remained as Charge Nurses: others went into private nursing, to the London hospitals or elsewhere, but very few went into the workhouse infirmaries. The living and working conditions at the new Infirmary were very good, better than those available at the local voluntary hospital, the Halifax Royal Infirmary. He reported that there was no shortage of candidates for training but that he felt their quality was deteriorating: he thought that compared with ten years earlier they showed less 'refinement of mind'. The Guardians sometimes tried to make the Matron take on unsuitable candidates but the Matron refused. He felt there was no need for a resident medical officer for the certificated training but did think there was a real need for some common standard of training and examination. He rejected the concept of two grades of nurses and felt that Poor Law nursing should be as good as any other. He then went on to discuss the Yorkshire Nursing Scheme which the Yorkshire Poor Law Board had designed and submitted to the LGB for approval.

Failing any national scheme, the Yorkshire unions planned a country-wide scheme to try to achieve a certificate of greater value for their nurses who, they felt, did not hold their infirmary certificates in any great standing. The examinations would be held by the Yorkshire College (later to become the Leeds University) and the scheme had the support of both the College and the Leeds doctors. The College involvement would give the resulting certificate the standing of any of those granted by regulated examining bodies and, consequently, would be held in national standing in the same way as the qualifications given by universities to doctors or other professions. The practical examination of the nurse would be held by a supervising committee of Superintendent Nurses, or if the LGB liked to appoint them, by Nursing Inspectors. It was felt that such a scheme would attract more candidates and it had the keen support of all the county except Sheffield and Dewsbury. Sheffield was holding back only because it did not feel sufficiently involved and wanted its own University College to have some part in the examinations.

In their annual reports, the LGB reported the scheme in some detail. It was supported by the Inspector for the area but the LGB made little further comment and nothing seems to have come of it. The scheme, however, was of considerable interest in its conception and was more ambitious than any other that was put forward for years after. It would have taken nursing into the general education system of the country and would have allowed British nurse education to keep pace with the American system and to supplement the apprenticeship system which has persisted until today: it was not until the Nurses' Act 1949 that experimental schemes were made possible and even then these schemes linking hospital and educational establishments did not materialise until the 1950s. Here, the

Committee missed its second great opportunity to establish the Poor
Law nurses within a national service with an enhanced and reinforced status and to set up a national system of training and certification for nurses which would have taken them into the mainstream
of general education and could have set the pattern for the training
and registration of all British nurses. State Registration had to wait
until 1919, and nursing is still outside the mainstream of general
education.

The Matrons or Superintendent Nurses who gave evidence all
felt that there should be resident medical officers for the training
schools but their reasons were not clear. Miss Gibson, in a rare
moment of confused thinking, said that there 'ought to be a resident
medical officer if there is to be a training school at all' because the
existence of 'a resident medical officer makes it necessary to a certain
extent to have a good superintendent nurse'. Mrs Wates felt that a
medical officer was necessary to train nurses. Miss Marquardt felt
that any full time medical officer should be resident anyway and
the nurse should not be required to accept the responsibility of
emergencies because he was not.

All the nurses who spoke on the subject accepted without question
the part which doctors played in the education of nurses; the doctors
gave the lectures, the nurses gave the practical training: the doctors
were responsible for the theory, the nurses for the skills. The discussion on nurse education by the non-nurses, the voluntary organisers,
seemed to accept the principle of nurses teaching nursing to probationers and did not concede so readily the need for doctors to take a
major part. This dichotomy in nurse training links with the various
reports made by Dr Edward Smith, *The Lancet* and the *British Medical
Journal* previously discussed. In none of them was there any discussion on nursing practice and not one comment on the activity of
nursing: the doctors evidently did not feel competent to do this;
there was therefore a split in the training of nurses between nursing
practice and theory which in any event related principally to medical
treatment. Nursing treatments had yet to be recognised.

The Committee also received evidence relating to the training for
probationer nurses at the Portsmouth Workhouse Infirmary given
by the Medical Superintendent, Dr Knott (Appendix 3). The
Yorkshire scheme as presented did not give details of a syllabus and
therefore cannot be compared with Dr Knott's scheme. His nurse
training certainly had the approval of the LGB and continued for

many years. It will be noticed that the scope of the nurses' duties (judged by the syllabus of training) had greatly increased. The 'common sense' discretions and responsibilities assumed by the nurse in Joseph Rogers' day (in fact he constantly complained that they were not assumed by the nurses he was given) might include noticing and reporting adverse reactions to treatments, changes in condition, the reading and interpretation of physical signs and symptoms such as pain for example. These responsibilities were being formalised slowly and made part of the nurse's accepted duties: 'What to observe and report to the doctor when patients were taking the above drugs and they were not agreeing with them.' It will also be noticed how the nurse was receiving a thorough training in subservience to the medical staff. In this syllabus there is no suggestion of the nurse as colleague, on the contrary the nurses were always taught 'respect to senior officers, respect to their own position, tact, self-abnegation', etc.

The Committee also took evidence about the starting age for probationers and their necessary qualifications: there was little of particular interest in the evidence and there seemed to be fairly general agreement that the quality of the probationers was not as good as it had been some years previously. In their report on this section the Committee recommended that the minimum age of entry should be 21, that candidates should be of good character and health and that they should have intelligence. They also recommended a preliminary trial period of six weeks to two months to the satisfaction of the Guardians. They drew up a plan for a formal recognition of a two-tier system of training for qualified nurses and trained nurses, the former to be trained in Minor Training Schools and the latter to be trained in Major Training Schools. The Major Training School should have a full time medical officer, be a separate Infirmary under the control of a trained Matron or Superintendent Nurse and give a three year course of training; it should give a certificate after the completion of training (involving theory and practice) and an examination by two independent examiners one of whom had to be a trained Matron or Superintendent Nurse of a recognised training school. A certificate of good conduct was also required. The trained nurse was eligible for promotion to the grade of Superintendent Nurse.

The Minor Training School was required to have a Superintendent Nurse or trained Matron and a medical officer available to give some instruction. The training course had to comply with a scheme laid down by the LGB. A certificate could be awarded after one year provided that a certificate of good conduct was also available and another certificate was forthcoming from a medical officer to confirm that the candidate was competent to undertake the ordinary duties of a nurse. The qualified nurse would be eligible to work under the supervision of a trained nurse and could, after one year's experience, undertake a further 18 months' training in a Major School to gain a certificate as a trained nurse. Thus a second tier of nurses would be officially recognised: the predecessors of the State Enrolled Nurse of today.

It was further recommended that the trained nurse should practice for one year before promotion and that every Superintendent Nurse should hold a midwifery certificate.

The Committee generally agreed that the training of Poor Law nurses was good and encouraged the idea of combined training schemes within a given area.

The third aspect of the Committee's remit was dealt with fairly briskly: they did not feel that there was any real shortage of Superintendent Nurses although there seemed to be a frequent turnover. They felt that the size of staff required by the 1897 Nursing Order (i.e. three nurses) was probably too narrow as a qualification for the establishment of the post and recommended that there should be a Superintendent Nurse post wherever there were 100 sick beds or more in a workhouse: the post could be optional in workhouses with 60 to 100 beds and, in these instances, the post could be combined with that of the Matron if an assistant matron (not necessarily also a nurse) were appointed. Thus the Committee removed the route by which Guardians could avoid the appointment of a Superintendent Nurse since many were in the habit of appointing assistant nurses instead of nurses in order to be able to circumvent the 1897 Nursing Order.

There was a considerable amount of evidence given on the last point investigated by the Committee: the possible need to define more strictly the respective duties of the Master and Matron of the workhouse and of the Superintendent Nurse. They looked at the situation from two aspects, the responsibility for the patients and their environment and the responsibility for the nurses on and off duty.

In relation to the patients, it was found that the 1847 General

Consolidated Order (Article 208) made the Master and Matron responsible for the discipline, care and nursing of the patients. The Superintendent Nurse was found to have no specific authority nor duties in connection with the sick except those which devolved on her indirectly under the 1897 Order. This had said that the Superintendent Nurse was to 'superintend and control the other nurses and assistant nurses in the performance of their duties' subject, as far as medical treatment went, to the direction of the medical officer and in all other matters, to the authority of the Master and Matron. She had no duty to do any actual nursing nor could she be dismissed or suspended by any other authority but that of the LGB.

Miss Wilson was in no doubt but that the duties of the three officers should be more clearly defined and that the Superintendent Nurse should be given greater and wider jurisdiction. She felt that nursing had become a specialised occupation which situation the workhouse Masters and Matrons had not recognised and that whereas the school teacher had always been recognised and given her own position and status, the nurse was still working under the same circumstances as when there had been no trained nurses. She claimed that the nurse should be in charge of her own department, in control of the supplies and the patients. The Master should remain as 'Captain of the ship' and have the right of entry to the sick wards but he should use this right with discretion. The Superintendent Nurse should have authority over the scrubbers (usually workhouse inmates) whilst they were working in the sick wards. She criticised the 1897 Order for lack of definition and explained that anomaly which left the Matron responsible for the sick and the Nursing Order which had not revoked this although it had placed the responsibility for nursing on the Superintendent Nurse.

Miss Wilson also criticised the current system which stopped the nurse from making any direct communication with the medical officer in an emergency. The Master was responsible for calling the medical officer and the nurse had to act through him. It was not uncommon for the Master (or Matron in the Master's absence) to overrule the nurse. Miss Wilson felt that the Superintendent Nurse should be responsible directly to the Guardians.

Miss Kett evidently had less vigorous views on this matter: she felt that the Master should remain supreme, that the Matron should control the workhouse labour (this necessarily meant the kitchens, stores, laundry and domestic staff since these all functioned through the workhouse administration and were primarily for the workhouse, although they serviced the sick wards in the infirmaries and the schools on the site) but should not interfere with the sick wards. The Superintendent Nurse should be entirely responsible for the sick. Her evidence, characteristically, was a little woolly and showed a propensity for accepting the status quo.

Another witness, Mrs Hawes, who was the Superintendent Nurse at Rotherham Workhouse Infirmary, spoke up strongly about the lack of sympathy shown to the work of the nurse by the Masters, Matrons and Guardians. She felt that the Guardians were unduly influenced by the two officers with whom they had most contact under the existing system. She suggested that the Superintendent Nurse should be on the same level as the Matron and, therefore, have the same opportunities for communicating and reporting to the Guardians. She complained of the Matrons' pettiness which kept the nurses short of clean linen, supplies and other equipment. Her opinion of the Matrons was that on the whole they were ignorant people, promoted from the ranks of the launderesses or porteresses with no understanding or knowledge of the sick in sick wards. She felt the need for the nurse to be wholly responsible to the medical officer, with a separate Nursing Committee for the infirmaries.

Other nurses also spoke of difficulties in their relationships with the Masters and, particularly, with the Matrons, they recounted experiences where there were complaints at the amount of linen used in the sick wards, at shortages of supplies, the deliberate withholding of supplies or equipment and the difficulty of obtaining nurses of any standing to work under these conditions.

Mr Tillotson confirmed that there was 'any amount of friction' between the Superintendent Nurses and the workhouse officers. He described how his Board of Guardians had laid down the rules which gave the Superintendent Nurse the control of clean linen for her domain, removed all responsibility for the sick wards from the Matron and insisted on the Master exercising his right of entry to the infirmary with consideration and restraint. The Master preserved the responsibility for all building work in the infirmary but the Superintendent Nurse was responsible for all other aspects and reported defects to him.

Many of them also discussed the problem of the Superintendent Nurse's authority over the nurses. Officially she controlled them only whilst they were on duty but had no authority over them when they were off duty, nor, usually, did she have any authority to grant them off duty since this was the responsibility of the Matron. This system was a relic of former days when the nurses were inmates of the workhouse and it had not been altered. Thus there was ample opportunity for the nurses to play the two officials off against each other and for the Matron to grant leave without consulting the Superintendent Nurse. Additionally, the nurses complained of inter-ference by the Matron during their off-duty, what they had of it. Many Guardians, but not all, had found it expedient to draw up additional regulations to re-define or clarify the duties, responsibili-ties and positions of the respective officers. Where this had been done adequately the situation was co-operative or, at least, contained, but where it had not been done the relationships were frequently strained. Clearly, the structure of the system took the nurse away from the power centre and removed any chance of her obtaining control over her own area except through unofficial and indirect manipulation or manoeuvring. With the growth of the nurses' professionalism, her expanding responsibilities and the increasing preponderance of patients over the able-bodied inmates the position was inflammatory.

On the other hand, the Superintendent Nurses were not necessar-ily equipped for administrative tasks and were not necessarily familiar with the systems of control exercised by the Poor Law authorities. The Masters were ultimately and statutorily accountable for the expenditure of public money and there was a considerable ésprit de corps amongst these officials, amply demonstrated in the *Poor Law Officers' Journals* of the day. Many were exasperated by the adminis-trative ineptness of the Superintendent Nurses and resented any in-fringement of their authority, curtailment of their power or reduction in their sphere of influence. The security of tenure enjoyed by Superintendent Nurses (which allowed dismissal only by the author-ity of the LGB) was an additional source of irritation, since the Guardians were not able even to suspend a Superintendent Nurse, as they were the Master or the Medical Officer. The Masters were anxious at the growing influence of the Nursing Superintendents and their evident, if tentative, groping after a greater cohesion and central organisation.

Mr White, the Honorary Secretary of the Workhouse Masters' and Matrons' Association felt that the status quo under the 1897 Order should be preserved since he felt that with ordinary tact there should be no need for friction. He said that Masters and Matrons were aware of changing conditions and the increasing progress of nursing. They were conscious of the change in the social climate and were trying to keep themselves up to date and to respond to these changes. He felt that greater care should be taken in the selection and appointment of all officers: 'In the appointment of Masters and Matrons and Superintendent Nurses, make the most stringent inquiries you can of every kind, even if you have to alter your form for the appointments; but having got the people, both Superintendent Nurse and Master and Matron, you will have to trust them.'

Mrs Richmond, the Matron of Luton Workhouse and a trained nurse, felt that the Superintendent Nurse should have absolute control of the sick wards, the nurses and her own stores but also felt that 'the nurses have been prejudiced by the heads of training schools and the Press against Masters and Matrons'.

Other witnesses spoke of incompetent administration by Superintendent Nurses which was a source of frustration and annoyance to Matrons who frequently had to prompt the former. This evidently pricked the dignity of the Superintendent Nurses for 'then she [the Matron] is distinctly told by the Superintendent Nurse that it is nothing at all to do with her; how is such bad management to be altered if the Matron is not to speak about it?'

Another Master had 'one Superintendent Nurse we were utterly unable to get on with in any circumstances whatever; she grossly insulted everybody; it was not a question of Master and Matron; it was the porter and porteress and every officer in the workhouse . . . she held out practically that not being able to be suspended by the Guardians brought her scarcely under the rule of the Board of Guardians'.

Several reports from the General Inspectors admitted friction between the nurses and the Matrons who felt as an affront the greater salaries paid to the nurses.

A resolution, sent by 'a large number of Boards of Guardians', asked that Guardians should be able to suspend the Superintendent Nurse and that she would take 'lower precedence' than the Matron to whom she should be responsible.

The memorandum from Louisa Twining suggested that all infirmaries should be separately administered under the control of the medical officer or head nurse. She also repeated her constant message that only people of better calibre and special training should be appointed as Masters and Matrons.

Florence Nightingale's memorandum written in 1897 was partially reprinted in the Appendix to the Report. This extract is interesting in that it shows how her thinking had by then begun to fall behind the mainstream of society with regard to the treatment of the able-bodied poor for she felt that the principle of less eligibility was right. However she also felt that this principle was not appropriate to the sick poor as the most sensible (i.e. economic) thing to do was to get them better as quickly as possible so that they could be returned to work and thus to independence. If this principle were recognised the administration of workhouse infirmaries could be improved, thus allowing improvements in workhouse nursing. She demonstrated the inappropriateness of having workhouse Masters and Matrons to administer infirmaries by showing that the best workhouse officers were those who were most successful at applying the less eligibility principle and must, consequently, be the worst at running the infirmaries or the nurses. She declared that the administration of infirmaries was quite different from that of workhouses and there must be an inevitable conflict between the attitudes of the Superintendent Nurses and the Masters and Matrons. Therefore she advised that there should be a new officer appointed to run the administration and finance of the infirmary and to be responsible to the Board of Guardians. All responsibility for nursing, internal management and discipline of the nurses should be vested in the head of the nursing staff.

The Committee acknowledged the ambiguous position of the Superintendent Nurse and the possible problems which might arise out of it. On the other hand, they found little evidence of friction and thought that with more time the situation would work. They recommended that the Superintendent Nurse should be made primarily responsible for the welfare and care of the sick, relieving the Master of all specific duties in connection with the sick in the sick wards. A duty was placed upon the Superintendent Nurses to consult with and report to the Master. The Master retained the right of entry to the sick wards; the Superintendent Nurse was to take responsibility for all stores, food, etc. after delivery. Similarly, the Matron was to be relieved of all responsibility for the sick wards except for the provision of cooked foods, clean linen, clothing, etc. and she should not have the right of entry to the wards.

The Committee also recommended that the Superintendent Nurse should have full jurisdiction over the nurses both on and off duty, full control over all domestic labour (paid and pauper) whilst they were on the wards but that the master should retain complete over-all authority. The Superintendent Nurse should arrange the supply of labour and hours of work for the attendants with the Master and report any deficiencies to him. She would be responsible for domestic maintenance of the sick wards and the Master would be responsible for building maintenance.

The Guardians were urged to build separate accommodation for their sick wards or infirmaries 'as an additional safeguard against future friction'. It seemed therefore that the Committee recognised their own recommendations and the resulting situation as being both imperfect and a compromise.

In studying the Report, one observation was outstanding: there was a remarkable lack of understanding between the four committee members and the witnesses. Misunderstandings abound, particu-larly with the Chairman (J. Grant Lawson, MP) but also with the other members (W. E. Knollys, Dr Arthur Downes, Dr Arthur Fuller). They did not seem able to comprehend the responses to their questions, often they did not appear to be attending, did not receive the replies, and on several occasions the same question was asked four or five times by two or three members of the Committee after which they still did not seem able to grasp the answer. There was understandable confusion over the term 'Matron' and it was sometimes difficult to grasp whether the discussion was about a workhouse Matron or a trained Matron. Sometimes it was clear that the several members of the Committee had placed conflicting inter-pretations upon the evidence.

Another observation was the small number of probationers who were received for training at the various institutions. Mostly, the Matrons of the separate Infirmaries (or the Superintendent Nurses) talked in terms of 10–12 candidates each year; Lewisham Infirmary with about 700 beds took 40 probationers a year. They trained only for their own staffing needs and did not have any idea of training for national needs. Indeed, this was also the normal practice of the voluntary hospitals and it was not until 1939 that the Interim Report of the Athlone Committee portrayed the concept of training on a national basis.

The Report discussed the use of beds in the Poor Law institutions and did not show surprise that about 30% were normally empty. The beds in separate Infirmaries were used at a slightly higher level but, in spite of this, the situation contrasted sharply with the state of overflow and overcrowding described in the 1909 Reports of the *Royal Commission on the Poor Laws*.

Again, in 1902, despite the evident shortage of trained nurses for the Poor Law institutions, the thinking evinced by the Report on the employment of nurses had not yet reached the stage where there was an official acceptance of the need to adjust to the situation. It is possible that there might have been more thought given to the idea of a centralised service if this had been the case, for, in that instance, the Committee might not have given so much weight to the rights of the Guardians to employ their own nurses.

There was a paternalistic and disciplinarian attitude displayed towards nurses by the witnesses (who were nearly all in the employing situation) and a constant discussion about who should be in authority over them (especially noticeable in the discussions about when the nurses were off duty). This attitude was no more, really, than a reflection of Victorian righteousness and the pious execution of a social duty to carry out voluntary work responsibly. The oversight and close control exercised over the nurse was similar to that exercised over domestic servants, and only slightly more than the oversight maintained on the medical officers who still had very little professional or clinical freedom except what was permitted by the Relieving Officers or the Guardians. It was a style of management current at the time (but becoming increasingly unpopular) and practised widely in commerce and industry. However, whereas other workers were able to shake it off in the course of time, and the doctors won professional independence, the nurses only exchanged their Masters for the doctors and the style was continued for many years even as it faded elsewhere. This managerial relationship slowly became the doctor:nurse relationship and the subservience was doubly enforced.

It is interesting also to notice the beginnings of a recognition of 'sapiential authority' of the nurse over domestic workers on the wards. This term was made explicit by the Salmon Report in 1966.

The Report was presented to Parliament in November 1902 but the LGB was noticeably reticent about it and made no reference to its proposals. In the ensuing years the agitation for a standardised form of training and registration of nurses grew in intensity and frequency and the Poor Law Nurses Report became enmeshed in this. Bills for the registration of nurses were introduced in 1902 and

1904 and a Select Committee was appointed to look into the matter. It is clear that the Government had taken fright after the 1902 Midwives' Act and particularly at the way the Central Midwives Board carried out its functions. It was anxious to avoid a similar situation arising out of any Nurses' Registration Act: the Poor Law institutions were not being registered as midwifery schools with sufficient speed. One of the qualifications for the Superintendent Nurse was that she should hold a midwifery certificate. The Poor Law authorities were therefore doubly embarrassed, or would be so when the period of grace expired, since it could not train its own midwives and could not produce nurses with the necessary qualifications for promotion. When this disaster struck there would not be enough candidates coming forward to train and to staff their infirmaries.

In 1905 the Select Committee reported in favour of registration and each year thereafter a nurses' registration Bill was put before one or other of the Houses of Parliament. The Government hedged on both the Poor Law Nurses Order (that it had promised as a result of the 1902 Committee) and on the registration of nurses; the CMB still delayed in approving Poor Law infirmaries and insisted on the policy of inspection which the Government could not accept. In 1906 *The Poor Law Officers' Journal* (29 June) complained about the CMB and subsequently commented about state registration for nurses: 'it will be little short of a public calamity if the Bill of the RBNA [Royal British Nurses Association] is allowed to pass through Parliament. At present there is going on a gradual appreciation of the value of Poor Law nursing and the services of Nurses trained under the Poor Law. This is exactly as it should be, for judged solely from the public point of view, it is in the highest degree desirable that the status both of the Poor Law infirmaries and of the Poor Law Nurses should be raised. . . . Our Poor Law infirmaries are our only real Public Hospitals and they should be allowed to develop to the very highest ends in association with the treatment of the sick. But as the National Poor Law Officers' Association point out, if this Bill were allowed to go through Parliament there would be nothing to prevent the proposed Central Nursing Board from declining to recognise Poor Law infirmaries as Training Schools under the Bill, or from so framing their regulations as to make it impracticable for the great majority of Poor Law infirmaries to qualify as Training Schools. We know what has already happened

E

in regard to the Central Midwives Board . . .' If the *Poor Law Officers' Journal* and the National Association knew and feared this, so did the Government, and it is reasonable to propose that this fear was at least one of the main reasons why the Government did nothing to help the nurses get through a state registration Bill.

In the meantime, public opinion was moving forward steadily: in 1903 the LGB began to give workhouses and infirmaries permission to dispense with central sanction for individual appointments of nurses, so long as the establishment was centrally approved. There was a growing acknowledgement of the need for a recognised nursing qualification and an increasing demand for hospital treatment. In 1906, at the annual general meeting of the Royal National Pension Fund for Nurses, Miss Sophie Morris of Bristol is reported as saying that the public was not supporting the voluntary hospitals enough to pay an adequate salary to their nurses. The *Poor Law Officers' Journal* (15 June 1906) commented: 'Is it not the fact that the public mind, especially in large cities of population, is tending more acutely towards the direction of State provided Hospitals. . . . It is not in accordance with the fitness of things that the respectable and self-supporting poor should in sickness be required to accept the hospital charity of the wealthy and be made the subject of medical experiment.'

This growing trend towards the greater use by the public of hospitals and in particular of the London Poor Law establishments was helped forward by legislation. It may be helpful to recall that at the turn of the century the weight of morbidity derived from the many infectious diseases including relapsing fever, smallpox, measles, whooping cough, scarlet fever, venereal diseases, zymotic enteritis and ophthalmia neonatorum.

After the establishment of the Metropolitan Asylums Board in 1867 it had tried to build new fever and smallpox hospitals but had been thwarted by local residents who were concerned to protect their own neighbourhoods from infection. A lawsuit against the MAB was largely responsible for the closing down of their Hampstead Hospital. On the other hand, the local sanitary authorities considered that the isolation of infectious cases was of the first importance and urged the MAB to extend their use of the fever hospitals to non-pauper cases so as further to protect the community. A Royal Commission was set up to review the situation and reported in 1882. It recommended that isolation hospitals (for fever and smallpox cases) should be administered separately from the Poor Law and that provision for infectious cases should include the non-destitute. In 1885 the Medical Relief Disqualification Removal Act was passed and in the words of Abel-Smith (1964) 'the sick pauper won the vote'. In 1889 the Infectious Diseases (Notification) Act was passed after which practitioners had to notify all cases of infectious diseases to their local Medical Officer of Health. As a result of this Act the number of admissions to MAB hospitals rose dramatically from 7809 in 1891 to 34431 in 1929 (Powell 1930). Also in 1889, under the Poor Law Act, the MAB was empowered to admit any person, irrespective of income, suffering from smallpox, diphtheria or fever. A Relieving Officer's signature was still required so there was still a distinction between the pauper and non-pauper. The 1891 Public Health (London) Law Consolidation Act confirmed previous enactments and made it explicit that every citizen of London suffering from an infectious disease, whether or not he was a pauper, had the right of admission to an MAB hospital, subject to a medical certificate.

The isolation of the diphtheria bacillus by Klebs in 1883 led to the development of antitoxin treatment for this disease which, at the time, was one of the most serious. This new treatment greatly reduced the mortality rate but increased the admission rate for the disease.

Thus the Poor Law, through the particular route of the MAB (which was in many ways an active, liberal and forward looking organisation) advanced towards the Public Health concept. Ayers (1971) says that this advance was conditioned by 'reforming endeavour, motivated by social maladjustments and aided by maturing public opinion, pestilence and the force of fear'.

One way and another however, the public was using its hospitals as it never had before. Not only more people, but different people, were accepting hospital treatment, whereas once it had been only the destitute, it later became the poor, then the lower middle class and, during epidemics, the professional class. However, the standards of accommodation, treatment, staffing and care varied considerably. The PL infirmaries, especially the separate ones, compared with the London voluntary hospitals, but the provincial infirmaries (except those in the very large cities) were still of an indifferent standard as indeed were many of the provincial voluntary hospitals. In the workhouse infirmaries medical supervision was often still given by local practitioners, on a part time basis, who frequently accepted contracts of employment requiring them to pay for the medicines which they prescribed, and there were still relatively few trained nurses. With the growing use of the infirmaries and asylums by a widening section of the public, the cry for a state medical system was increased. The definition of destitution became more difficult to maintain as did the preservation of the distinction between pauper and non-pauper patients. Where there was both a voluntary hospital and a Poor Law infirmary the patient might have a choice, but the former only took 25% of all the patients in the country, were highly selective and were sited in towns and cities. All other hospital patients had to accept Poor Law accommodation. Furthermore, as has been mentioned previously, the large infirmaries too, were becoming more selective and were increasingly trying to admit a larger proportion of acute cases (particularly operative cases), thus crowding out the other patients into the small infirmaries There was also a growing trend in the large infirmaries to take non-pauper patients as paying patients. The status of acute medicine was subordinating the needs of the aged and chronically ill patients.

REFERENCES

Abel-Smith, B. (1964), *The Hospitals, 1800–1948*. London, Heinemann, p. 130.
Ayers, Gwendoline M. (1971). p. 105.
Departmental Committee on Nursing the Sick Poor in Workhouses, 1902, Cd. 1366, Vol. xxxviii.
Poor Law Officers' Journal, 29 June 1906, pp. 22–23; 15 June 1906, p. 574.
Powell, Sir G. A. (1930), *The MAB and its Work, 1867–1930*. London, MAB. Chapter 30.
Royal Commission on the Poor Laws, 1909, Cmd. 4499.
Select Committee on Registration of Nurses, 1904, Cd. 281, Q1437, 1438. 1905, Cd. 263, Q250, 251.

8

THE ROYAL COMMISSION
ON THE POOR LAWS: 1909

Dissatisfaction with the state of medical care increased with the growing social expectations of the public, the rising political power of the Trades Unions and the Labour movement and the trend towards a state welfare policy which was demonstrated by a spate of social legislation previously described.

In 1905 the Government set up the *Royal Commission on the Poor Laws* which finally reported in 1909. The Commission consisted largely of representatives of the Charity Organisation Society, the LGB, Poor Law Guardians and other 'orthodox' thinkers. There was, however, a minority section comprising Mrs Beatrice Webb, the Rev. Russell Wakefield, Francis Chandler and George Lansbury who were against the principle of less eligibility and the general ethos of the Poor Law. In the end they insisted on dissociating themselves from the Majority Report and issued a Minority Report. The Commission looked at the whole area of the Poor Law and received a vast amount of evidence from a host of witnesses. It also received evidence from its special medical investigator, Dr McVail, and compiled a stupendous amount of statistics. The evidence was published in 37 volumes and the two reports took up three further volumes.

The Majority Report (dealing with medical relief) described the increasing costs of infirmary treatment since 1878 and published a table (Cmnd 4499, Vol. I, p. 313):

Cost Per Head Per Annum in Metropolitan Infirmaries

Years ended Lady Day	Average	Ranging from
1878	£37	£28–54 (exclusive of loan charges)
1888	£36	£21–69
1897	£48	£36–77 (inclusive of loan charges)
1906	{ £60	£43–95 (inclusive of loan charges)
	{ £50	£36–75 (exclusive of loan charges)

They described how some urban workhouses sent operation cases to General Hospitals but how in the larger Infirmaries, 'the most delicate surgical operations are now performed by the medical staff'.

About 3000 operations per annum were done in London's Infirmaries: the rate of recovery in provincial Infirmaries was better than in the general hospitals and they described the growing availability in the London Infirmaries of X-ray equipment and electrical treatments. All these factors they ascribed to 'the growth of aseptic surgery and public demand for improved methods' but also to the fact that 'the Guardians have been obliged to train their own nurses in order to maintain an adequate nursing staff, which alone has necessitated a certain amount of surgical work; and in the second place the pressure on the accommodation of the voluntary hospitals has driven into the workhouse infirmaries many persons needing surgical treatment' (Vol. I, p. 314).

In discussing the widening scope for medical relief they believed that the policy of deterrence had decreased so that it was possible, frequently, for patients to be admitted to separate Infirmaries and discharged without going through the workhouse: they felt that the poor gladly received treatment and that the District Medical Officers no longer found it so difficult to persuade their patients to enter the infirmaries. They added that some poor actually travelled from their rural homes into a town to use the urban workhouse infirmary. There was also evidence of patients of a 'higher social stratum' using the infirmaries who were referred directly by their general practitioners: costs for these patients were wholly or partially recovered according to their means but the use of the infirmary beds by them, it was claimed, was driving off poor people into the workhouses again. On the other hand, there were still people who preferred not to use the infirmaries because of the pauper label; especially was this noticeable with the maternity cases. Mothers did not wish to have the place of birth of their children registered as 'X Workhouse'.

It was confirmed that the 1885 Medical Relief Disqualification Removal Act had done much to encourage poor people to use the infirmaries, as had the Public Health movement.

There was an increasing tendency for the voluntary hospitals to transfer patients to infirmaries: this was said to be due to the advance of medical science which allowed patients to be put on the road to cure more quickly. Additionally, of course, there was a preference on the part of the voluntary hospitals for the patients who were lucky enough to be suffering from one of the diseases for which there was a specific treatment, since the new or most recent one could be tried.

Those patients who did not suffer from such diseases were less likely to be admitted or more likely to be transferred. In many areas where there was no voluntary hospital, patients were 'destitute' of the necessary medical facilities and some Guardians were beginning to accept this definition. (The LGB officially adopted the extended definition, in a circular dated 18 March 1910, that a person might be 'unable to provide for himself the particular form of medical attendance or treatment of which he is in urgent need'.) This took the definition of need away from a purely economic criterion into the social area, a change of emphasis which had far reaching effects and which led to a flood of patients from the middle classes into the infirmaries. The test had moved from pauperisation and less eligibility through destitution and lack of means to social need.

As far as the separate Infirmaries were concerned, those in the metropolis and the large industrial cities (Camberwell, Woolwich, Poplar, West Derby–Liverpool, Birmingham, etc.) were increasingly having to accept street casualties and industrial accidents since they were situated in areas where these were likely to occur and where no general hospitals were equally convenient. These Infirmaries were therefore more and more doing the work of the general hospitals.

As far as outdoor medical relief was concerned, it was found that more District Medical Officers were referring patients to the infirmaries. Although the Guardians were empowered to employ district nurses, few, in fact, did so although many subscribed to their local nursing associations.

There was an evident expansion of the use of cottage nurses (untrained) employed by voluntary agencies to help the sick poor in their rual homes. Sometimes these nurses actually lived for a period with the household, doing routine, non-technical work, domestic work and helping with the cooking. Some workhouse nurses spent part of their time working in the district. There was still a considerable deterrent quality attached to outdoor medical relief.

The Majority Report looked at a comparison of numbers of beds in Poor Law establishments (excluding MAB asylums) and in voluntary hospitals (1908) (Vol. I, p. 328) and discussed the overlapping of Poor Law and Public Health functions. They found that public health hospitals run by the local authorities under the Public Health Acts of 1875 and 1891, existed for the treatment of serious acute infectious diseases; there were occasional domiciliary nurses. The Acts of 1875 and 1891, in giving power to the public health

City	Beds, Voluntary Hospitals	Beds, PL Infirmaries
London	10224	16300
Liverpool	1172	2000
Manchester and Salford	1270	3250
Birmingham	838	2200
Leeds	450	1000
Sheffield	559	800
Newcastle	417	350
Cardiff	235	500
Leicester	200	500

authorities to build hospitals for the sick in their districts, had placed no limitations as to the disease or economic status of the patients. The local authorities could also provide medical assistance and medicines for the poorer inhabitants of their districts, although in practice this was usually limited to instances of epidemics or infectious diseases. The distinction between the Public Health service and the Poor Law service was that the former was preventive in its objectives and the latter was curative.

Reviewing the system of medical relief to the poor, the Committee reported (Vol. I, p. 342) 'We can say that the sick poor were probably never so well looked after as they are at the present day. But at the same time we have received much evidence to the effect that the system of Poor Law medical relief suffers from palpable defects and requires recasting and enlarging.' There were only two medical inspectors for all of England and Wales and one of these was specifically for London; there was no system of inspection for outdoor medical relief, many District Medical Officers still paid for their own prescriptions; there was overcrowding in some sick wards, especially in rural areas: there was defective ventilation, lighting, water supplies, bathing arrangements and sanitary facilities. Perversely, they also criticised the signs they had seen of extravagance and over-elaborate structural design.

The Majority then discussed the problem of overlapping in institutional care: they found a lack of co-operation in planning services; the sick poor were treated freely at the voluntary hospitals but were charged variously by the Poor Law infirmaries whilst being treated as paupers. Industrial accidents received free treatment at the voluntary hospitals, were charged by the Poor Law Infirmaries and had free treatment from the Municipal Hospitals (i.e. Public Health Hospitals), all depending on the location of the place of work.

Tubercular cases were sometimes treated by Poor Law infirmaries, sometimes by public health hospitals: sometimes they were charged and sometimes they were not. The system of disenfranchisement depended on a decision by the revising barrister and could be capricious. Relationships between the voluntary hospitals and the Poor Law authorities were openly hostile; whilst the voluntary hospital doctors were specialising more and more, the Poor Law doctors were unable to do so.

The report (Vol. I, p. 351) on Poor Law nursing in the infirmaries made the point that 'it appears that the great improvement in workhouse nursing, which has taken place since the issue of the Nursing Order of 1897 has led many Guardians to suppose that very little more remains to be done'. The Commissioners did not entirely agree with that supposition. In the rural workhouses Dr McVail had reported 'that the nursing arrangements are, with few exceptions, inadequate. A number of witnesses hold similar views expecially as to the inadequacy of the night nursing'. They reported difficulties in recruitment experienced by the Guardians for all the same reasons so frequently given on previous occasions: inadequate salaries, unsatisfactory accommodation, long hours, monotonous work, professional isolation, dislike of rural life. In the urban infirmaries they reported that the nursing establishments were inadequate but that the quality of the nursing appeared to be of a high standard. They also commented on the high standard of nurse training and reiterated the need for a revised superannuation system for nurses.

With regard to outdoor medical relief, specifically the nursing side of it, they commented that nursing associations were not ubiquitous and there was not always a nurse available when the need for one arose; few Guardians had appointed district Poor Law nurses and the provision for nursing the outdoor sick was inadequate; they felt that 'the want of proper nursing for the outdoor sick paupers especially in rural districts, is a serious defect on the present system of medical relief and that this has a prejudicial effect on the health of the paupers'. They expressed reservations about the usefulness of the cottage nurses who had to work under the supervision of trained nurses. They felt that voluntary associations should be encouraged, especially where they were not already in existence, and that the Guardians should pay a more realistic subscription for the nursing services they receive from them. They felt that frequently the indoor nurse could be used for outdoor cases and that urban areas specifically should consider the usefulness of employing their own staff of outdoor nurses.

They considered that the organisation of an outdoor system of nursing was one of first priority and that any such system should be subject to routine inspection by the central authorities. Evidently they had been impressed by the evidence of neglect: 'Many cases die simply from want of proper nursing. . . . I cannot speak strongly enough on this point. It is one of the medical officers' greatest drawbacks that he cannot obtain efficient nursing for his outdoor cases' (Vol. I, Q 34803).

'Indeed', they wrote, 'in many instances the sick are still left to the care of some neighbour or casual helper, frequently underpaid, whose services the Guardians are able to obtain. And it not infrequently happens, that a sick person may even be left without any nursing or attendance whatever.' On the other hand, where there were trained nurses, there were also occasional difficulties since 'owing to prejudice and ignorance, the poor often resent the intrusion of a trained nurse whose ideas of cleanliness and order are not in accord with their habits'.

In their general conclusions and proposals the Majority accepted the theory of the pauperising nature of sickness but could not subscribe to the idea of a completely free medical service because, they felt, a free preventive service already existed which had successfully reduced the death rate due to preventable disease and had, therefore, diminished pauperism due to preventable diseases. Furthermore, it would be well-nigh impossible to confine any free medical service to the very poor, or even to the poor. As the limits of the class that was able to avail itself of such a service grew, so prejudice against using the service would decline; 'each beneficiary recruits several others from amongst his friends, and what was at first an arithmetical soon becomes a geometrical progression in numbers' (Vol. I, p. 373). A free medical service would destroy all the voluntary agencies and hospitals and private medical practices; the cost would be prohibitive and the comparatively well-to-do would absorb the best accommodation to the exclusion of the very poor.

They were also against the transfer of medical care to the sanitary authorities because of continuing the existing duplication of staff and relief (they felt that the bulk of medical treatment was based on the need for an adequate diet and therefore both the Poor Law authorities and the medical authorities would be dispensing food relief). Furthermore, as the able-bodied would be cared for by the Poor Law authorities and the sick by the medical authorities there would be a steady transfer in an out of each, and under which would lie the responsibility for the aged and infirm?

The Majority felt (Vol. I, p. 377) that there must be limits to the practicable in the reform of medical relief: 'treatment of every human being from the cradle to the grave' was not envisaged and would lead to the development of too many hypochondriacs. 'Good health is no doubt a matter of the greatest importance to all, but it is not the sole aim of life, and it is possible to exaggerate the part it plays in the attainment of human welfare . . . moreover . . . it must be remembered that a complete defence against illness does not at present exist even for the millionaire.' On the other hand, they did feel that 'all methods for the prevention and cure of disease which have been generally approved by science' should be universally available with or without payment according to the citizen's circumstances.

They felt that the quality of medical care had shown enormous improvement over the years but still had defects; there was a need for medical representation on management committees, a need for local requirements to be surveyed and the deficiencies made good. There should be better co-ordination of services.

They disagreed with the long held view that medical relief was the cause of poverty, rather, they argued, it was sickness that was the cause of poverty. Medical care should be divorced from workhouses and should never be the reason for disenfranchisement; the need for investigation of a person's financial situation should not have to precede nor be permitted to delay treatment. The means test should continue; there should be a continuing need for independent provision against sickness and the recovery of the cost of treatment should be enforced.

The Majority Report therefore set out a scheme of reform which included the reorganisation of medical assistance on a provident basis: better definition of responsibilities and better co-operation between all agencies both statutory and voluntary; better central inspection; the establishment of a Public Assistance Authority to take over the powers and duties of the Boards of Guardians and to co-ordinate medical care, develop an adequate nursing service for out-door medical care, and control and report on medical provisions. There should be a Medical Assistance Committee to advise the Public Assistance Authority in re-organising or co-ordinating all Poor Law medical services and other agencies.

It has been the trend, at least in some quarters (Ryder and Silver 1970) to decry the Majority Report as orthodox and conservative, seeking to perpetuate the fundamental principles of 1834 and strengthen the principle of deterrence, of taking a moral stance rather than a social view of poverty. Others (Titmuss 1963) complain that it was founded on 'outer' rather than 'inner' observation, that there was no attempt to treat the underlying causes of poverty or study the 'mainsprings of behaviour', that it was 'dressed with assumptions about how people ought to behave', and was lacking in insight. Be that as it may, it is only fair to accept that the attitudes displayed by the Majority Commissioners were those extant in the Edwardian society in which they lived, that the social sciences were still young and had not permeated into the thinking of the political and ruling strata and that the philosophy of the report reflected the philosophy of a proportion of society of the time. It is also interesting to note that, with the passage of time, many of the hesitations, reservations and fears expressed in the report have substantially come to pass: sickness due to 'preventable' diseases (if it can be assumed from the context that infectious diseases were referred to) has been largely overcome in the United Kingdom; the fears of a geometric progression in the numbers of people using the free medical service have not proved unfounded when translated into the current terms of social security and the National Health Service; the values that gave pre-eminence to acute medicine ousted geriatric and chronic-sick care; the voluntary hospitals were absorbed (although many of the voluntary agencies were able to find new roles for themselves and consequently survive, and there is an interesting current resurgence of private medicine) and lastly the cost of the Welfare State, specifically the National Health Service and Social Security, have exceeded even Beveridge's calculations. There is, in fact, a trend towards a return to some form of means test, some form of selective charging for medical and dental treatment; an 'in and out' situation persists for some people between the National Health Service and the Social Services and the problem of the aged and infirm has not yet been successfully settled between the two services. The philosophy of the pre-eminent importance of the maintenance of life is giving way to the concept of the need to consider the quality of life. It is possible that the Majority Report contained elements of a social philosophy which will be more acceptable to a society in ten years' time than it was in the past 70 years, even if the commentary and rationale remain dated.

The evidence (Cmnd. 4499, Vol. I, p. 34) that the infirmaries were all full to overflowing was interesting: it was also reported that as fast as new extensions could be built they were filled. This situation contrasted strongly with the evidence given in 1902 when the infirmaries were 30% empty. The cause of this is given as 'the increased attractiveness of the workhouse infirmaries and partly to the want of accommodation at the voluntary hospitals'. This factor, in association with the evidence also given about the wards 'quite equal to those of a first class general hospital', the ornamentation of structure and the elaboration of equipment: the 'steward's room is more expensively furnished and decorated than the writing rooms of a first class hotel or club' tempt an application of Marx's theory of 'embourgoisement' to the Poor Law institutions of the day.

Apart from the Minority Commissioners, there were five memoranda of dissent to the Majority Report, making a total of 9 dissenters out of 18 Commissioners.

Turning to the Minority Report, the Commissioners looked at domiciliary treatment under the Poor Law and noted that medical orders were still granted or refused at the discretion of the Relieving Officer, that the District Medical Officer had no power to order a domiciliary nurse to be provided and also commented on the paucity of domiciliary nursing provision throughout the country. Even in the dispensaries there was no establishment for a nurse. There was, consequently, the recurring problem of how to ensure that the sick poor carried out the doctor's orders. Since there were practically no records kept by the District Medical Officers it was not possible to know what were the diseases they treated, what treatments they gave, the numbers and frequency of attendances and the outcome of their treatments. There was no inspection of their work, no control over their function and no stimulus or encouragement offered them. Unnecessary expense was incurred by the patients' delay in seeking the help of doctors which, in turn, was caused by the persisting policy of deterrence. This delay in treatment was the cause of otherwise unnecessary admissions to infirmaries, over-long hospitalisation and increased mortality. The District Medical Officers had to treat their patients at home, they were not able to order dressings nor bandages and could do nothing to remedy the social causes of the illnesses they were treating. 'The majority of the cases that he has to attend are, moreover of the most disheartening kind – largely old people with chronic complaints, or persons of more than the average degree of ignorance, carelessness, intemperance and above all, grinding poverty, with the drawbacks of bad housing, the poorest kind of clothing, insufficient and unsuitable food, inadequate attendance and an almost total absence of skilled nursing' and they quoted some of the evidence which had been given, 'there is practically no sanitary supervision of phthisis in the home of the patient. . . . Phthisis cases are maintained in crowded unventilated houses. . . . Diabetes cases live on the rates and eat what they please. Infirm men and women supported by the Poor Law are allowed to dwell in conditions of the utmost personal and domestic uncleanliness' (Vol. III, pp. 175, 178).

With regard to institutional treatment, they commented that many Guardians had failed to implement the policy of the LGB. Rural workhouses included very mixed and unclassified populations, many of the buildings were old, unsuitable, badly ventilated and heated and lacking in plumbing. None of the rural workhouses, they had found (App. no. lvii to Vol. IX), had a resident medical officer and there were still scores of establishments where there were no nurses, either trained or untrained, available for night duty. There were even some places where there were no paid nurses, and they felt that the numbers of pauper nurses were actually increasing. Dr McVail had reported (App. Vol. XIV, pp. 28, 29) that the staff of nurses was insufficient in the majority of workhouses; he had quoted one nurse on call day and night in an establishment with 24 beds of which 16 were occupied.

Of the 300 urban workhouses half had from 50 to 100 sick beds and the other half had from 100 to 400 sick beds. The standard varied considerably, some of them being old, ill-designed, ill-equipped and badly staffed. Some of them (four) with between 200 and 300 sick beds had no resident medical officer and one with 352 sick had none. In one Inspector's district of 40 unions there were two workhouses with more than 50 sick who did not have a Superintendent Nurse, 12 had no paid trained nurses on night duty (in two cases for 35 patients and in another case for over 50 patients), 12 had over 50 patients to each night nurse and 12 had over 25 patients to each day nurse. The total number of nurses for 300 town workhouses with 70000 to 80000 patients between them was 2646 (163 Superintendent Nurses, 1390 nurses, 1093 probationers). This contrasted with the nursing level in the separate Infirmaries which was 2490 for 40000 patients. Such was the overcrowding in some workhouse infirmaries that the general part had to be used for convalescent patients and this exacerbated the difficulties between the nurses and the Matrons.

As regards the separate Infirmaries, about 49 of these had nurse-training schools and the other infirmaries mainly obtained their nurses from these sources. The metropolitan Infirmaries turned out over 400 trained nurses each year, certificated for a three years' training. The Minority repeated the evidence (but with greater strength) that the separate Infirmaries had become largely surgical having daily operating sessions under general anaesthesia; they were therefore no longer devoted to long-stay cases and were increasingly doing the work of general hospitals.

In the London area, in spite of the extensive provision of voluntary hospitals, there were 32 infirmaries (including one children's infirmary at Carshalton) varying from 242 beds to 793 beds, totalling 17000 and about three times as many as all the voluntary hospitals put together.

In Liverpool the number of Poor Law beds was also about three times those of the voluntary hospitals. The largest infirmary was Mill Road with 900 beds, one visiting consultant, three resident doctors, 56 paid nurses on day duty (1:11 patients) 22 on night duty (1:27). It was specially designed and equipped and had become largely used by people who were far from destitute.

Crumpsall Infirmary in Manchester was virtually separately administered if not formally, had 1400 beds for the sick and 400 for lunatics and epileptics and was probably the largest hospital in Great Britain. It boasted three resident and two visiting doctors, 78 paid nurses on day duty (1:12) and 24 night nurses (1:48).

The Birmingham Infirmary had 1400 beds, several resident doctors, three visiting physicians and one visiting surgeon. It treated about 4500 cases a year.

In their book deriving from the Minority Report, the Webbs (1910) have described the new Infirmaries: 'the structure tends to be elaborate, ornate and expensive. The lighting and heating, the ventilation and sanitation, the operating room and the dispensary, are all of the most costly if not always of the most useful character. On the other hand, it is clear that in the proportion of doctors and nurses to patients, and in the variety and specialisation of the staff, even the best Poor Law Infirmary falls markedly below the standard of the London hospitals.' They quote as their source the evidence given by Dr McVail, and they continue from him, 'my general conclusion is that even where Guardians provide excellent, and perhaps extravagant modern building, and equip these most elaborately with the most modern medical and surgical appliances, and furniture and furnishings, yet when they come to the appointing of staff to do the work of these fine institutions, liberality of policy fails them, and parsimony takes its place. They may have most advanced views as to the manner in which the poor should be housed and fed but when they come to medical work they are likely to adopt unknowingly a policy of sweating both as to the amount of work required and as to the payment made in it.' To this parsimony the Webbs have also added that the lack of interest manifested by the LGB had removed all stimulus and challenge from the work of the doctors. There was no opportunity to specialise, there were only a few visiting consultants and no contact with medical teaching.

The Minority was strong in its criticism of the philosophy of Poor Law medical relief and repeatedly complained that its dominant concern was 'relief', that it was curative only and paid no regard to prevention, had no concern with the domestic conditions of the patients, nor the promotion of medical science and no contact with medical education. For all this it cost over £4 000 000 each year.

The Minority looked at the voluntary agencies whose work impinged on the Poor Law. It may be helpful, at the risk of some repetition, to demonstrate their feelings about some of these so that their expressed criticism of medical relief may be put into some kind of perspective. They were no less critical of the outpatient departments of the voluntary hospitals; they found them slipshod in their work, overburdened, giving gratuitous (i.e. unwarranted) treatment and missing many serious cases. 'At present', they quoted from a medical practitioner, 'the outpatient department of the voluntary hospital is to a large extent a shop for giving people large quantities of medicine' (Webb 1910, p. 134). They were equally critical of the medical missions, medical clubs and Provident Associations and of the voluntary hospital inpatient system they wrote 'the voluntary hospital is not concerned with the treatment of disease; what it treats, and treats so magnificently, is collapse from disease'. They discharged their patients too early, causing an undue amount of chronic illness which ultimately ended up in the Poor Law institutions.

But the Minority was not critical of everything: they found points to regret about the detail and the local administration of the public health services but they had an unreserved admiration for their concepts and work. As they explained, local authorities were charged with the health of their populations: for the provision of medical advice, attendance or treatment for as many (certainly of the acute cases) as were under the Poor Law medical service. They even sometimes treated the same diseases. The municipal hospitals treated smallpox, scarlet fever, diphtheria, enteric fever, etc. They admitted patients from all sections of society – even including the professional classes. There was no legal sanction of what cases these hospitals could take, there was no central inspection nor audit of these hospitals, no official knowledge of that branch of civic activity and, once again, there were no statistics kept.

There was a limited but growing outdoor service; contacts of notifiable diseases were examined; Health Visitors were widely used for the notification of cases.

The local authorities had also undertaken the care of school children at the request of the education authorities and here again the Health Visitors played an active and important role. Parents were made responsible for the implementation of advice given at the school clinics under sanction of school exclusion orders. This work was regarded as hygiene work and was not looked on as 'relief'.

In addition to all those services the public health authorities also provided the maternity and child welfare services and the mortality rate had recently begun to decline. This, the Medical Officer of Hackney had remarked, was because public health measures were being taken into the homes by the Health Visitors and lady volunteers. There were milk dispensaries and milk banks but these charged a small fee and therefore many pauper mothers could not take advantage of them since the Guardians would not repay the fee as 'relief'.

Health Visitors, 'the friends of the family', visited every house to look at its hygiene and sanitary arrangements, see to disinfection, watch over child rearing, feeding and the source of the milk supply.

They also visited homes where an infantile death had been reported from any infectious disease or tuberculosis, or where sanitary defects had been reported; they followed up infectious disease contacts, visited school exclusion cases, cases of erysipelas and discharges from municipal hospitals.

Thus the local sanitary health services covered a wide area always seeking to prevent disease, seeking to achieve early diagnosis and giving education in the healthy way of living.

Whereas the Poor Law, they reported, was deterrent by philosophy and tended to destroy the individual's independence, the public health authorities created in the individual an enhanced sense of personal and social obligation, heightened parental responsibility and raised personal standards. Unfortunately some local authorities were apathetic and the services were not always available, the scope of work was sometimes limited, for instance the Health Visitors only looked after babies up to 12 months, there was no antenatal care, the school medical service was restricted, there was no treatment of the venereal diseases: there was a deficiency of volume and geographic spread.

Therefore, the Minority felt, there was a need for a unified service even if it did run counter to medical thinking which preferred to maintain the dichotomy between curative and preventive medicine; Dr McVail, the special medical investigator, had thought that there should be a State service, or at least a unified service under public health administration. These sentiments had been supported by Dr Newman, the Medical Officer to the Board of Education, Dr Leslie MacKenzie, the medical member of the LGB for Scotland and Dr Newsholme, the Chief Medical Officer of the LGB. There should be a central office and a strong Inspectorate including medical and hospital experts. Medical care should not necessarily be free but charges should be based on a scale of fees to be prepared by Parliament. Under the unified service all medical services should be included: the MOH, Hospital Superintendents, School Doctors, District Medical Officers, Workhouse Medical Officers, Dispensary Doctors, Medical Superintendents of Infirmaries: each in his appropriate sphere, all under a County Medical Officer.

They did not discuss the organisation of the Nursing Service.

The Minority Report has probably received more discussion and note than did the Majority Report: it was privately printed and circulated by the Webbs who also took every opportunity to speak about it, write about it and publicise their ideas. The Minority wanted the Poor Law organisation to be broken up, they wanted its functions to be distributed between various committees or authorities which would consequently be able to apply specialist knowledge: Health, Pensions, Employment, Education and Public Assistance; each category previously classified by age would be re-classified under needs, thus the aged and infirm would be distributed between the Pensions Committee (if they received pensions), the Public Assistance Committee (if they did not have an income nor a pension), the Health Committee (if they required substantial medical or nursing care).

The Minority Report was no less condescending in its language than was the Majority Report; it was as unrealistic in its utterances, as remote in its perspectives and as manipulative in its social techniques, but unlike the Majority Report it did try to establish some policy that could aim at dealing with the sources of poverty and illness, it accepted the challenge of social changes (and, for that matter, of scientific changes) and tried to meet them. Beatrice Webb had a host of connections and friends amongst the social reformers, she was married to a socialist, had worked with Booth, had (with Lansbury) taken part in social relief in the East End of London, and knew at close quarters the daily life of the urban workman. She drew on these experiences, was passionately involved in her social convictions and used the findings of social research that had become available over the years. In this respect the report was forward looking and tried to avoid conventional thinking.

In the event, however, the Government took no action on either report and social legislation during the next 40 years probably drew from both reports dealing with the needs of categories of people and disease in an ad hoc fashion.

It is remarkable however that both reports continued to neglect the nursing infrastructure of the medical service to which they had given so much consideration. No significant recommendations were made to support or develop the nursing service, no recommendation was made for a central service or for a nursing inspectorate. Whilst several recommendations were made to help in the development of the medical service the Commissioners did not find it necessary to give equal consideration or, indeed, any consideration to the nurses. They wanted an adequate supply of trained nurses, they deprecated the use of untrained nurses, they accepted that the care of the sick depended on the nurses and they spent many hours hearing evidence pertaining to the nurses but they did not conceive of the need to make any recommendations aimed at the development or the strengthening of the nursing service. In their discussions on the reorganisation of medical care the Minority never mentioned the deployment of nurses. They commented on the exploitation of medical and nursing staffs by the Guardians, of their 'parsimony' and 'sweating' policy. They recommended increased opportunities for professional development for the doctors but they made no similar proposals for the nurses. They were as guilty of neglect as were the Guardians.

And the shortage of nurses for the Poor Law establishments continued.

Looking at the Minutes of Evidence, one is struck by the comparatively small amount of real thought that was given to the nursing service: certainly there is little new thinking, little real analysis of the system and how it worked or why it did not work. There is some discussion on a central nursing department and a Poor Law Nursing Service, there is discussion on training, numbers of nurses, conditions of work, status, availability of recruits, etc. but the thinking demonstrated by the evidence was, at the time, orthodox and there did not appear to be any analysis in depth nor was there any evidence of an attitude that nursing had a central place in the administration of medical relief. A great deal of evidence, by contract, was received on the work, payment, conditions of service, responsibilities and position of the medical officers.

The Nursing Order of 1897 was said by several witnesses to have been responsible for a marked improvement in the conditions of the workhouse infirmaries by increasing the employment of Superintendent Nurses over a wider range of infirmaries, increasing the numbers of nurses and decreasing the numbers of pauper nurses. There was still however a common avoidance of the Order by Guardians and medical officers who resisted the requirement to appoint Superintendent Nurses for a staff of three nurses or more; they did this quite simply by failing to appoint nurses and by using attendants instead. Thus the decrease in the use of pauper nurses was often nominal only, since the pauper nurses had become pauper attendants or assistant nurses. Furthermore by that time, the relative understanding of the late 19th century of the meaning of the terms 'certificated nurse', 'trained nurse', 'qualified nurse' and 'nurse' had become very cloudy indeed, and confusion reigned. The certificated nurse could be one who had trained for three years in a hospital or infirmary of considerable standing or it could mean that she had been granted a certificate by a doctor after a perfunctory training in, perhaps, a cottage hospital. The trained nurse was probably one who had received some training in a hospital but who did not possess a certificate (sometimes she had prematurely terminated a three year training). The 'qualified nurse' was usually qualified by experience only but was frequently accepted by the LGB as an alternative to the certificated nurse in a rural infirmary (and could even be confirmed as a Superintendent Nurse) provided that she 'satisfied' the medical officer. 'Nurse' meant anything, from the pauper neighbour looking after an outdoor sick person to the upgraded inmate avoiding the stigma of pauperdom by earning her keep. The position was further confused by the term 'assistant nurse' who could be officially so described after one year of a three year structured training in a reputable infirmary (whilst still continuing her training), or she could be a wardswoman. The 'Minor Training Schools' which were still lacking official recognition under the Poor Law could also produce assistant nurses or trained nurses after a one or two year training course. The LGB also preferred the term 'assistant nurse' to 'qualified nurse' and sought to promote it in that sense.

Thus the recommendations of the 1902 Committee had frequently been adopted without official sanction and the new system ran parallel to (or was overlaid on) the older, simpler one. The position was even more confused than it had been ten years earlier.

It was said by several of the Inspectors who gave evidence (Qs. 107828, 2340, etc.) that there were 'trained' nurses in almost every workhouse but others quoted instances where the Guardians, medical officers or Masters avoided their appointment. It was confirmed that there were not enough nurses and this was blamed on the reluctance of Guardians to increase expenditure on establishments, although it was also made clear that 'a medical officer cannot now complain that the nursing is insufficient: if it is, it is his own fault' as he could requisition additional nurses, but 'medical officers sometimes preferred attendants to nurses'. The rising costs of the infirmaries were blamed substantially on the establishment of an adequate number of trained nurses together with their accommodation and maintenance.

Mr Raw, the Consulting Physician from Liverpool who was also the visiting Medical Superintendent at Mill Road Infirmary, pleaded eloquently for a National Nursing Service.

The British Medical Association representatives had very little to say about nursing at all: their only point was to call for greater medical control over the district nurses since, they complained, 'they became a kind of unqualified general practitioner for the district for children's ailments and medical matters generally' (Q 393252).

Whilst there was general agreement that the quality of nursing had improved in the infirmaries there was a complaint from Birmingham about the state in which patients were sent to them by the charity hospitals: 'some abominable cases of bed-sores'.

There was also considerable discussion on the numbers of nurses, especially the nurse:patient ratio. Everyone agreed that this was a very difficult problem and depended on the state of dependency of the patient and also on the physical environment. Miss Stansfield (Q 14603) (a Lady Inspector appointed in 1897 to the Metropolitan District) felt that, because of these difficulties, she could not give general agreement to a ratio of 1:8; Dr Downes agreed with her; Dr Anderson of the BMA felt that a weakness in the infirmaries was the 'excessive' number of probationers on the nursing staff. The 1902 Committee had earlier heard that it was cheaper to use probationer nurses than assistant nurses and this seemed to be a continuing trend as an economic preference. An interesting table of the relative ratios of nurse:patient and probationers:trained nurse had been drawn up by Dr McVail for his evidence (Appendix 4). This showed a comparison for the voluntary hospitals (teaching and non-teaching) and the infirmaries. The numbers of patients per nurse ranged from 2·1 to 4·7 for the voluntary hospitals and from 7·2 to 22·2 for the Poor Law infirmaries. As for the ratios of probationers to trained nurses, these ranged from 1·2 to 5·2 at the voluntary hospitals and from 0·6 to 5·7 at the infirmaries. There were therefore many more nurses per patient at the general hospitals, but the proportion of trained to untrained nurses was roughly the same in both areas. The term 'trained nurse' is used in the tables generically and no further more specific definition is available. Similarly, the meaning of the term 'nurse' is not clear and the possibility that it might have included assistant nurses should not be excluded.

Whilst there was difficulty in obtaining Superintendent Nurses in some infirmaries due to resistance from the Guardians, Medical Officers and Masters, it was also claimed that possible candidates were put off by a continuing lack of definition of their position relative to the Master; Matrons of the large Infirmaries were frequently appointed from nurses from the general hospitals, as sometimes were ward sisters. Miss Stansfield felt that this practice was mutually beneficial as the Poor Law nursing in the metropolitan Infirmaries had modelled itself as far as possible on that of the general hospitals but on the other hand, she felt that the quality of nursing in the infirmaries, where the patient turnover was slow and the cases difficult and demanding, was much better than it was in the general hospitals. She felt that there was little reason to be concerned about the supply of probationer nurses: 'No I do not think the stream of probationers will ever run dry. I think there will be quite sufficient applications. I think as Poor Law Nursing becomes more readily recognised it will hold an increasingly good position. It is only a question of time, and I think there will be less and less difficulty.'

There was also some discussion on training and its status relative to that in the general hospitals. Here Miss Stansfield (Q 14599) had this to say: 'I am obliged to admit I do not think it does rank as high. I do not think it would be so if the public understood how excellent the training under the Poor Law is, how Poor Law nursing really requires the best women, how it is infinitely finer work to nurse a poor bed-ridden woman who continually wants lifting and feeding, or to watch a chronic case, than it is to assist in one of those great accident cases in one of the general hospitals.' She also felt, as far as the private nurse was concerned, that a Poor Law trained nurse was an infinitely more effective and satisfactory nurse than one trained in a general hospital. She thought that 'the nurse in the Poor Law institution is really worthy of a higher status than the nurse in a general hospital'.

There was much discussion about a register for nurses: mostly it related to a State register but there was also talk of a register for Poor Law nurses, presumably as an alternative measure. Miss Stansfield felt that 'State registration alone will entirely establish the Poor Law nurses' position' but a Poor Law nurses' register would help to encourage the devoted Medical and Nursing Superintendents who put so much work into nurse training. She felt that publication of the examination results would help to grade the infirmaries in order of success thus assisting candidates in their selection of training schools. Dr Fuller of the LGB (Q 10666) felt that a register would help to control nurse training schools, 'there are places where they have absolutely no regulations for their [the probationers'] instruction and what is more, where there is no instruction obtained at all, except what they may happen to pick up by rule of thumb from the superior officers, whoever they may happen to be'. He added that that situation was not restricted to Poor Law institutions. He felt that probationers should not be trained in the small workhouses but maintained that there were no regulations forbidding this. He felt that the proposed system of Minor Training Schools, if accepted officially, would allow the Medical Inspectors to regulate the position.

Dr Downes (Q 23147) talked of the excellence of the training of Poor Law nurses: 'nursing and treatment which you get is not second to any hospital . . . the infirmary trained nurses may even be preferable to the hospital trained nurse.' Referring to the 1902 Committee, he reminded the Commission that it had recognised two grades of nurse in the Poor Law: the certificated nurse and the qualified nurse. He said that the qualified nurse would be a product of the Minor Training School but the LGB was concerned that the term 'qualified' might mislead people into believing that the nurse had greater training than she had actually received. The LGB therefore preferred the term 'assistant nurse'. However, the recommendations of the 1902 Committee had not yet been implemented. The LGB did not envisage that the assistant nurse would practise alone but that she would act under the supervision of a Superintendent Nurse.

Dr Downes referred to the 1905 *Select Committee* enquiring into the *State Registration of Nurses* and regretted that it had not availed itself of any evidence from Poor Law bodies.

There was further evidence of an anxiety over the possible registration of nurses: Mr Charles Spurrell (Q 23487f) who was the spokesman for the Infirmary Medical Superintendents' Society referred to the matter and was of the opinion that Poor Law infirmaries were bound to be accepted as training schools under any future legislation. There was, he said, already an interchange of staff between the hospitals and infirmaries but unless legislation was very carefully framed the results could be prejudicial as they had been under the 1902 Midwives Act. To date there had been only 11 Poor Law infirmaries accredited for midwifery training although 'a considerable number of other institutions of not greater importance had been recognised'. Up until the Act the flow of midwives from the Poor Law infirmaries had been considerable but 'now that had ceased'.

Legislation for State registration would have to avoid the situations introduced by the Midwives Act where several authorities had the power of inspection over the same institutions sometimes giving irresponsible advice. (By 'irresponsible' was meant the fact that the CMB was not statutorily responsible to any authority.) If a similar situation grew up under State registration for nurses it would affect more nurses than had the Midwives Act and might possibly affect the administration of the whole infirmary (rather than just the maternity units). He was referring particularly to the situation of the Whitechapel Infirmary which was one of the greatest Poor Law Infirmaries, one of the largest and one of the best. This Infirmary had had its application for recognition as a midwives' training school delayed over several years because the CMB objected to some relatively minor details of lay-out in the maternity unit. The delay was the cause of great bitterness on the part of the Poor Law authorities.

Other witnesses, all Guardians of large, well respected unions, gave evidence on the need for a standardised nurse training and system of examinations, the appointment of nurses as lady inspectors of infirmaries and nursing, the need for all patients to be under the supervision of certificated nurses of three years' training, the need to maintain the status of Poor Law nurses, of the Poor Law nurses' certificate and of the need for an adequate establishment of nurses. The witness from Huddersfield Union, Miss Siddon, regretted that nothing had come of the Yorkshire Nurse Training scheme described to the 1902 Committee.

Dr McVail's report (App. Vol. XIV) was similar in many ways to the report of the 1894–6 *BMJ* inspectors but demonstrated some considerable development in his understanding of infirmary design, lay-out, expectations for amenities and general standards. It also demonstrated a considerable advance in achievements and attitudes on the part of the Guardians over the intervening period of 10–12 years. He took as his sample 16 rural unions and 13 urban workhouses and infirmaries which had been selected on the grounds that no one else would be giving evidence on them. They were dispersed throughout the country (England and Wales). He found cause to complain about deficient water supplies, some defective sanitary conveniences, and accommodation for married inmates and staff. He did feel however that not all married inmates actually wished to live together on their admission to a workhouse.

In the rural unions he also criticised a continuing absence of medical records of patients' daily temperatures, pulse and respiration rates, treatments and diets. He found that Guardians frequently expected the medical officers to provide their own equipment such as ophthalmoscopes and laryngoscopes and that modern conveniences such as telephones were often not used even if they were available. He acknowledged the difficulty in distinguishing between the aged and infirm who might not need medical treatment and those who might and the resultant difficulties in adequate classification and warding. For this reason he found that medical treatment was not widely needed, but where it was given he found it fairly satisfactory and that the medical officers still paid for their prescribed medicines.

Commenting on nursing in these rural unions Dr McVail also acknowledged the problem of keeping a nurse adequately employed when there were no patients or only a few patients over a period of time and, conversely, of finding a nurse when an inmate needed nursing and where none was regularly employed. He found, on the whole, that the nursing was deficient and that pauper wardsmen or wardswomen were used. He seemed to take the presence or absence of bedsores as a criterion for his judgement of nursing.

He found the condition of the beds and mattresses to be usually satisfactory and consisting of hair, flock or straw filling. Lockers were usually available, there was a supply of bed linen but sometimes the size of the sheets was wanting. As for the food, he found this of good quality but served badly and poorly stored.

In the urban areas he found a continuum of standards ranging from those similar to the better rural areas to the well developed and separately administered Infirmaries doing the type of work usually done in the general hospitals. He cited the Camberwell Infirmary as an example of the best. He had noted, however, a difference in the age of the population of the infirmaries as compared with the general hospitals: in the infirmaries the patients aged over 60 years accounted for from 25% to 72% of the population, whereas in the general hospitals these patients accounted for only 5%–6% of the total. In the developed infirmaries there was an increasing trend towards taking more of the younger age groups with a tendency to 'draft' the aged inmates into adjacent workhouses. In the Camberwell Infirmary there was a total number of 800 beds of which there were 500 'hospital type cases'. There was also an increasing trend to accept cases described as urgent which did not require an order from the Relieving Officer; thus the Medical Officers were more and more controlling the admission of patients into their infirmaries. All the infirmaries were full to overflowing although patients who were not paupers and who could be expected to pay for at least part of their treatment were accepted and he cited the Whitechapel Infirmary as an example of this practice.

In the urban unions, he found the buildings nearly all excellent, they were well designed, had good beds and bedding, were well ventilated, well heated, enjoyed a hot water supply and bathrooms, although he frequently complained of a lack of safety keys for the hot water taps. From all these causes for satisfaction Dr McVail had to exclude Hope Hospital in the Salford Union which had older buildings, a rougher finish and was not so well supplied with amenities: a little imaginative expenditure, he felt, would easily have put things right.

Whilst the physical environment was, on the whole, good, Dr McVail was less pleased with the staffing standards. He found that the medical staff were insufficient and overworked. He gave as an example the staff at three Infirmaries: Whitechapel where there were three medical officers for 590 beds, Camberwell where there were six doctors (some of whom also worked at other institutions) for 819 patients, and Hope where there was one part-time and two full-time medical officers for 800 patients.

Dr McVail also published his tables for the nurse:patient ratio and for the ratio of probationers to trained nurses. He had observed, he said, that the better class of nurse was more drawn to the bright, clean and well-managed establishment whereas the inferior class of woman went to the dingy establishment where the training was poor, where there were few operations and which was generally lacking in appeal.

Dr McVail also reported on the maternity units which he had found to be 'models of comfort and cleanliness, the nurses well trained, the instruments and appliances are beyond criticism and medical assistance is available whenever required'. He was concerned, however, to note that sometimes the babies were allowed to sleep in bed with their mothers, 'which is now regarded as objectionable' and that dummies, comforters and tube feeding bottles were sometimes still in evidence. But, he felt, the Poor Law maternity units were excellent training schools for midwifery nurses.

In his discussion on outdoor relief, Dr McVail confirmed the paucity of nursing, 'Quite unquestionably in some rural districts the want of sick nursing of paupers is a serious defect in the present system of Poor Law medical relief.' Although there was a similar deficiency of outdoor nurses in the urban districts, the problem was not so acutely felt as the urban sick poor were more willing to be admitted to the infirmaries: there was real evidence of a continuing antipathy towards the rural infirmaries where admission was still through the gates of the workhouse. The unions sometimes subscribed to the nursing associations but not so generously as to ensure the supply of a nurse every time one was required.

An interesting piece of evidence demonstrated by Dr McVail tended to disprove the long-held belief that medical relief still caused pauperism: only about 1% of rural sick had medical relief before they received general relief, and in the urban areas the figure was about 3·2%. This evidence, corroborated by other evidence, gave rise to the statement by the Minority that medical relief was not the cause of pauperism: rather, they felt, it was sickness that gave rise to poverty.

Dr McVail made many recommendations some of which were for a reorganisation of the local administrative units so as to achieve larger areas which could more easily rationalise the instruments of medical relief; a greater degree of central control by the LGB and more inspection of medical relief agencies; the need for compulsory detention of certain cases; the requirement that District medical officers should report unsanitary situations to the Public Health authorities and that medical relief should be conditional on the patient carrying out the treatment as prescribed by the District medical officer.

McVail's outline for the reorganisation of the medical relief system was based on the existing service and did not suggest any new organisation: he based his proposals on the existing Scottish system in which there were full time Medical Officers of Health with the Diploma of Public Health. He felt that the Poor Law medical service should be combined with the Public Health medical service to form a single unified service. Each medical officer should have the specialist qualification appropriate to his function, either curative or preventive, and the service should be biased towards the prevention of disease and the promotion of good health.

McVail added a memorandum to his report in which he philosophised on the merits and disadvantages of a free medical service.

He felt that the cost of improving physical health would be the weakening of moral fibre under such a free system: 'Good health is not the only important thing in this world. A free medical system could not justly be compared with a free educational system since the latter was finite and limited by the school leaving age whereas medical care continued from "childbirth to the grave". If free treatment were given it would be necessary to give free medicines, but much medical treatment involved an adequate diet so free medicines would also involve free food. It was likely that free clothing would also become necessary, then free housing; the need for full employment, regular annual holidays and freedom from all material worries would all be argued as necessities for good health, and there would be no end to it.' He felt that there was still much to be said for personal payment for personal services received but as payment was not always possible when the services were needed it was wiser to pay beforehand, on an insurance basis. He therefore felt committed to the idea of health insurance through the Friendly Societies.

It will be seen that the Commissioners were impressed by McVail and that his report was influential in the compilation of the two final reports, both of which incorporated many of his ideas. His proposals were not innovative however, neither, it can be said, were either of the final reports. One was orthodox and the other was a reflection of the newer trend of social thinking which had been developing over the past few years. The Majority Report sought to bolster the Poor Law, the Minority Report sought to break it up. The Majority Report did not consider in too great detail the trend of disease and the Minority Report reflected the current preoccupation with preventable disease, What neither report considered was that infectious diseases had already been largely controlled by the time of the Commission, and the incidence curve of these diseases was on a downward slope. It was probably rather early for the increase in the number of deaths from cancer and other diseases now labelled 'behavioural diseases' to be observed, but there was such a trend. If these two factors had been observed and noted it may be that the Reports would have given less weight to Public Health, then in its hey-day. Another factor which could have been noted was the significant increase in the population of the over 60s. Very little attention was paid to this and no provision made for it in the Reports. Although a large number of statistics were studied, these factors did not emerge for the Commissioners.

Another observation which can be made was the lack of any evidence given by nurses. Whereas in 1902 there was a balance of professional witnesses between the medical officers and the nurses (the nurses had been represented by both prominent and obscure nurses, senior in rank and status and junior, nurses from the great Infirmaries and nurses from the small workhouse infirmaries), there was no Poor Law nurse to give evidence to the Royal Commission. What evidence was given on nursing was given by Guardians and Inspectors, but mostly by the medical officers. Whereas in 1902 there had been Miss Wilson of the Workhouse Infirmary Association, Miss Kett of the Northern Workhouse Nursing Association, Mr Tillotson of the Yorkshire Poor Law Nursing Board, letters from the declining Florence Nightingale and Louisa Twining, Miss Lee and a variety of voluntary workers interested in and to some extent leading the direction of nursing, by the time of the Royal Commission these people were no longer in evidence and the medical officers were very clearly in charge of their field. The nurses were subordinated and the doctors spoke for them. Thus the surge of popular interest in nursing had declined; the status brought by the 'Ladies' of the 19th century had not, in effect, been ascribed to the profession: the charisma of Florence Nightingale and the influence of Louisa Twining had given way to bureaucracy, and their concepts and teaching had become routine (Gerth and Wright Mill 1974).

No nurse had emerged to take over the leadership of the profession which was by then fractionised: the Poor Law nurses and the voluntary hospital nurses, the pro-registration nurses and the anti-registration nurses, the trained (certificated) nurses and the untrained (qualified, assistants or 'experienced') nurses. The nurses in the Poor Law had never really been able to gain a place in the lines of power: they were not allowed to report directly to the Guardians, they had no representative in the LGB nor were there any nurses in the central Medical Department. All negotiations and all reporting on nursing matters were made for the nurses by the doctors. Nor had the nurses yet isolated any indigenous function for themselves. They were subject to the medical officers, to their prescriptions and orders. Without doubt the competent nurses were the doctors' right hands and first lieutenants, but that was all; they never saw themselves as being in control of their own function or even of their own careers. No nurse could receive a certificate of training without a testimonial from a doctor, no nurse could obtain a post without a similar testimonial and no nurse could gain promotion unless she had evidence of pleasing her previous medical officers. Such was the power of the doctors over the nurses that it is small wonder that leaders who were independent or forward thinking did not emerge. One nurse who overlapped Florence Nightingale and was also an independent-minded, free-thinking spirit was Mrs Bedford Fenwick, who was comfortably married to a sympathetic doctor and did not need to work. This enforced dependence on the doctors subsequently became an established precept and 'well-disciplined' and 'amenable' became the hallmarks of a good nurse.

So much for the Royal Commission. It was shelved by the Government who, by then, realised that any evolution of the Poor Laws must be contingent on a complete revision of the local authorities. The ideas and ideals of the two reports were not completely lost, however, since they were revived and resuscitated in subsequent social legislation. The Commission had very little effect on Poor Law nursing except indirectly: more unions paid larger amounts of money to the nursing associations thus expanding the district nursing services, and the Public Health hospital service, with its reputation suitably burnished, continued to expand, particularly in the care of acute cases.

REFERENCES

Gerth, H. H. and Wright Mill, C. (Eds) (1974), *From Max Weber*. **London,** Routledge Paperback. Chs IX, X.

Royal Commission on the Poor Laws, 1909, Cmnd. 4499.

Ryder, J. and Silver, H. (1970). pp. 123–4.

Titmuss, R. (1963), *Essays on the Welfare State*. **London, Unwin University** Books. p. 19.

Webb, Beatrice and Sydney (1910), *The State and the Doctor*. **London,** Longmans. p. 109 f.

9

ADMINISTRATIVE CHANGES
AND SOCIAL UPHEAVAL:
1910–1919

After the Report of the Royal Commission on the Poor Laws, the Government sought to tidy up and consolidate the administration of medical relief and the Poor Law.

There had been a spate of social legislation and social attitudes had, by then, begun to erode the principle of deterrence in the Poor Law. There was still a general feeling that the poor had only themselves to blame and that the able-bodied unemployed should not be encouraged to rely too heavily on parish relief, but the distinction between the 'deserving poor' and the 'undeserving poor' was more generally accepted. The aged and infirm and the sick poor came into the former category and their situation and conditions were more sympathetically examined. Moreover the Royal Commission had thoroughly ventilated the whole of the Poor Law. Lastly, the Royal Commission had shown that it was not only the destitute who went into Poor Law infirmaries: the poor, the middle class and, often, the professional classes were obliged to use the Poor Law infirmaries for want of anything else in their localities, and even sometimes preferred the infirmary to the hospital.

In 1910 the LGB reported that the use of case papers for all patients (including the sick poor) was to be made compulsory and that the Relief Book and Medical Relief Book were to be abandoned. The respective duties of the Master, Matron and Superintendent Nurses were classified with some responsibilities being transferred to the nurses. Thus their status slowly became better established.

In 1909 the MAB hospital at Carshalton was officially opened for sick children. Originally it had been built for infectious cases and convalescents but as soon as it was completed it was discovered that the decline in infectious diseases was such as to make it redundant. It was therefore decided to convert it for the use of sick children and a nurse-training school was included. This was actually the first nurse-training project started by the MAB and they paid their probationer nurses on a higher scale than other nurse-training hospitals.

In 1910 the Infirmary Medical Superintendents' Society circulated a proposed scheme for uniform training and examination of Poor Law probationers. They made the comment that 'it is very important that the interests of Poor Law nurses should be carefully safeguarded, so that whatever legislation may be brought forward in the future their position may be as advantageous as that of Nurses trained in the general hospitals'. It was considered that the proposed scheme, if implemented, might have put the Poor Law nurses in a stronger position. The Medical Superintendents sent a copy of the scheme to the Association of the Poor Law Infirmaries' Matrons who accepted the proposals providing they were applied nationally and were not restricted to the metropolis. It will be noticed that the scheme was drawn up by the medical officers and not by the Matrons; the Matrons were reported as holding their meetings in the pleasant gardens of the infirmaries in a tea-party atmosphere of the bourgeoisie: their meetings were concerned with details of the micro-environment whilst the medical officers were concerned with the broader picture. This distinction is reminiscent of the Victorian family: the wife concerning herself with household matters and the husband with the family finances, the City and Imperial Preference. Both functions required some knowledge and skill but the former was localised and restricted and the latter was wider-ranging; at the same time each side was ignorant of the other's skills.

During this period there was a consolidation of the system of providing certificated training at Major Training Schools within the Poor Law nursing system and the term became more widely used. The Minor Training Schools also developed and provided assistant nurses. The syllabus of lectures given at the Mile End Infirmary was given in the *PLO Journal* (1911, Vol. XX). The Medical Superintendent gave the lectures on hygiene and 'materia medica', the Matron lectured on elements of general nursing and invalid cooking, the Senior Assistant Medical Officer taught surgical nursing and bacteriology and the Junior Assistant Medical Officer was assigned elementary anatomy and physiology. It will be noticed that there were no lectures mentioned on medical nursing which may have been included in 'elements of general nursing'. Presumably the allocation of subjects to the officers might have reflected a 'hierarchy' of knowledge.

Also in this year, the *Poor Law Officers' Journal* made a series of comments about nurses' accommodation, including the wards and

F

equipment. There was a campaign for separate nurses' homes, better equipment in the wards, greater distinction in the status of certificated and assistant nurses, better differentials between the two grades in the scales of pay and in the work. It was reported that the less well-endowed establishments were finding it much more difficult to recruit nurses and there was a resultant up-grading of many old nurses' homes and the building of new ones. An example of such a new home was at Burnley where fireproof materials were used, the nurses had separate bedrooms and there were separate sitting rooms, a breakfast room and a library.

The conditions of work of the Poor Law nurses gradually improved but their hours of work were still very long. In 1906 Miss Stansfield had given evidence to the Royal Commission that she was seriously worried by the situation: 'I am not at all satisfied with the nurses' hours of work. I think they are far too long.' She discussed the impossibility of introducing a three shift-system because of its need for extra nurses to cover the wards, said that the problem was not confined to the Poor Law infirmaries and mentioned the recent suicides of two nurses from London, one of whom worked in a general hospital. The *Poor Law Officers' Journal* reported that nurses were indulging in drugs because of overwork and long hours. Their exhaustion was further exacerbated by indifferent feeding. A scheme for a six-day week for nurses at the Bethnal Green Infirmary (where most of the patients were tubercular) was referred by the Guardians back to the sub-committee because it required extra nurses. Those in favour of the scheme argued that there was a real need for better conditions for the nurses who should be moved from time to time to a different ward in order that their interest be stimulated by nursing different cases; nurses, they said, were exploited by the public and were being lost to the authorities because of their catching tuberculosis from their patients.

Off duty varied and, possibly, those institutions with the better hours were the ones to be reported but at Booth Hall Infirmary, Blackley, it was said that the senior nurses had two hours off duty daily, an evening off from 6.00 p.m. to 10.00 p.m. once a week and a half day from 2.00 p.m. to 10.00 p.m. once a month. Every three months they had from 10.00 a.m. to 10.00 p.m. off; on alternate Sundays they were off from 10.00 a.m. to 12.30 p.m. or from 1.30 p.m. to 4.00 p.m. or from 5.00 p.m. to 10.00 p.m. The junior nurses had two hours off duty daily, 6.00 p.m. to 10.00 p.m. once a week,

2.00 p.m. to 10.00 p.m. once a month and the same Sunday off duty as the senior nurses. There was enough evidence to assume that the nurses went off duty at 10.00 p.m. but no hint of their morning starting times was given.

The Matron of the Lambeth Infirmary at Booth Street is reported to have pleaded for more nurses: she reported that there were two nurses looking after over 31 patients on day duty and after 2.00 p.m. there was only one nurse. On night duty there was only one nurse to 34 patients. The Guardians responded by resolving to raise the salary of first year probationers from £7 to £10 per annum in order to attract more recruits and in the meanwhile to increase the nurses' off duty to two hours each day with a half day off weekly and a full day off each month. Unfortunately the LGB blocked their plans to recruit six extra staff nurses and 14 additional probationers as they felt that the Infirmary was already sufficiently well staffed.

It was at this time also that many general hospitals and infirmaries increased the training period from three to four years in order to provide more nursing staff for themselves.

An interesting picture of the social mood of the period is gained from a study of the House of Commons debate on the Poor Law on 27 April 1911 (Parliamentary Debates 1911). On the one hand, Members complained that there was overlapping of the different health services, of diseases such as phthisis being allowed to spread, the continuation of deterrent measures rather than preventive action, an overdose of discipline in the workhouses rather than kindness, the need to abolish the mixed, general workhouses, the desirability of handing Poor Law administration over to the County Councils, the need to give free medical relief to the sick irrespective of means, the problem of maintaining children in general workhouses and the need for a better and stronger lead from the LGB.

On the other hand, there were Members who asserted that the basic cause of destitution was physical, moral and mental defects in the individual. The problems were heredity ('we are breeding from defective stock'), the need to control breeding in these defectives, that the infirmaries were as good as general hospitals, that the paupers were being demoralised and undermined by over-easy and over-generous relief.

Mr Burns, the President of the LGB, said in reply that his Board was being blamed for economic and industrial problems which were operating socially, that many of the problems were inherited through the generations, that the Government could not be expected to do anything when neither the Royal Commission nor the Members could come to some sort of agreement. More and more was being loaded on to the County Councils and it was questionable whether they could also take on Poor Law work. Any change from the present system of Poor Law could be expensive and the House was constantly complaining about cost. Although there had been no legislative changes, much had been achieved through administrative change. The issues of the problem were changing very fast; to the Minister's mind the Majority Report was archaic and the Minority Report was obsolete.

The administrative changes referred to by Mr Burns was the *Departmental Committee* set up in 1911 *to examine the Orders of the Poor Law Commission, the Poor Law Board and the Local Government Board* and to consolidate and amend them. A series of recommendations had been made by this committee which did not finally report until 1913, although interim reports were issued.

It may be helpful to remember that during this period other social legislation had been enacted: in 1906 the School Meals Act had been passed, in 1908 the Old Age Pensions Act had 'helped 1 000 000 potential paupers', and in 1911 the National Insurance Act had been put on the Statute Book. This Act dealt with insurance against sickness and disability in the worker (but did not cover the families) and also dealt with unemployment. The new administrative arrangements for sickness in the insured man effectively set up yet another medical care system involving the 'panel' doctors, the Insurance Committees and the Approved Societies, and eventually used more nurses, also obtained through the nursing associations by subscription.

By 1913 the Athlone Committee was preparing to report: rumour and counter rumour flourished. Mr Burns confirmed in the House of Commons that the Committee had consulted the Poor Law Unions' Association and 'some other bodies', Miss Stansfield (by then the Principal Lady Inspector over a corps of Lady Inspectors, mostly trained nurses) told the Annual Meeting of the PL Infirmary Matrons' Association that they had been consulted by the LGB on the proposed Nursing Order. The President of the Association, Miss Barton, said that they had been able to influence the Government on the Poor Law Institutions Order. They had also insisted that any scheme for training nurses should include the PL nurses and not keep them shut out. At the end of the meeting a memorandum was sent to the LGB asking that the status of the Superintendent Nurse be secured under the draft Order so that the standard of nurse could be maintained. Evidently there was still some overlapping of duties with those of the Matrons and friction in spite of the recent adjustments.

The shortage of nurses increased: many unions reported an inability to recruit and Bath proposed to abolish the grade of assistant nurses, styling them staff nurses in order to attract candidates. Mr Burns, in reply to a question about this, said that it was a national problem and beyond his control. He agreed that the National Insurance Act and the setting up of tuberculosis sanatoria by the local authorities had increased the problem. The debate on nurses' hours of work also continued but when a motion was put to a general meeting of the Infirmary Matrons that nurses should have one day off duty each week they decided that it would cost too much and rejected the motion. It is interesting however to note a lecture given by Miss C. Seymour Yapp, Superintendent Nurse of the Tynemouth Infirmary. In this lecture she contrasted the work of the Poor Law nurse with that of the general hospital nurse. She maintained that the PL nurse had shorter duty hours and more off duty than her counterpart; she was also better fed.

In July 1913 the first report of the Departmental Committee together with the draft Orders were tabled in the House of Commons. In December the LGB circulated an explanatory letter to all Boards of Guardians. There were two Orders issued concurrently: the Poor Law Institutions Order 1913 and the Poor Law Institutions (Nursing) Order 1913. For the first time an official document relating to the Poor Law avoided the use of the term 'pauper' and preferred instead to refer to the 'poor' or the 'destitute'. This avoidance of the term 'pauper' became official policy from then onwards.

The Nursing Order rescinded the Nursing in Workhouses Order 1897 (and therefore the General Consolidated Order of 1847 which was the first and last occasion when the duties of the nurse had been prescribed) and came into operation on 31 March 1914. It was the Order under which all Poor Law nursing was controlled until the Local Government Act of 1929 and was therefore of considerable importance. It ordained that every institution of over 100 beds should appoint a Superintendent Nurse; all institutions in which three or more nurses were employed should appoint a Head Nurse (unless it was over 100 beds), all Poor Law institutions were to employ a certificated nurse on its staff or submit proposals to the LGB for obtaining such a nurse when it might be necessary. No person was to be appointed Superintendent Nurse or Head Nurse unless she was already in the post of Superintendent Nurse on 31 March 1914 or unless she was a certificated nurse having trained at an approved school and was also a certified midwife under the Midwives Act of 1902. No one but a certified midwife should be appointed as a midwife; only those people who had received 'such training in nursing as may render him or her a fit person and proper person to hold such office or perform such duties' should be employed as nurses, excepting female assistant nurses (serving under a Superintendent Nurse) or probationers nurses. The Superintendent Nurse should not be dismissed without the consent of the LGB but could be suspended. So long as the nursing establishment (excluding the Superintendent Nurse), the scales of salaries and the qualifications to be required were agreed by the LGB, individual appointments need not be approved by the Board, and the continuation of appointment of those Superintendent Nurses already in post on 31 March 1914 was guaranteed. The Order excluded from its terms the separate Infirmaries.

In its Circular Letter the Board made additional points: it said that in 1893 there were some 3000 nurses in the Poor Law nursing service and in 1913 there were 7600, an increase of 150% 'without any similar increase in the number of persons under treatment'. It also maintained that the population of trained nurses was greater. They reminded Guardians to take up references of all nurses before appointment, that no inmates could be employed in any nursing capacity without the specific approval of the MO; the Superintendent Nurse was to perform those duties usually performed by the Matron in the sick wards and would be required to make reports; the Head Nurse was also required to be a certified midwife and would act under the MO in all matters relating to treatment and nursing of the sick unless the Matron of the institution also possessed those qualifications required of a Head Nurse.

Thus, yet another level was added to the nursing hierarchy and the position of the Superintendent Nurse was established even if it left the position of the Head Nurse slightly indeterminate.

The Order appeared to be much more authoritative than previous orders and was aimed at tightening up the appointment and quality of nurses. Nevertheless there were a number of exceptions made by the LGB during the ensuing years which established many anomalies in the posts of Superintendent Nurses. Nurses who were uncertificated but who had served unions for many years were approved as Superintendent Nurses and were therefore in a position of authority over more recently employed certificated nurses.

The Departmental Committee of 1913 had been asked that the Superintendent Nurse should be allowed to make her report directly to the Guardians and that she should be allowed to be present at their meetings. The Committee had preferred to recommend that her report should be presented by the Master but suggested that the House Committee should consider reports from Principal Officers (including the Superintendent Nurse) with the officer present.

The Committee saw the Superintendent Nurse as an administrator or manager but regarded the Head Nurse as a 'forewoman' of a small institution. They had made her subordinate to the workhouse Matron because, they argued, there was an increasing number of Matrons who were themselves trained nurses.

Although the 1847 Order listing the nurses' functions had been rescinded, the 1913 Order, in fact, did not make any new prescription nor was one ever attempted thereafter and the duties of the nurse were never again described.

The amendments introduced by the Order were very conservative and demonstrated a persisting preoccupation with dietaries. It will be observed that the Superintendent Nurse's duties included actual nursing. This could well have been included in deference to views expressed, after the 1897 Order, that she was not actually required to do any nursing.

There was still a discrimination between Poor Law Infirmaries and general hospitals. In Article 1 (Definitions) of the Institutions Order, the Committee could have defined the Infirmaries as hospitals, but they elected not to do so.

The Committee also persisted in requiring a resident physician or Surgeon as one of the prerequisites of an approved training school, in spite of the recommendations of the 1902 Report.

The first Order, the Poor Law Institutions Order 1913, was divided into three parts. The first related to the management of the institution and made provision for the use of record papers for the inmates of the sick wards, the setting up of House Committees and Women's Committees and provision for the engagement by the

Master of an additional nurse in an 'emergency' which was to be defined by the MO.

The second part related to the duties of the Matron: she was to be responsible for the implementation of all orders from the MO for the treatment of the sick, for all nursing, heating and ventilation of the sick wards, provided that there was no Superintendent Nurse and no Head Nurse who might otherwise be responsible for these functions.

The duties of the Superintendent Nurse included those listed above and, additionally, she was 'to assist the Master and Matron in supervising the discipline in the institution, instruct the Assistant Nurses and Probationers employed in the institution in the nursing of the sick and take such part as may be practicable in the nursing of the sick'.

The duties of the Head Nurse included performing her duties as nurse, and, subject to the provisions listed above (relative to the Matron), superintending the other nurses and assistant nurses in the performance of their duties.

In 1914 the *Poor Law Officers' Journal* gave some instances of the immediate effect of the Orders on the nursing situation in the country. It spoke of nurses in several unions who had given many years' service but who had had to be dismissed in order that trained nurses could be employed. At the South Infirmary, St Pancras, they had had to take on an extra medical officer and at Hartlepool Infirmary the medical officer, acting on the advice of the Superintendent Nurse, had increased the nursing staff, reorganised their deployment and had recommended to the Guardians that the accommodation should be improved and a training school set up.

In the same volume of the *Journal*, there was an ominous note of the impending war: Poplar and Stepney Sick Asylum was arranging to accept military nursing orderlies for training.

In the *Annual Report* of the LGB for 1913–14 there are accounts from the inspectors of the nursing situation in their respective districts. They showed continuing difficulties in obtaining trained nurses and a continuing use and expansion of the district nursing services. The opinion is expressed that the voluntary hospital beds were totally inadequate for the growing demand and that the position would have been very difficult but for the Poor Law infirmaries. A table is given of the numbers of beds and nurses in the East and West Ridings of Yorkshire for 1913:

	Beds	Nurses	Unions/ Hospitals
East Riding Infirmaries	1387	96	10
West Riding Infirmaries	5624	477	35
TOTAL	7011	573	45
East Riding Voluntary Hospitals	534	144	7
West Riding Voluntary Hospitals	2775	676	33
TOTAL	3309	820	40

The Local Government Board did an audit of accommodation and found that there were 271 Poor Law infirmaries used only for the treatment of the sick poor. The sizes of these institutions varied considerably:

	Workhouse infirmaries	Separate Infirmaries
Less than 100 beds	330	144
100–200 beds	36	41
200–300 beds	16	27
Over 300 beds	18	59

These figures excluded all MAB beds but included beds for chronic, acute and all cases under medical care but not needing active or continuous treatment nor special nursing.

The President of the LGB in anticipation of the imminent war, declared (Parl. Debates 1914) that the Government no longer felt that it could hold itself aloof from the private societies who were engaged in work of health or of nursing, the provision of hospitals or of dispensaries. It was therefore seeking to co-ordinate the work of these societies in order that officialdom and the societies could work hand in hand. There was no complete information available on hospital accommodation throughout the country and he was acquiring information through his inspectors. He was setting up a Central Council in London to secure the overlapping of nursing agencies and to make good any deficiencies detected. An Intelligence Department was to be set up in the LGB and in future all infirmaries would be visited by women inspectors. Asked about the total number of trained nurses in the United Kingdom, he had to reply that there were no figures available but that in England and Wales there were approximately 9000 under the Poor Law. Moreover no criteria had been laid for the standard or content of the training for nurses and there was no information available as to the training given by municipal hospitals and sanatoria.

This lack of information and standards appeared as a glaring omission in the light of the preparations then being made for the forthcoming war. Poor Law institutions were being requisitioned for barracks and military hospitals and the Army Medical Corps moved into the latter. Medical Officers and nurses volunteered for war service and were joined by colleagues from the voluntary hospitals. The numbers of medical and paramedical staff fell far short of the numbers the authorities felt they would need and a recruitment drive brought in volunteers from all classes and walks of life. About 80 000 VADs were enrolled, mostly untrained (Abel-Smith 1964). Voluntary hospital consultants found themselves posted to infirmaries and were dismayed by the shortage of equipment and staff. The military authorities had to renovate and equip specialist departments in many of the more backward infirmaries. Often they took over an entire infirmary complete with the nursing and medical staff, requiring the sick poor to be moved to other Poor Law establishments, but even so the shortage of nurses was remarkable by their standards since the nurse: bed ratio for military hospitals was 1 : 19 compared with the Poor Law ratio 1 : 44. There was a profound upheaval of medical and nursing personnel, social classes, trained and untrained personnel and patients. Many PL nurses went to the front and received a status which they had never before known, others were in the services at home and abroad; those remaining in the infirmaries worked with the voluntary hospital doctors or army medical officers and those who were not looking after wounded servicemen trained VADs and RAMC orderlies. Some looked after the flood of Belgian refugees: all who remained in the infirmaries had to struggle with untrained and inefficient staff.

There were frequent complaints by the Poor Law medical officers and nurses who were working alongside military colleagues receiving better salaries and allowances. At the same time there were serious shortages of staff and more women doctors were being employed. In order to allay the discontent of the Poor Law medical and nursing staffs, their salaries were increased and in some cases, doubled. This made the nurses in the voluntary hospitals discontented and forced up their salaries.

By 1916 the number of beds handed over to the military authorities by the Poor Law authorities was 52 000 and the number of

VADs in 1917–18 had risen to 120 000. Also in 1916 the Government set up the Ministry of Reconstruction, with Dr Christopher Addison as the Minister in charge. The new Ministry, convened a *Local Government Committee* to look into *the transfer of the functions of Poor Law Administration in England and Wales*, under the chairmanship of Sir Donald Maclean and with Mrs Beatrice Webb as one of the members. In the same year, the Commons were told that the health of the country was being well maintained, there was a decrease in enteric fever and cerebrospinal fever and there had been no small-pox. Maternity and child welfare work was pressing ahead; there were 900 Health Visitors in employment and the infant mortality rate was dropping and was down to 11·10% in 1915.

In 1917 the Financial Secretary to the War Office spoke of the contribution to the war effort of the nation's women: 'In view of the man-power situation, we have continued and developed the employment of women in substitution for men wherever possible . . . the forms of employment are clerks, motor drivers, cooks and female labour of various kinds. In speaking of the women's part of this war – and it is great and growing – I cannot omit a reference to the brave and devoted service of the nurses.'

In 1917 the Maclean Committee reported. It had, said Dr Addison, made a 'reasoned attempt to secure reforms in harmony with those indicated by the Royal Commission which reported on the subject in 1909, without reviving the controversies which then centred round the Majority and Minority Reports of that body'. The Report repeated that it had found overlapping and conflicting principles of administration and it therefore concentrated on centralising in one (local) authority the administration of all expenditure from public funds. There were to be a Public Health Committee, and Education Committee, a Mental Deficiency Committee, a Prevention of Unemployment and Training Committee and a Home Assistance Committee. The Public Health Committee was to be responsible for the sick and infirm, maternity, infancy and aged requiring institutional care and for all institutions appropriate to these. The direction of its policy should be both preventive and curative. The Home Assistance Committee was to be responsible for vetting the home conditions of all people receiving public assistance, identifying special needs and referring those people for specialist help.

All Poor Law Officers (including doctors and nurses) should be taken over by the local authorities with their rights fully protected.

General mixed workhouses were to be abolished. In general, all relief services should be administered from County Council level but there should be District Committees. The report stressed the importance of complete unification of all services, free of the principle of deterrence or the Workhouse Test. Their recommendations included the abolition of the Boards of Guardians.

The Committee in its Report showed a wider recognition of distinct categories of 'deserving poor' and, moreover, they officially recognised these groups. Amongst the new categories which they listed were persons in distress because of the war, soldiers' dependents and discharged soldiers. They also included amongst the 'deserving poor' old age pensioners and families whose children were in receipt of school meals. All these were put under special administrative arrangements. Unfortunately this had the unintentioned effect of stressing the 'undeservedness' of those categories remaining with the Poor Law.

The London County Council had also set up a *Special Committee* to look into the *Health Administration in London* and their Report was published in December 1917. The LCC had experienced considerable problems from the fragmentation of the Poor Law medical services between the many unions of the metropolis and had been anxious to centralise the administration of all Poor Law matters in order to equalise the rates, but this required legislation which the war had prevented. The report of the Special Committee therefore substantially agreed with the Maclean Report but expanded one or two details. They proposed that the health functions of the Poor Law authorities should be divided between the LCC (as the central authority) and the metropolitan borough councils, that the cost of the Public Health services of an environmental or local character should be borne by public funds but that the cost of the prevention of the spread of infectious diseases should be split equally between the Government and local funds. They also proposed that the cost of other medical treatments should be borne, as far as possible, by the individual or by an insurance agency such as a Friendly Society. In order to co-ordinate the different hospitals in the metropolis they proposed the formation of a Central Council of London Hospitals.

In the meantime plans were laid for a Ministry of Health to replace the LGB and reshape the Poor Law, and throughout 1918 there was considerable discussion in Parliament about the proposed Bill, with clear evidence of opposition from members who preferred to return to pre-war conditions. There were those who had been born and brought up in an atmosphere of peace and who, whilst being considerably shaken by the war, remained secure in the conviction that life would soon be put right and that the old life would return with few changes. On the other hand, others, Dr Addison included, realised the extent of the blight caused by the war and the need for change. At the second reading of the Bill (Parl. Debates 1919) he spoke of the high war casualty rate, the need to safeguard the lives of the people and the terrible destruction of the 1918 influenza epidemics. He described the armies of disabled people lost within the community, the loss of recruits to the forces and production capacity to industry. There were, he said, too many people and too many authorities dealing with health (1800 in all) and there was a need for one central authority to be responsible. It was time to disentangle the treatment of sickness from any relationship with the Poor Law; health could not be related to destitution and must only be considered in relation to sickness. Housing and the environment were also of importance. Under the Bill it was proposed to abolish the LGB and to set up a number of Advisory Committees. A wide extension of health facilities was envisaged including nursing, midwifery, diagnostic units and hospitals: there were many sections of the community (including the middle classes) that did not have the use of those services; the middle classes were particularly unfortunate since they could not afford the fees but preferred not to be the recipients of charity. There were half a million children in schools suffering from malnutrition who would become the problems of the future.

During the ensuing debate, members spoke variously of the splendid work done by the Guardians and of the high standards of the infirmaries which represented some of the best war hospitals in the country. It had taken a war to bring home to the people the need to do something for the health of the nation, the need for a change from the spirit of the Poor Law, the realisation that what was good enough in 1914 was not then tolerable to the people. Some speakers wanted the voluntary hospitals to be taken over, a research department to be established in the new ministry, the General Medical Council to be absorbed, and more stringent powers with which to deal with the laggard local authorities. It was recalled that over the previous $8\frac{1}{2}$ months only 40% of all recruits examined by the Army could be classified as A1 and that industrial and agricultural workers were less fit than the better paid miners. One Member felt that there was a need for better hospitals and that every citizen had a right to free hospital treatment.

In the meantime there were official congratulations in the Commons on the splendid work of the Poor Law infirmaries during the war, and the military authorities repeated these.

Eventually after considerable political manoeuvring Lloyd George managed to get the Ministry of Health Bill on to the Statute Book with Dr Addison as the first Minister of Health. Hopes were high and the plans drawn up for the new Ministry were extensive but the economic climate changed and many of these never came to fruition.

REFERENCES

Abel-Smith, B. (1964). p. 235.

Departmental Committee of the LGB, Poor Law Orders, 1935. Cmd. 6938, Vol. XXXVIII, 241.

Ministry of Reconstruction, *Report of the Local Government Committee*, 1917, Cd. 8917, Vol. XVIII. (Maclean Committee).

Parliamentary Debates 1911, Vol. XXIV. 1980 f. 1917, Vol. XC, 2186 f. 1919, Vol. 112, 1828 f.

Poor Law Officers' Journal 1911, Vol. XX, p. 16. 1914, Vol. XXIII, pp. 416–547. 1914, Vol. LXIII, 1339 f.

10

POLITICS AND THE POOR
LAW NURSES: 1919–1948

The war had brought many changes to the country, it had tested social institutions and had forced re-organisation in many areas. Whilst changes were already in the air during the first years of the century, the war had halted some and hastened others. Priorities had had to be reassessed, old inadequacies had been highlighted and the emergency had forced an acceleration in the trend towards collectivist economic and administrative policies. The social and economic upheaval of the war years had contributed to a change in social attitudes. The underprivileged groups of pre-war years, who had been taken very much for granted, suddenly became vital to the war effort. The war had highlighted the critical need for labour in the armed services, in the factories and on the farms. This shortage of manpower, which worsened as the war went on, strengthened the market position of the working classes, gave them an enhanced self-consciousness, better bargaining power and brought them higher material standards. What had been unobtainable before the war became commonplace: attitudes changed, values shifted and beliefs were challenged. Some of these social changes were formalised by legislation and others were manifested informally by alteration in the general way of life (Marwick, 1974).

The Church of England was not prepared for the social upheaval of the war and its attack on the Christian gospel of love and forgiveness. For years it had rested on the stability of Victorian society and prosperity and had not anticipated such a crisis of beliefs. It was therefore unprepared and unable to give a message nor offer any leadership. Many Churchmen led the country in prayers for the ultimate victory of good over the wholesale evil of the German enemies and called the clergy to volunteer for combatant duties. There were also those who shrank from this and felt that a more restrained way was preferable.

The breakdown in the settled way of life was, from the Church's point of view, most noticeable in the collapse of Sabbatarianism and the increase in divorce. A large number of people were, by then, out of touch with organised religion; congregations became even smaller and a new generation was growing up totally ignorant of the Christian faith. In the years after the war, during the slump of the 1920s, the Church took an interest in the unemployed but was unable to do much in the problem. The drift from the churches continued (Moorman 1954, Wakeman 1914).

The budding social policy of pre-war days had not only been halted but in some cases had been reversed. Education grants were suspended, school medical services were cut, teachers and school children left their schools to take on war service. Housing conditions deteriorated, many people flocked to the cities where most of the munitions were manufactured and there was gross over-crowding. In all this welter of problems, the people discovered new leisure time pursuits. They bicycled, and some even had cars; they travelled to nearby resorts, visited the cinema and went to dances where the emancipated women flaunted their freedom and openly danced with men whom they had not previously known. Those who could afford it went to night clubs, and underwrote the Roaring Twenties.

The population of England and Wales had grown to 37·9 millions by 1921. By 1941 it was an estimated 41·7 millions and in 1951 it was 43·7 millions. But the birth rate was beginning to flatten out after the post-war peak and in 1921 it was 21·8 per 1000, in 1941 it was 15·3 (estimated). By 1951 it rose again to 17·3. The death rate continued to fall from 13·5 to 12·4 and then 12·3. The tables for age distribution showed a continuous process of ageing in the population with a rise in the age group over 64 years, from 53 per 1000 in 1911 to 105 per 1000 in 1947 and a drop in the age groups 0–14 from 308 per 1000 to 215 (Stern 1962).

The birth rate was falling, families were smaller, migration was breaking up extended families and leaving the aged and the younger nuclear families as separate units. The change in values and attitudes, the break up of the extended family, the loss of Church influence and the emancipation of women all contributed to develop changes in sexual morality. Treatment for the venereal diseases was more readily available (if not particularly efficacious); Dr Marie Stopes preached the right of women to use contraceptives. The movement of people around the country and women's employment (which gave them independence) also provided opportunities and helped to allay fears.

In 1918 women over 30 were enfranchised and in 1919 Lady Astor became the first woman MP.

The public, seeking a 'Country fit for Heroes', encouraged their representatives to pass the Ministry of Health Act in 1919 which put medical relief under the newly formed Ministry and relegated it in importance below the Public Health Department and to Part III of the *Annual Report*.

Collectivist policies were thought to be the panacea and the Government was gradually forced by circumstances to take more responsibility. In 1924 Old Age Pensions were raised to 10/– per week. In 1925 The Widows, Orphans and Old Age Contributory Pensions Act extended to widows and orphans the benefits of the 1911 National Insurance Act and introduced the contributory principle to old age pensions. Not until 1937 was a substantial portion of the country covered by national insurance and in the gross unemployment of the 1920s and 1930s the Government had to provide 'uncovenanted dole'.

In 1929 the Boards of Guardians were abolished under the Local Government Act and their functions taken over by the County Councils and County Borough Councils. The Poor Law was broken up between local authority committees but survived this legislation and remained, for many, the basis of relief until 1948. In 1934 the Unemployment Assistance Board was established under the Ministry of Labour to function alongside the Poor Law. In 1941 the Determination of Needs Act abolished the household means test and established the 'needs test' era.

The era of laissez faire had died and the era of 'universality' was born; the era of human rights was passing into the era of individual rights.

In 1936 the local authorities were empowered to build new general hospitals, including, for the first time, outpatients' departments.

In 1942 the Beveridge Report was published. Based on the assumptions of full employment and a nationally available health service, it reiterated the philosophy that personal initiative should not be stifled by state help and that state help should be based on the insurance plan. Benefits should be paid to the unemployed, the sick, widows and the old people and would cover everyone 'from the cradle to the grave'. The plan accepted the idea of a national minimum level of subsistence first propounded by Booth and Rowntree. Insurance benefits were to be supplemented or, in the case of the few uninsured categories, to be provided by a National Assistance Board which was to replace the local Public Assistance Committees. Thus, relief was to be removed from the local authorities and made a national responsibility.

There was a rise in the number of women workers, salaried workers and local government staff and a commensurate fall in domestic workers. Factory work overtook domestic work in social esteem but between 1920 and 1938 unemployment reached a level of 10% of the working population. The trades union leaders became more militant and social conflict was a feature of the inter-war years.

In the world of science, there was phenomenal progress. Rutherford made advances in splitting the atom, Banting isolated insulin in 1922 and medicine was thenceforth able to control most cases of diabetes mellitus which had previously been an irreversible disease. In 1925 the vitamins B_1 and B_2 were isolated and in 1926 liver extract was successfully used for the treatment of pernicious anaemia, another previously irreversible disease. In 1927 vitamin C was isolated and insulin shock therapy introduced. The electron microscope, introduced at the same time, enabled an impressive advance in biophysics by allowing the inspection of tracer elements and isotopes. All this while the medical experiences of the war were being developed and refined: there was an advance in the widespread use of innoculation, war wounds had given new ideas for wound treatment, including the use of irrigation techniques and wound suturing, reconstruction surgery, orthopaedic surgery and plastic surgery. These reconstruction techniques generated the early concepts of multispecialist teams in the operating theatres. In 1928 Fleming isolated penicillin and between 1929 and 1935 chemotherapy advanced with giant strides: the constitution of thyroxine was discovered, vitamins A and D were discovered, pure vitamin C was manufactured together with the successful synthesis of many other vitamins. In 1929 electro-encephalograms were used, in 1933 the first total pneumonectomy was performed and in 1935 the first prefrontal lobectomy. In 1936 cortisone was isolated and in 1938 sulphapyridine was synthesised.

This last drug was the forerunner of the sulpha drugs which revolutionised the treatment of many infections and allowed physicians to master bacterial pneumonia. More advanced surgery could be tried as the control of postoperative infections was now available. Thus the era of infection control was to take over (for a few years) from the era of infection prevention which had been the doctors' main defence for so long.

In 1939 nuclear fission was discovered and the atom was split.

In the next 10 years, many of the early antibiotics were discovered and subsequently synthesised, starting in 1940 with penicillin. In 1944 quinine was synthesised. Advanced surgical techniques such as heart surgery for 'blue babies' was established.

Another development from the war was the use of psychology and the increasing understanding of psychiatry. The behavioural sciences began to play a more important part in the diagnosis and treatment of many diseases.

Medicine was increasingly influenced by social concepts such as living conditions, working conditions and the environment. As the infectious diseases abated there was a rise in the behavioural diseases such as ischaemic heart disease, cancer of the lung and obesity. Health education became a panacea and non-medical staff were taught to teach 'the healthy way of life'. This delegation of medical matters was not limited to health education and could also be seen in the handing over of such aspects as hygiene inspections to school nurses and an increase in the teachnical tasks allowed to hospital nurses. As the doctors moved forward into more scientific and complex medicine they relegated many of their routine functions to other people.

In 1919 the new Ministry of Health was responsible for an immense complex of duties including the Poor Law and Public Health. On its inception it took over the Medical Department of the Local Government Board with its large staff of skilled and experienced administrators. Housing became a prime concern but the policy of 'homes for the heroes' suffered considerably from the rising costs of the post-war era and from the economic blight of the 1920s. Infant life protection was further developed and in 1936 the Public Health Act was passed, replacing the great Public Health Act of 1875. The new Act embraced both environmental and personal hygiene aspects and covered a very wide field.

The Public Health authorities were on a two-tier basis with wide powers available at local level, shared between the county councils and county districts. The county boroughs carried out all the usual public health functions in their areas. The Medical Officer of Health was responsible for all functions including the environmental, personal and local authority hospital services.

Soon after the war, in 1919, the Consultative Council on the Medical and Allied Services had been set up under the Chairmanship of Bertrand Dawson (later Lord Dawson of Penn). By May of 1920 an Interim Report was published.

In the debate that followed there was evidence of growing anxiety over the financial affairs of the voluntary hospitals, a growing realisation of the need for a state hospital system and some discussion on the municipalisation of the Poor Law Infirmaries.

The economic depression of the 1920s had begun to make itself felt by the time the Dawson Report was received. It made the point that organisation of medical services had become 'insufficient' and failed to bring the advantages of medical knowledge within reach of the people. Any improvement would require a new and extended organisation distributed according to the needs of the people, who could no longer be expected to provide for themselves. The growing cost of medical treatment was reducing the numbers who could afford it. There was a need to bring together preventive and curative medicine and to take them into the sphere of the general practitioner who should be concerned with communal, as well as individual health. Any scheme of services should be available to all classes of people although this did not necessarily imply a free medical service. It recommended Primary Health Centres equipped for curative and preventive medicine at the general practitioner level and to include an efficient nursing service. A group of the Primary Health Centres should be supported by a Secondary Health Centre where medical staff of a consultant or specialist level could take over the care of the patient from the general practitioner. The Secondary Health Centre should, in turn, be related to a Teaching Hospital having a medical school. There should also be Supplementary Services, in relation to the Primary and Secondary Health Centres, with special staffs for the care of patients suffering from such diseases as tuberculosis, mental diseases, epilepsy, certain infectious diseases and orthopaedic conditions. All these institutions were to be jointly co-ordinated by unified local health authorities.

This was the first sketch of a National Health Service but was shelved because of the growing national economic recession and because it was realised that Local Government would have to be reorganised before the health services could be tackled.

The emancipation of women arising out of the war had led to their continued employment in many jobs not considered suitable or not existing before the war. Women were being employed as sales assistants, telephonists, bus conductresses, in the service occupations, the Civil Service and schools. All these occupations vied with nursing for the available women and inevitably there was a decline in the numbers electing to take up nurse training which was long (usually four years), arduous, poorly paid, lacked status and was subject to rigid discipline. This last aspect was an increasing problem in an era when women were for the first time enjoying their freedom and, it will be recalled, the new leisure time pursuits. It is not surprising therefore to find some debate on the economic position of nurses compared with other females in employment. Miss Seymour Yapp wrote to the *Poor Law Officers' Journal* (1919) that the best women were coming forward for nursing; she felt that they would not be the best if they waited for better conditions. She felt that nursing was not the worst paid women's profession but there remained the problem of how to improve conditions without attracting those who were less devoted or sacrificing the ideals of the profession. Nursing compared favourably with other occupations, she maintained; the nurse had free training and trained nurses, except those in the higher grades, received a salary comparable with the teachers. She said that nursing was not only a profession but a calling and needed a professional body such as the College of Nursing to deal with questions of salary, etc.

The College of Nursing had been founded in 1916 and in 1919 it published a report on nurses' salaries. The figures given in the report were based on average salaries in hospitals and infirmaries of more than 500 beds in average daily occupancy (*Poor Law Officers' Journal* 1919).

In the same year a survey (*Poor Law Officers' Journal* 1919, Vol. XXVIII) of nurses' hours of work was made with a sample of 514 hospitals, including 81 Poor Law Infirmaries: the longest hours were day duty 71 hours and night duty 84 hours, and the shortest day duty $52\frac{1}{2}$ hours and night duty $59\frac{1}{2}$ hours.

The Minister of Health, weary of the continuing disagreement in the nursing profession about State Registration and faced with the problem of a flood of demobilised VADs, finally introduced his own Bill and steered it through to the Statute Book. Thus in 1919 the nurses of the country, including the Poor Law nurses, achieved legitimacy with a General Nursing Council of 25 members. It was the aim of the Minister to make the Council as representative as possible

Hospital/Infirmary

Number considered	London General 5	Provincial General 2	Scottish General 3	London Infirmary 11	Provincial Infirmary 11	Scottish Infirmary 3	Irish Infirmary 2	College of Nursing Suggested
	£	£	£	£	£	£	£	£
Matron	310	260	250	126	156	183	120	350
Assistant Matron	78	100	87	60	70½	75	65	130
Home Sister	65	90	65	47	57½	57	61	100
Night Superintendent	62½	65	70	44	53	57	75	100
Ward Sister	54	50	48	39	43	45	46	30 beds £75 20 beds £60
Other Sisters	52–108	45–50	60	59–60	51–75	—	50–55	60
Staff Nurse	37	37½	40	30	35½	34	40	Charge Nurses
Probationer								
Year 4	28	30	31	25	28	—	18	50
Year 3	25	24	26	22½	22	24	10	30
Year 2	19	19½	21	19	18½	21	6	22
Year 1	13	14	18	15	15	18	5	18

of all sections of nursing and four Poor Law nurses were included: Miss A. Dowbiggin, Matron of Edmonton Union Infirmary, Miss C. Seymour Yapp, by then the Matron of Ashton-under-Lyne Infirmary, Miss Constance Worsley, Matron of the Infirmary for Children, Liverpool and Miss Susan Villiers, Matron of the South Western Hospital (MAB). However, only one of these nurses, Miss Seymour Yapp, had actually received her training at an infirmary and the others had been trained in voluntary hospitals.

In an account of the work of the Ministry of Health up to 1920 (Parl. Debates 1920), Dr Addison reported that the preventive health services had in the past suffered from a lack of policy and forward planning but he was satisfied that the public health services were functioning well and that they had been instrumental in stopping the spread of epidemics then current on the continent. He reported that tuberculosis and venereal diseases were both still problems and that his department, learning from the lessons of the war, were encouraging early treatment of mental illness. The infant death rate had started to fall, after remaining stationary for many years:

1900 – 154 per 1000
1901 – 154 per 1000
1906 – 132 per 1000
1918 – 97 per 1000
1919 – 89 per 1000
1920 – 78 per 1000

He felt this satisfactory trend was due to better nursing, midwifery and other facilities arising out of the efforts of the previous few years. However, he also reported that 40% of school children were found to have physical defects during their school medical examinations.

He reported the passing of the Act for the State Registration of Nurses 1919, and said that well-paid nurses were necessary for all these measures.

Dr Addison (*Ministry of Health Annual Report* 1919–20) confirmed that all Poor Law accommodation lent to the military authorities had been returned. He also gave an account of nursing in the Poor Law institutions.

The Ministry of Health recognised as Major Training Schools 26 London and 54 provincial institutions. There were also 24 Minor Training Schools, all but one of which were in the provinces. Many training schools combined with others to give greater breadth of experience for their probationers, many also trained midwives. Some institutions made their training extend over four years with the nurses graded as Charge Nurse for the last year and studying an option such as ophthalmology, theatre work, midwifery or sick children as a speciality. An even greater shortage of nurses was noted, particularly in the rural unions. The Minister reported that he had encouraged the unions to improve the salaries of their nurses; there was also a general tendency to reduce the hours of work to 48 per week. In order to help in the recruitment of nurses, there was an experimental scheme to lower the age of entry (still 21) of probationers and to allow some probationers to be non-residential. Both these schemes remained tentative pending receipt of the views of the GNC.

The Minister had laid down certain standards for Poor Law Infirmaries throughout the country: any institute which employed a resident medical officer should be properly staffed and all institutions with over 200 beds were expected to appoint visiting specialists for medicine, surgery, and children's diseases. The proportion of nurses to patients should not be less than 1:6 for both day and night duty. The ratio for the infirm wards should be 1:9. Every institution should aim at training as many probationers as possible. The eight-hour day should be applied to the nurses. Any institutions with more than 200 beds for the sick should appoint an Assistant Medical Officer. All nurses going on holiday should have an allowance paid to them in lieu of the cost of their board. All probationers, as far as possible, should receive surgical and midwifery training.

The return of many infirmaries to the PL authorities gave an opportunity for re-organisation and development, particularly in London.

Some Poor Law authorities were re-designating their infirmaries as hospitals: the Archway Road Infirmary was to be renamed the Holborn Hospital, and a report from Oxford described a plan to convert their workhouse (recently handed back by the Military who had used it as a hospital) to a public hospital to be used in collaboration with the City Council who also needed a new one. Reports of progress abounded, 'more additions are reported week by week to the schemes which bring Poor Law hospitals into full utilisation for the sick who need hospital treatment; they are, in fact, so considerable now in number as almost to reach beyond description at any length' (*PLO Journal* 1920).

It was also claimed that the burden of the 1911 National Insurance Act was falling on the Poor Law infirmaries. In 1912 Lloyd George had said 'the main work of the voluntary hospitals was not touched by the Act' and that was felt still to be true in 1920. Guildford, Wolstanton, Burslem and Eccleshall Brierlow substantiated this assertion and the Medical Superintendent of the Wigmore General Hospital (Infirmary) had said that 80–90% of their discharged patients were insured persons.

Additional Medical Superintendents were appointed, outpatients' services were developed in order that the turnover of patients could be increased, the acute cases were retained in the infirmaries, the chronic cases were kept in the workhouses and the convalescent cases were also transferred. Some institutions were upgraded and provided with X-ray departments, operating departments and lifts. It was found that the very different type of work undertaken during the war by the staff had had beneficial results: gunshot wounds were rather different from the usual run of infirmary cases which were predominantly respiratory problems and the nursing of these wounds had developed into orthopaedic nursing. Other specialities such as ear, nose and throat and ophthalmic work were also developing. The growing tendency towards medical and nursing specialisation was reported as creating difficulties in general nurse training and meant that the probationers had to circulate between institutions (in the manner described by the Minister in his report) and also between infirmary and voluntary hospital. However, the infirmaries were able to offer a quid pro quo as the post-war 'baby boom' meant that their maternity units were very full and busy and the voluntary hospitals were able to send nurses to them for maternity experience. One Inspector reported that this growing specialisation had also involved the necessity to make added appointments of specialist nurses such as nurse masseuses and Sister Tutors. Other specialities included nurses who were skilled in electric treatments such as Faradism. More consultants were appointed for these specialist units and the quality of work increased and improved. There was also in many areas an increase in spare accommodation, and the tendency to take paying patients, which had started before the war, spread. Patients were accepted from general practitioners in spite of complaints from the medical organisations. Some infirmaries themselves became specialist units and the Southmead Infirmary took only acute cases, the Crescent Road Infirmary in Manchester took only venereal diseases, Booth Hall Infirmary (Manchester) and Alder Hey Infirmary (Liverpool) became units restricted to children's diseases. Where this conversion happened there was a co-operative agreement made between unions for the admission of inmates and patients across union boundaries and some workhouses became institutions only for the able-bodied, transferring their sick to another union. More and more Infirmaries were being granted Orders for separate administration thus removing them from the lay administration of the Poor Law and putting them under medical administration.

The numbers of Major Training Schools grew to 30 in the metropolis and 89 in the provinces. The GNC accepted a starting age of 19 but the proposal to allow non-resident probationers was rejected because of fears of loss of ésprit de corps, discipline and health.

In spite of these developments, the uncertainty of the Ministry's plans for the future of the health services contributed towards the delay of a great deal of work that might have taken place in the period of post-war social reform. The Minister was slowly moving in the face of continuing opposition and the costliness of his policies frightened many politicians and added strength to his opponents' criticisms. In the end Addison was moved from the Ministry of Health and the majority of his policies were never implemented. With the new Minister, development of health services slowed down considerably and was further delayed by the Government's plans to reform Local Government (which did not finally materialise until 1929).

Addison however was able to make some ground and during his office he set up the *Consultative Council on Medical and Allied Services*, with Bertrand Dawson as the Chairman. He also developed the School Medical Service and the Maternity and Child Welfare organisation by, amongst other means, regulating the training of Health Visitors.

The financial plight of the voluntary hospitals prompted the Government to set up the Voluntary Hospitals Commission with the duties of distributing Government grants, initially one of £250000, and trying to promote a more co-ordinated hospital service.

The 1921–22 *Annual Report* of the Ministry of Health talked of the need to establish cost effectiveness of health management schemes and administration and anticipated that 'the development of health services on proper lines will be facilitated by . . . the compilation of the Register of existing nurses under the Nurses Registration Act, 1919'.

In the Report of 1922–3, it was said that the Poor Law Department of the Ministry of Health had kept in touch with the proceedings of the GNC to avoid difficulties inherent in the existence of different bases of qualifications in the nursing service. In 1922 there were over 1000 certificates of training issued by the Poor Law authorities to their nurses and it is possible that the Ministry of Health was still apprehensive about a statutory registration since these certificated nurses were not *ipso facto* registered by the GNC. Indeed, in 1923 a question was asked in the Commons (Parl. Debates, 1923) about a five to nine months' delay in registration and, at a later date, about the position of the nurse training schools which were likely to be discontinued by the GNC.

It was said that the registration of nurses had reduced the numbers of candidates coming forward for training and that the policies of the GNC were exacerbating this situation. Although the certificated nurses of the Poor Law Infirmaries had been registered by the GNC, as indeed had many 'existing' nurses under the conditions for registration laid down by the Act, there were still many unregistered nurses practising under the leeway allowed by the Act. But the increased attractiveness of other occupations was more and more taking away suitable candidates from the profession. Nursing was more definitely under the control of the medical profession although there was a faction led by Mrs Bedford Fenwick who tried to establish the profession under its own authority. The voluntary hospitals and the College of Nursing were afraid of the large number of Poor Law nurses taking over control of the profession and the small hospitals were fighting to retain their nurse training schools so as to be able to use probationers as cheap labour.

The first Council appointed by the Minister, the Caretaker Council, had drawn up a draft schedule for approval of all nurse training schools. There was to be a 'one portal entry' with a preliminary examination at the end of the first year of training and a general standard of nurse education for all training schools. The principle of a Preliminary Training School was expected to be accepted; the period of training was to be clearly prescribed, and only hospitals (or infirmaries) with an appropriate number of beds and an adequate amount of clinical material could be approved. Finally, a minimum standard of general education was proposed for all candidates (Bendall and Raybould 1969).

A draft pamphlet setting out the proposed syllabus of lectures and demonstrations for general nurse education was circulated to all hospitals including the Poor Law infirmaries. This scheme was based on the system then current at St Thomas's Hospital. The Poor Law infirmaries were alarmed by this syllabus as many of them could not meet all the requirements. The Poor Law Infirmaries were currently running a two-tier system of nursing between the Major Training Schools and the Minor Training Schools; if the one portal system were accepted they would lose their second tier which provided the assistant nurses who were of critical importance to the smaller and rural workhouse infirmaries. Similarly, a general standard of nurse education would cripple these smaller infirmaries and therefore seriously hamper the Major Training Schools who used assistant nurses as ward staff on a non-officer level. The installation of a Preliminary Training School would be a serious blow to the economics of many infirmaries who, it will be remembered, based their nursing organisation and nurse training on the cheapest system possible. (Nurse training was given not for philanthropic reasons but because it afforded the least expensive means of obtaining nurses. This philosophy was shared equally by the general hospitals: probationers were cheaper to employ than assistant nurses.) Many of the smaller infirmaries (and the smaller general hospitals) could not hope to contend with a minimum requirement for beds and clinical material. Lastly, whilst the principal separate Infirmaries took in candidates with an adequate educational level it could not be said that the other infirmaries were so selective; indeed, by now, they were glad to take in anyone who applied, as were most of the provincial voluntary hospitals.

Reaction to the draft circular was epitomised in the *British Journal of Nursing* (9 July 1921) which reported a meeting of the Hackney Board of Guardians (cited by Bendall and Raybould 1969 p. 46). The Guardians had received a recommendation from their committee to apply for approval as a nurse training school and to adopt the curriculum laid down by the GNC. 'We regret to note that Rev. A. H. Dacombe [why are the clergy so reactionary?] said that if the Board adopted the recommendations it would put them under the coercive and tyrannical option of the General Nursing Council. Having alluded to the success of their present régime and the substantial cost that the appointment of a Sister Tutor would entail, he moved the reference back of the recommendation, which was supported and carried.

'We have no doubt wiser councils will prevail as the Clerk pointed out that running of the Infirmary was carried out economically owing to the large number of probationer nurses on the staff and in the event of the infirmary not being recognised it would be difficult to attract probationer nurses and that would eventually mean the employment of a highly paid staff of trained nurses.'

A conference of Poor Law Nurse Training Schools sent a delegation to point out to the GNC their problems and suggest that the syllabus aimed at a too high standard.

At the end of 1921 the Caretaker Council had to be reconstituted after the resignation of two-thirds of the members. The Second Caretaker Council then published their examination syllabus. The Poor Law authorities were more agreeable to this whilst remaining disturbed at the training syllabus and the proposed standard of general education. They wrote to the Minister of Health about these points and it was subsequently suggested that the training syllabus should be retained only as an advisory instrument.

In 1922 the GNC published their list of approved training schools which included 25 infirmaries in London (out of 30 Major Training Schools) and 37 infirmaries in the provinces (out of 89). Twenty-five infirmaries were excluded because they did not employ a resident medical officer.

The rules for approval of nurse training schools which the GNC laid down included a minimum number of beds (250 for the Poor Law infirmaries and 100 beds for the voluntary hospitals), a resident Medical Officer and the availability of experience in medical, surgical, gynaecological and paediatric nursing. Hospitals or infirmaries were allowed to group together in order to aggregate experience in these areas of nursing for their probationers; affiliated training was also permitted.

Partly because of the problems of the small rural workhouse infirmaries in obtaining nurses, partly because of the anticipated disqualification of their use as nurse training schools and the consequential need to employ more expensive nurses, the Ministry of Health decided to develop a plan to centralise the care of the sick in the larger infirmaries. The Chief Medical Officer argued the case in his *Annual Report* in 1923 (*On the State of the Public Health*). It was felt that this proposal would allow for better classification, the better use of resources and it would be more possible because of the use by many authorities of motor ambulances. There was no discussion about the convenience or inconvenience to the inmates and their visitors.

The *Annual Report* for 1924 gave up more space to the Poor Law Medical Service than in previous years and provided some interesting figures.

There were 650 Boards of Guardians in all with an average population of about 60000 and a range between 10000 and 1 000 000.

The figures (1923) of beds of Poor Law institutions were admittedly inaccurate but there were reckoned to be 70 separate Infirmaries with a total of 36547 beds and 629 workhouse infirmaries with a total of 83731 beds, making a grand total of 699 infirmaries and 120278 beds.

Of these infirmaries, there were 66 with over 500 beds, 100 with 200 to 499 beds and the remainder had well below 100 beds, several with fewer than 20.

Five per cent of all Poor Law beds were occupied by tuberculosis patients (2% of these were non-pulmonary). As the Poor Law Infirmaries were not designed for 'sanatorium treatment' their tubercular cases were invariably of an advanced nature since they had been admitted as a last resort. It will be remembered that the Public Health authorities also provided accommodation for tuberculosis and took the bulk of these cases.

Ninety infirmaries had been approved as training schools for nurses by the GNC. Of these there were 18 Associated schools, 4 Affiliated schools, 3 were provisionally approved, 2 were male nurse schools and 3 were for the training of Sick Children's Nurses. 'The facilities afforded in recent years for the training of sick nurses in Poor Law Infirmaries have done much to raise the efficiency of these institutions.'

There was also a continuing development in the specialist departments, providing 'highly complicated apparatus' for, amongst other things, electrotherapy including artificial sunlight, ionisation, deep-ray, radiant heat, Begonie treatment, high frequency currents and 'various applications of X-ray both for diagnosis and for treatment'.

In 1924 a *Select Committee* was set up to report *On the GNC*. Mr L. G. Brock, the Principal Assistant Secretary, Ministry of Health, spoke of nursing being 'ancillary to medicine' and, therefore, that there was a need to ensure a training that would secure a nurse whom the doctors would find acceptable. There was therefore the need to preserve a medical element in the composition of the Council. He thought that there was a risk that a particularly well organised section of the profession 'might sweep the board. . . . It is conceivable for example that the Poor Law nurses, if they felt that there was a divergence of interest between them and the nurses in the voluntary hospitals, or in private practice, might attempt to carry all the seats and might succeed in doing so – there is always that danger.' He confirmed that the Poor Law nurses were more numerous than those of the voluntary hospitals, and better organised.

The voluntary hospital nurses were probably not at all organised: they worked in separate units throughout the country and there was no unifying link between them or their hospitals. Some of them belonged to the College of Nursing, but only a minority. The Poor Law nurses also worked in separate units throughout the country but in a sense they were united by the Poor Law and many of them belonged to the National Association of Poor Law Officers in which there was a nursing section. There is no evidence nor even suggestion that they wanted to 'sweep the board'. Indeed, it is more likely that the Poor Law nurses, who were trying to gain acceptance from the rest of the profession, were more wanting to model themselves on the voluntary hospital nurses than to control them. Mrs Bedford Fenwick in her evidence, disagreed with Mr Brock and did not feel that the Poor Law nurses were likely to come together to 'nobble' the Council, and Maude MacCallum, Honorary Secretary of the Professional Union of Trained Nurses, thought that the largest block of nurses was not so much the Poor Law nurses but the private nurses.

It is interesting, however, that the Ministry of Health which had at one time (as the LGB) refrained from supporting any Act for the State registration of nurses in order to protect the interests of the Poor Law nurses (or, more probably, to protect the interests of the Poor Law Infirmaries) was now afraid of the power represented by the numbers of Poor Law nurses and was actively seeking to allay it. It is also a demonstration of the political naivety of the Poor Law nurses that they did not appreciate the power that was available to them if they had chosen to wield it. But, it has already been shown, they were more interested in achieving a social status than a political status and did not take their opportunity.

Arguments against a prescribed syllabus of training centred around the small hospitals, who could not have hoped to achieve that standard, rather than around the Poor Law infirmaries who had by then come to terms with the training requirements of the GNC by appointing tutors, grouping themselves and taking in more acute cases. Miss MacCallum and Mrs Bedford Fenwick both took the view that the hospitals were primarily interested in managing their patients and had no real interest in training nurses except as an expediency. Indeed this has been an argument ever since for the removal of nurse training from the hospital agencies and the need to put it into the education system, but the removal of so many probationer nurses from the hospitals would have paralysed their service, as well as bankrupting them, and the Government did not feel able to do this.

In 1925 all except one of the Poor Law Nurse Training Schools had been approved by the GNC making a total of 121 compared with 168 for non-Poor Law establishments. In the preliminary examinations held in July and October 1924 and in January 1924, the figures were as follows:

	July 1924	October 1924	January 1925
Total number of passes	1526	1110	1043
Number of PL nurses	650	542	496

The CMO seemed anxious about the attempt, in some quarters, to shorten the working hours of the nurses. Although the Minister had reported in 1920 that the nurses were working a 48-hour week, a paper given by Miss Roberts, the Matron of the West Derby Infirmary in Liverpool, belied this. She agreed that 'benefiting by a sympathetic public opinion, which nurses created by their work during the war, Guardians generally are granting increases of salary on fairly liberal terms' (PLO Journal 1920 p. 657). She also thought that conditions of service, recreation facilities and working hours were improving in some quarters but said that the 56-hour week was still fairly general. Sir George Newman, the CMO, and Miss Roberts agreed that a shorter working week would be prejudicial to the patient. Miss Roberts, in common with many of her colleagues, thought that a vocational sense in candidates for nurse training was the best quality to look for in selecting probationer nurses and the hard conditions for training and throughout any nurse's career were well known. Any woman lacking the desired quality was easily put off and there was therefore no problem about selection. Sir George, on the other hand, had the responsibility of maintaining the services and as economically as possible. He took a more pragmatic view of the discussion: 'Some reform in the hours of work was undoubtedly overdue, but it is questionable whether there is a tendency for the pendulum to swing too far in the other direction. As in the case of doctors, there are obvious difficulties in adopting a 48-hour week for nurses. It is not good for the patient to be subjected to unnecessarily frequent changes of nurses, and it is also difficult to fix responsibility for neglect when the duty for carrying out special treatments is shared by several nurses. Shorter hours entail more extended absences from the wards with consequent loss of interest in the work and lessened opportunities of watching the progress of the illness and acquiring professional experience. It is also stated that the health of the nurses has not been improved by the shorter hours. Whether this is so or not, a 48-hour week entails administrative difficulties without equivalent compensations, and it is suggested that it would be in the best interest of all concerned that any desired decrease in the working time of nurses should be effected by increased yearly leave rather than by curtailing the daily hours of work' (*On the State of the Public Health* 1925).

In this sentiment he was supported by the voluntary hospitals who could not afford the extra staff that would be necessary for a shorter working week for the nurses, by the College of Nursing whose membership was predominantly from the voluntary hospitals, and by the GNC who had felt that it would be undignified to allow nurses to be associated with the Eight Hours Bill introduced for the benefit of labourers and artisans in 1920.

By 1926 40% of all newly registered nurses were from Poor Law training schools, 79% of Poor Law entrants for the Preliminary examination and 71% for the Final examination passed. This was more or less the same pass rate as that of the general hospitals. The increase in the unemployment rate had increased the numbers of people accepting treatment from the infirmaries. The Minister of Health explained that the demand for institutional treatment had also caused an added load on the infirmaries since the voluntary hospitals continued to be unable to satisfy the demand, 'Thus the public is less concerned with who runs the hospital than with the nature of the treatment available to them from the hospital'

G

(Ministry of Health *Annual Report* 1926–7). The suburbanisation of the London population had effectively removed local patients from the situations of the London voluntary hospitals. This phenomenon was repeated in the provincial conurbations whose residents took it for granted that they could be treated in their local infirmaries. Extensions, renovations, enlargements or new buildings were reported from all over the country including West Bromwich, Wirral, Bucklow, Walsall and Wolverhampton, Chester, Altrincham, Macclesfield, Stockport, Birkenhead and Cannock. This in spite of the restrictions imposed by the economic crisis and the pending re-organisation of local government.

In 1928 the Local Government Bill was published. Under this the Poor Law medical services were to be absorbed by the local authority Public Health services and the major local authorities were given the responsibility of administering the Poor Law, including medical relief. Thus, it was hoped, the overlap of services and the dual systems would be merged into a unified service.

The Bill also required an early general survey of the minor authorities (District Councils) with a view to re-organising their boundaries for the better implementation of their powers, including their sanitary functions. There was to be a County Medical Officer and a Medical Officer of Health at District level.

All local authorities as far as possible would be required to take over existing Poor Law medical services and general relief under an Act other than the Poor Law Act, which was not, however, to be repealed. The alternative Acts available for medical relief were the Local Government Act 1888 and the Maternity and Child Welfare Act 1918, the Public Health Act 1875 and the Public Health (Tuberculosis) Act 1921. Thus, it was hoped, all medical or health care could be given outside the aegis of the Poor Law. 'A clear direction is thereby given that the process known for the last 20 years as 'the break up of the Poor Law' shall be put in hand in a practical manner and carried so far as the existing law and the prevailing circumstances allow' (*On the State of the Public Health* 1928).

Each major local authority had to appoint a Public Assistance Committee. Each County had to subdivide itself into areas for the administration of relief by local sub-committees (or Guardians Committees) of the main Public Assistance Committee. The Medical Officer was to advise the local authority of the desirability of discharging certain of the transferred functions through specialist sub-committees such as a Public Health Committee. He was also to advise the local authority which services could be implemented through the alternative Acts rather than via the Public Assistance or Poor Law Acts. Where total transference of all institutions under one of the alternative Acts was not possible he was to advise on the need to transfer at least one institution for hospital use.

The Chief Medical Officer wrote that 'the Local Government Act will fail in its purpose if its operation is limited to the transfer of Poor Law powers en bloc to the Public Assistance Committees' (*On the State of the Public Health* 1928).

There was also a requirement that the local authorities should consult with local Committees and voluntary hospital authorities. The relationships between the old Poor Law authorities and the voluntary hospitals were, however, so antagonistic that this requirement was never implemented in anything more than a perfunctory manner in spite of frequent exhortations.

In February 1928 the census of Poor Law beds showed that there were 37500 beds in separate Infirmaries (4933 of which were unoccupied) and 84000 beds in the workhouse infirmaries. No final census of Poor Law nurses was given.

In an editorial the *Poor Law Officers' Journal* (1929) deplored the move of power from the periphery to the centre and reported that in the House of Commons all the clauses relating to public health, hospitals, midwives, etc. were passed, without any discussion, under the Guillotine set by the Government. It reported a discussion, printed in *The Times*, in which it was claimed that the 'pauper taint' would continue to linger and that the change in terminology from Poor Law Infirmary to Municipal Hospital would help only a little. *The Times* also suggested that the middle classes would stand to gain the most from municipalisation (See Eckstein 1970). The *Journal* resented the allusion to the 'pauper taint' and claimed that treatment from the voluntary hospitals was just as much charity as treatment from an infirmary (only £800000 of the total voluntary hospitals' income of £3¼ million came from patients' contributions). The *Journal* could not see how a change in terminology could disguise the receipt of free or charitable treatment from a municipal hospital which had previously been an infirmary.

Advice was liberally given by the Chief Medical Officer to the medical officers on the necessary arrangements to be made in anticipation of the transfer of services. There was advice on calculating the anticipated requirement of beds, the classification of destitute and hospital accommodation, administrative problems such as the route of admission of patients and the possible advantages of a district nursing service as a way of relieving pressure on the hospitals. Also on the need to review the aged to determine where he or she should be lodged – either in a hospital or a workhouse; the need for chronic wards in hospitals, 'their presence in the hospital can be calculated to lower medical and nursing standards throughout the hospital', and the need to improve standards in the municipal hospitals, the 'great traditions of English medicine as exemplified in the voluntary hospitals and in the best type of medical practice must become increasingly the routine practice in all these institutions'. The overriding need for unification; treatment of patients without deterrence; and a new emphasis on statistical data, scientific medicine, efficiency, progress, uniformity of standard and the need for competent, reliable doctors, were all discussed.

Not one word was written about the organisation of the nursing service nor, indeed, whether they should be organised. They, like the aged, were to be allocated.

The discussion that centred around the Local Government Act was predictably polarised. There were those who feared the growth of collectivism and thought that the new Committees would be run by people appointed to them rather than people who had been elected; the Guardians argued that the County Councils and District Councils were too remote from the people (they termed them 'frigid bodies'); Josiah Wedgwood wrote to his constituency in Stoke that 'we are being centralised into servitude'. There were complaints that the proposals were delaying health schemes already planned by many unions and Lord Dawson complained in the Lords that the proposals were 'defective' because the local authorities had no expertise in curative medicine. The plans, he said, should have centred around the voluntary hospitals. The *Poor Law Officers' Journal* thought that the outlook for the hospital service for the poor was not a happy one.

On the other hand, there were those who felt that the Act had not gone far enough, and that the administrative areas should have been larger; that the allocation of institutional care between the various Acts would preserve the division of the medical services. It was also said that Committees were not suitable to look after institutional health work and that there was a need to make a complete divorce between the medical services and Public Assistance. One speaker said that the Bill perpetuated a mixed system of dealing with destitution – and was proved right in the event. Another speaker complained about the distance that people would have to travel to arrive at the institutions which would be located somewhere in the administrative district but which would no longer be 'local' to the bulk of the parishes and unions within the district (*Parl. Debates* 1928).

In retrospect, it is possible to see that the delegation of duties between the Major and Minor Authorities was done without very much thought and in an arbitrary way. The power to provide institutional treatment was given to the smaller authorities who could not do this with the same rationality as the larger authorities, covering larger populations. The range of services appeared comprehensive but they were legislated for under permissive statutes. There were Treasury grants, but notwithstanding these the principal method of financing the services depended on local taxation, and the amounts available depended on the wealth of the areas concerned. Those areas which were well-populated, well-industrialised and affluent could afford more and better services, but conversely, those areas which were poorer and in which the people were in greater need could least afford the services. There were therefore great disparities in the number of services and in their quality from one local authority to another. Furthermore, the new arrangements depended more heavily on the general practitioners whose standard of practice and dispersal was also very variable. The best practitioners tended to cluster in the wealthier urban areas; there were fewer and less good practitioners in the poorer areas. The National Insurance of the day still only covered the working population, and not all of them, and left out the wives and families who could not afford to pay for a general practitioner but who possibly needed his services more than did the worker.

The provision of services depended also on the will of the councillors, many of whom were indifferent to the medical services in the same way as had been the antecedent Guardians: medicine and health had to take its place in the queue and was not always given much priority. The Ministry of Health had delegated the health services to a local administration which was not invariably efficient and did not always enjoy a well developed social conscience, but the Central Government had no means of influencing local administrative discretion.

As for the nurses, they were left roughly where they had always been. Many changed their masters and came wholly under medical direction but they were still without power or authority. The nursing hierarchy stopped at the level of the hospital: the Matrons had to report to the Medical Superintendent and had no say in major decisions or planning. They had no representatives on the Health Committees and none at the Ministry.

The appropriation of the infirmaries was slow and uneven through the country: the LCC took over all but 12 of the separate Infirmaries, the county boroughs took over 76 infirmaries, and of the county councils only Salop appropriated any infirmaries. There were difficulties in taking over the mixed workhouses and many members of the new Public Assistance Committees were ex-Guardians who actively discouraged the transfer. Then, too, there was the enormous cost involved in upgrading the infirmaries for use as general hospitals. Theoretically, it was planned that the hospitals should be operated by the Health Committees under the Local Government Act 1888 or the Public Health Act 1875. The aged and infirm, who were not thought to require either continuous medical supervision or skilled nursing care, were to be maintained in residential accommodation under the Public Assistance Committee and the Poor Law, but the theory was not put into practice and Abel-Smith (1964) has described how the majority of beds for the sick were still administered under the Poor Law in 1938. In the event, a larger number of local authorities simply did nothing. They left both the infirmaries and the workhouses under the Poor Law and allowed the dichotomy between the Public Health authorities and the hospital services to continue. The one important difference after 1929, however, was that the Poor Law had been officially relegated as an undesirable means of dispensing relief (medical or general) and was therefore even more despised and the target of controversy. In 1932 the estimated expenditure of Poor Law authorities on the sick was £6 770 628 compared with the expenditure on hospitals by the Public Health authorities of £10 750 000. In 1926 there were 1114 Poor Law institutions of all kinds and in 1934 there were 1034. During the eight intervening years, 125 institutions had been closed or transferred but 47 institutions had been erected or acquired.

For most authorities therefore, the Local Government Act 1929 made very little impression on the medical care of the sick poor, except that their best infirmaries were the ones that had been appropriated and their least good ones were those that had been re-tained. In a very general sense the sick with financial means were able to take advantage of the municipal hospitals and the poorer sick were once again relegated to the workhouses, by then re-styled Public Assistance Institutions.

This development caused the establishment of a third force of nurses: the voluntary hospital nurses, the municipal hospital nurses and the remaining Poor Law nurses. But, lulled by the brave intentions of the 1929 Act, the public simply forgot about the last group and they were never again referred to by official sources.

The LCC had wanted for years to centralise the administration of the medical services and were well prepared for the transfer. They had set up a Special Committee on Health in London which had looked into the reorganisation of health services and reported in 1917 along very similar lines to those of the Maclean Committee. There were, of course, problems of organisation which were peculiar to the LCC but their plans were approved by the Minister of Health and they were able to proceed.

Some time before vesting day they set up two new committees, the Public Assistance and the Central Public Health Committees. They also appointed a Matron-in-Chief, Miss D. E. Bannon. As a result of the reorganisation, they became responsible for the control of 141 hospitals, mental hospitals, institutions, residential schools and various types of homes. The total number of staff who were trans-ferred was 26 000: the LCC had inherited an enormous task. Early on it had taken the decision to appropriate all Poor Law Infirmaries into the Central Public Health Department in order to remove them from Poor Law administration. These infirmaries, hospitals and sick asylums from the Poor Law and the MAB covered a wide range of purposes.

It was obvious that a huge outlay would be needed for improve-ments and the LCC therefore decided to make a survey of all accommodation. One of the first exercises in extensions and upgrad-ing which the Council undertook was at the nurses' home at the Archway Hospital.

About 8000 female nursing staff were inherited and a Nursing Committee consisting of Miss Bannon, two Principal Matrons (Miss Butler and Miss Cordell) and two Matrons set to work to consider conditions of appointment to the grade of Sister. Earlier the Central Public Health (Staff) Sub-Committee had begun to draw up a

MAB	No. of Institutions	No. of beds
Infectious diseases hospitals	14	8700
TB sanatoria and hospitals	9	2057
Special children's hospitals	5	2400
Special diseases (VD, ophthalmia)	3	132
Epileptic colonies	2	705
Total	33	13994

Board of Guardians	No. of Institutions	No. of beds
General hospitals	28	17350
Institutions allocated as hospitals	11	9620
Children's infirmary and nursery	1	200
Total	40	27170
Queen Mary's Hospital, Sidcup Tooting Home (St Benedict's Hospital)		820

(LCC *Annual Report* 1929)

common salary scale, conditions of service and hours of work. They had been reminded by the GNC about the problems of unregistered nurses (many of whom were still practising) and it was subsequently decided that State Registration would be a condition of permanent appointment to all nursing positions under the control of the Central Public Health Department of the grades of Ward Sister and above. A similar requirement was made for male nurses of the Charge Nurse grade and above.

With regard to hours of work and leave, it was agreed that there should be a 56-hour week for day duty and a 66-hour week for night duty with a gradual reduction to 56 hours as soon as the staffing situation could be settled. Matrons were to be allowed five weeks' annual leave, Assistant Matrons and all grades of Sister were to have four weeks and probationers were to have three weeks. There was a proviso agreed, in the interests of health, that any probationer showing signs of strain certified by a medical officer might be granted an additional week of leave after six months' service. All nurses were to have one day off duty each week and time off duty in lieu of overtime. Furthermore, it was decided that appointments were to be made to the LCC nursing service rather than to hospitals so that nurses could be interchanged.

These settled conditions of service, the opportunity for wide experience because of the possibility of movement through all the LCC hospitals, and the good opportunities for promotion offered by being a member of an extensive nursing service are to be contrasted with the timid rejection by the various Government Committees looking into Poor Law nursing from 1902 onwards. It was reported that the LCC enjoyed a considerable number of applicants for training in their hospitals in comparison with the difficulties experienced at the time by other hospitals.

There was, however, still a shortage of nurses in many LCC hospitals which was difficult to alleviate because of the acute shortage of accommodation. But the Council authorised the employment of 500 extra nurses for all the general hospitals, some of whom were to replace the 'co-operative institution' nurses, who were hired on a temporary basis. In addition an extra 100 Sisters were also appointed. It was decided that nurses should be allowed to become non-resident in order, originally, to help with the shortage of nurses' accommodation. This was an experiment and was offered rather tentatively, but it was received warmly and became such a popular feature of the LCC nursing service that it soon became an established right. The Council was the first organisation to introduce non-residence and the innovation was not repeated by other hospitals for many years.

The quality and quantity of applicants increased quickly and in 1931 it is reported that 3042 nurses were engaged. A Board of Medical and Nursing Examiners was set up to help achieve a more uniform standard. There were to be two hospital final examinations each year consisting of two papers of three hours each and covering aspects of medical, surgical and special nursing and general nursing, materia medica and dietetics, an oral examination given by medical examiners and a practical examination given by nurse examiners. All training hospitals were divided into seven groups and within each group a gold medal was to be awarded to the best all round nurse with an aggregate mark of not less than 85%, and not less than 75% in the practical examination. In 1931 708 candidates took the GNC final examination paper and 506 passed. It was decided also to make a survey of the facilities and equipment available in each of the recognised training schools.

The number of acute beds grew quickly. The LCC promoted

policy of appointing consultants and specialists and in 1933 the British Postgraduate School of Medicine was established at the Hammersmith Hospital. Considerable emphasis was put on the specialist departments and many new ones were set up.

Whereas in 1921 there had been 38000 acute beds there were, 12 years later, some 53000. Even as the population grew older, the number of long stay beds diminished from 84000 (1921) to 54000. In 1910 the proportion of acute chronic cases was 20% and in 1930 the proportion was 80%. Similarly, the length of stay for the patient was changing: in 1909 it was 63 days, in 1919 it was 53 days, in 1928 it was 34 days. But, paradoxically, the number of people in London aged over 65 years had increased by 55% over the previous 30 years although the introduction of the Old Age Pension and other social measures had allowed a reduction in the rate of demand for residential accommodation for the time-being.

If progress in London and several of the large provincial cities was impressive, it was disappointing in the counties. The hospitals and institutions were visited only by the Committees of Guardians and there was little evidence of any effort at co-ordination or rationalisation. Not surprisingly, there were complaints of varying standards of nursing, standards of nurse:patient ratio and of nurse training, and the euphemistic report of the Chief Medical Officer of the Ministry of Health (*On the State of the Public Health* 1933) that most of the differences between the municipal and voluntary hospitals had disappeared could not be substantiated. Similarly his inference that the voluntary hospitals and municipal hospitals were more and more working together was not borne out by any other sources.

By 1933 there was a comprehensive scheme of training for all branches of nursing in the LCC and the duration had been lengthened to four years. The salaries had been standardised at £30 for a first year probationer, £35 for a second year probationer, £45 for the third year and £50 for the last year (*LCC Annual Report* 1933).

New hospital blocks were built, most of the service departments were refurbished, re-equipped and modernised and the hospital service settled down. Other routines were also standardised, such as the daily schedule for patients, costing for dietary allowances and the organisation of the district medical services. The nursing establishment was again increased and the hours of work reduced to 54. As a broad generalisation the nurse:patient ratio for an average ward was fixed at 1:4 and ward orderlies were employed in each ward. The total nursing staff established for the 12 general hospitals under the LCC (*Annual Report* 1935) was described as:

Matrons	12	Staff Nurses	640
Assistant Matrons	12	Probationer Nurses	1472
Night Superintendents	12	Assistant Nurses Class 1	5
Sister Tutors	12	Nursery Nurses	8
Sister Housekeepers	10	Charge Nurses (Male)	4
Home Sisters	12	Staff Nurses (Male)	62
Food Supervisors	12	Probationer Nurses (Male)	22
Administrative Sisters	12	Ward Orderlies Class I	
Departmental Sisters	34	(nursing) (Male)	31
Sisters	262	Service relief Sisters	10

But from 1927 onwards there was a general fall in the intake of probationer nurses in the former Poor Law Infirmaries.

Nothing was done about the shortage of nurses and in 1930 *The Lancet* published a letter from Dr Esther Carling complaining of the growth of agencies supplying untrained nurses to hospitals and the disappearance of trained nurses into work where their conditions, salary and status were better. It was useless, she wrote, to appeal to the idealism of young girls since their parents and teachers only knew of the long hours and wear and tear of the nurse's life. This letter was followed by a reply from a graduate nurse, Gladys Carter, who claimed that nurses were discontented with overwork and lack of educational facilities. She maintained that there should be a rationalisation of nursing: what was the proper function of a nurse? How many nurses did the country need? She said that it was time to design a proper career for nurses with adequate salary, training and conditions of work. There was a third letter from R. C. Wingfield who supported Miss Carter and said that there was need of a highly qualified grade of nurse who had to be paid appropriately.

The Lancet decided to set up a *Commission to enquire into the duties, pay, diet and recreation of hospital nurses*. The Commission used the services of a statistician, Professor Bradford Hill, a sprinkling of nurses and a majority of eminent doctors all from well-known hospitals. They issued an *Interim Report* in 1931 and a *Final Report* in 1932 but between the collection of their data and the *Final Report*, the depression had bitten into the economic life of the country and there had been an influx of recruits into the nursing profession. They showed that there was a relative shortage of nurses (particularly probationers and staff nurses) and a lack of educational quality because of a wider choice of occupations for women with better career prospects, better pay, conditions, hours of work and less discipline. The demands of maintaining a service in hospitals militated against the provision of a good training and, once trained, the nurse felt the need for additional training so did not remain in her hospital as a staff nurse. They recommended a better status for nurses and nursing representation on the Management Committees.

They also suggested the need for closer links between nurse training and the education authorities and proposed the establishment of some nursing schools in universities. They wanted a shorter period of training and the recognition of two grades of nurses with a simplified system of registration and student status for probationers.

The Report generated considerable discussion, especially over the proposals that the Preliminary Examination should be in two parts, with the first part taken in the schools before the candidate started her training. On the whole there was a fair amount of agreement with the report and many of its recommendations were independently implemented. The conditions of service however were not considered to be so urgently in need of improvement because of the influx of candidates after 1931.

As soon as the depression showed signs of lifting there was another recession in the recruitment figures and by the end of the 1930s, the position was again worrying. The Government set up an *Inter-Departmental Committee on Nursing Services* (the Athlone Committee) in 1938 which never completed its work because of the war, but did issue an *Interim Report* in 1939.

In this *Interim Report* the Athlone Committee made the point that nursing was a service of outstanding national importance and deserved better status, better salary and better conditions of service. There was a need to help the voluntary hospitals financially and, it was anticipated, these grants would offer a means of controlling them. All hospitals (voluntary and municipal) should also be given grants in order to encourage and improve nurse training.

It also reported a shortage of trained nurses and the high proportion of probationer nurses who were being employed to make up the deficiency.

But recruitment of trainees was falling off, despite the rise between the years 1931 and 1933 during the slump, and this could not be without significance. There was also a significant waste of probationer nurses: about 25–30% left in their first year.

The Committee felt that the real cause of the shortage was that the demand exceeded the supply: new treatments were requiring more nurses and shorter working hours also increased the demand. It felt that the shortage of nurses was not a temporary phenomenon since the demand was likely to continue. The Report made the point for the first time, that hospitals recruited only to provide themselves with staff; they did not think in terms of supplying a national need. There should be a 'regularised and ordered system of recruitment and training in which the national needs receive equal consideration with the needs of the individual training hospital'. There was a call to measure the needs of the nation and a requirement for a central recruiting authority.

Recruits should preferably have a secondary education but, as this would not provide enough candidates, girls with an elementary education should also be accepted.

The hours of work were too long and were 'deleterious to health'; they should be shortened. Domestic and other non-nursing duties should be reduced and married nurses should be employed.

The Committee called for the position of the Assistant Nurse to be regularised by the establishment of a Roll of Nurses under the control of the GNC. It also recommended that it should be an offence for any person to practice nursing for gain who was not a Registered or Enrolled Nurse. It called for a national scale of salaries for nurses negotiated by a Salaries Committee, a minimum of four weeks' annual leave and medical supervision of nurses' health.

By the time the Report was published, the country was at war and no official action was taken on it.

The war in 1939 brought a general standstill to all further development. Once again there was a cataclysmic mix up of staff and patients, once again the professionals from the voluntary hospitals were drafted into the municipal hospitals or Poor Law Infirmaries. Again the public from the better off areas were evacuated to hospitals and institutions in the rural areas which had not enjoyed the generous treatment afforded by the LCC and other more forward-looking authorities. And once again there was dismay at the standards of accommodation and facilities that were found and disbelief that these could still exist.

In the 1930s and the early 1940s, as part of its preparation for post-war reorganisation, the Ministry of Health undertook a hospitals survey in the country and sent out officers to help and advise in their administration. The Sankey Report had recommended grouping hospitals, including both municipal and voluntary, into regions and this subsequently became policy.

Hospital surveys were made in different parts of the country, each of which was selected as a basis for the ten envisaged regions. Generally, the surveys were made in 1941 but were based on figures available in the late 1930s, and the reports were not published until 1945. It was reported (Ministry of Health, *Hospital Surveys* 1945) that the voluntary hospitals were foundering for lack of finance and it was obvious that they could not continue without Government help. The rise in scientific and technical medicine had further increased the cost of medical treatment. The public were no longer content with home treatment and demanded hospital care: as hospital patients came from the higher social strata they demanded higher standards of accommodation and the hospitals' resources in terms of nurses and money were drying up. More patients required more nurses, more sophisticated treatments enabled a faster turnover of patients and consequently a larger staff of nurses; the public health services employed more nurses as did the other non-hospital fields, and the shortage of nurses was exacerbated.

The surveys demonstrated a wide spread of hospitals over geographical areas and quality ranges. They showed that the voluntary hospitals were as a rule small, and mostly located in the city centres and therefore incapable of extension. They were usually badly planned, noisy, drab and inconvenient. On the whole, they had been built during the period 1870–90.

The municipal hospitals, many still under Poor Law administration (i.e. the workhouses) were often older than the voluntary hospitals, dating before the 1870s but they were more spacious and had more land available for extensions. The infirmaries, on the other hand, were often newer than the voluntary hospitals but lacked outpatient departments and had only rudimentary operating and X-ray departments.

Nursing ratios were better in the voluntary hospitals than in the municipal hospitals, where accommodation was inferior.

Generally, it was reported, hospital accommodation was highly unsatisfactory, out of date and not designed for modern medicine.

There was a shortage of space, and a shortage of many specialities: there were, for example, enough general surgeons but not enough paediatricians. Some of the accommodation was so bad that it should not have been used.

The chronic sick were particularly badly off as many had been pushed out of the better accommodation to make way for acute cases. The staffing ratio was inadequate and there was a need for separate accommodation, away from the hospital, for the aged who did not require medical attention.

In 1947 the Ministry of Health set up a *Working Party* under the chairmanship of Sr Robert Wood to look into the *Recruitment and Training of Nurses*. Again there was a minority report signed by Dr (later Professor) John Cohen. The Wood Committee used a volume of contemporary methods of statistical analysis but Dr Cohen did not feel that the study had been sufficiently scientific or that the problem could be studied by the traditional method of 'exchanging views, supplemented perhaps by written or oral evidence'. He called for a study of manpower and regretted the lack of objective methods in assessing staffing standards.

In the main report, one of the interesting observations was that the voluntary hospitals were rapidly increasing their intake of student nurses from 7950 in 1937 to 10050 in 1945, whilst the municipal hospitals were virtually standing still in this respect (3800 in 1937, 4050 in 1945), and whereas in 1929 there had been about twice as many Poor Law nurses as voluntary hospital nurses, by 1945 the position was very different.

In 1942 the Beveridge Report had been published. It was based on an assumption that there would be a comprehensive health service. In 1946 the National Health Service Act was passed. On vesting day in 1948, 1145 voluntary hospitals with 90000 beds were taken over and 1545 municipal hospitals with 390000 beds (80000 of these were still administered under the Poor Law) were also handed over. The LCC handed over to the NHS the largest and most comprehensive hospital system under a single authority that existed in the world. It had lost many hospitals during the war and its staff, depleted by war service, had not been recouped. Altogether it gave up 98 hospitals with a pre-war bed complement of 70120 and a total staff of 20000. In 1939, before the outbreak of war, its nursing complement had totalled 10552.

There is no evidence of the numbers of nurses working with the

80 000 Poor Law beds when they were handed over. They were still employed by the smaller authorities but there was no central record maintained and no reports of them were found.

In the nineteenth century the Poor Law nurses had been paupers; during the years of the reform of nursing the Poor Law nurses never quite achieved the status of the voluntary hospital nurses although they deserved it. Theirs had been a harder life, they had fought a more bitter battle for their patients, they came from further behind to win recognition as nurses, they worked for deprived people in deprived conditions, their load was heavier, their hours were often longer, their salaries often lower. They were slighted by their voluntary hospital sisters, bullied by the Poor Law Masters and Matrons, frequently despised by the doctors, tainted with the public detestation of the Poor Law. And in the end, they were almost forgotten. But not quite.

REFERENCES

Abel-Smith, B. (1964).

Bendall, E. and Raybould, E. (1969), *A History of the General Nursing Council for England and Wales, 1919–1969*. London, Lewis and Co. Ltd. Chapter 3, also p. 46.

Eckstein, H. (1970), *The English Health Service*. Cambridge, Mass., Harvard University Press. Chapter 2.
    In this Eckstein argues that the National Health Service in 1948 was a 'middle class rather than a lower class service' for the same reasons, i.e. the poor were already served by a health service of which the middle classes could not avail themselves for economic reasons. See also p. 3 of his book.

Inter-Departmental Committee on Nursing Services. Interim Report, 1939, London, Ministry of Health.

The Lancet, 1930, Vol. 2, 826, 937, 993. 1931, Vol. 1, 451 f.

The Lancet Commission on Nursing, Final Report (1932) Supplement. London, The Lancet Ltd.

LCC. *Annual Report*, 1929, p. 134. 1933, Vol. 1 (Part 1), p. 169. 1935, Vol. IV (Part 1), p. 73. Note the elongation of the hierarchical structure, also the increase in specialisation as the base of the pyramid broadens.

Marwick, A. (1974), *War and Social Change in the 20th Century*. London, Macmillan Press. Chapter 1.

Ministry of Health *Annual Report*, 1919–20, p. 35. 1925–6, 1926–7, p. xxii.

Ministry of Health *Hospital Surveys* (1945). London, Ministry of Health.

Moorman, J. A. H. (1954), *History of the Church of England*. London, Adam and Charles Black. Chapter XXII.

On the State of the Public Health (Report of the CMO, Ministry of Health) 1923, p. 126. 1925, 1928, pp. 71, 72. 1938, p. 193.

Parliamentary Debates, 1920, Vol. 131, 2639 f. 1923, Vol. 161, 1081 f.
    1928, Vol. 223, 2450 f. 2646 f. 2680.
Poor Law Officers' Journal, 1919, Vol. XXVIII, pp. 877, 452, 640. 1920,
    pp. 633, 657. 1929, p. 9.
Stern, W. M. (1962). Chapter 2.
Wakeman, H. O. (1914), *An Introduction to the History of the Church of England*
    (Revised Ollard, S. L.). London, Rivingtons.

11

REPRISE

The Poor Law nurses developed from the pauper nurses at about the same time as the voluntary hospital nurses developed from the ward maids in the period 1860 to 1890. As the voluntary hospital nurses developed and became more professional they, with the doctors and voluntary hospitals, moved away from the poor and the incurably sick towards the wealthier sections of the community and the acute sick. In this sense, the voluntary hospitals advanced with scientific developments and abandoned those people whom science could not help. The Poor Law nurses formed an alternative group of nurses who stayed with the paupers and incurables and cared for them in spite of the pressures of an advancing society. If there had not been Poor Law nurses, another organisation would have had to be developed to look after these people. They might have been left alone, but the social conscience of the later 19th century would not have accepted this for long. The Poor Law nurses did not voluntarily remain with the incurables: they stayed with them because that was their role, which was therefore one of bedside nursing and, largely, it remained thus through to the National Health Service. Whilst the voluntary hospital nurses followed the scientific and technological progress of their doctors and moved further away from the caring role of the bedside nurses, the Poor Law nurses remained there. This freezing of their role gave a stability and permanence to the roots of nursing whilst the 'advances' of the voluntary hospital nurses widened the gap between the point of departure and the goal and gave breadth to nursing. But because of the Poor Law nurses, the profession did not lose its caring role entirely.

Nursing is beginning to look at itself more critically and there are those nurses now who feel that a return to bedside nursing is necessary. It is possible that such a return to its roots is still available to the profession because the Poor Law nurses were there for so long preventing the void from being filled by another group of workers.

With the development of science, scientific medicine and 'scientific' nursing, most people said that the aged and infirm did not need skilled nursing but only kindly attention. Neither, they said, did the chronic sick need skilled nursing but only some rudimentary nursing care. Some of the Poor Law nurses who had been caught up in the challenge of medical progress felt the same way, but there were also many who were not afraid to think differently and who had the courage to speak up in public, contradicting their medical officers and nursing colleagues. These nurses were available to defend the interests of the long-term sick, the old and the demented. They insisted on these categories having, as far as resources would allow, the same quality of care as was given to the acute sick. In the past 20 to 30 years we have been able to appreciate their perspicacity and understanding. They treated the long-term sick as people and individuals rather than as cases or write-offs, and they were proved more humane in their understanding of their patients' needs.

The voluntary hospital nurses were, obviously, located in the cities and their hospitals cared for only a fraction of the sick poor. The voluntary hospitals gave care only to the selected cases. In contrast to this, the Poor Law nurses were located in almost every parish or union in the country: they were in the cities, they were in the country towns and they were in the villages. It was not possible to be selective in the cases that the infirmaries accepted, they had to care for anyone who was in need of medical relief, and as the definition of destitution broadened over the years, the catchment of patients grew. Once an individual was admitted to an infirmary, he could not be discharged except as he was fit. The voluntary hospitals were quite free to discharge any recalcitrant patient and often did so. The terms under which the two sections of nurses did their work were therefore quite different. The voluntary hospital nurses gave their care under the charitable cover of the hospital which included not only the Lady Bountiful ethos but also the privileged position of the donor; there was a social and status division of some degree between the nurse and the patient which not only separated the two but gave an added authority, backed by the social structure of the day, to the nurse over the patient. In contrast to this, the Poor Law nurse had only such power over the patient which any able-bodied attendant would have over a disabled person (however temporary) but lacked the space between herself and the patient which the private charity hospitals gave their nurses. Granted that both hospitals gave charitable care, the Poor Law infirmary *had* to give relief to the sick under a statutory obligation and was financed by local taxation to which many of the patients might have contributed at some time or other.

The Poor Law nurse was therefore not accorded the vicarious status given to the voluntary hospital nurse and had to win her position from a situation which was already disadvantaged by the lingering image of the Poor Law institutions. Her task was very much harder, and was made even more difficult because she had no sanction available against the patient: he could not be discharged. Other sanctions which might have been available to other Poor Law officers, such as the Master or Wardsmen, were barred to her because of her nursing ethics.

The Poor Law nurse was the local nurse in the sense that she worked in the community from which her patients came. She therefore gave a service, however good or indifferent it may have been, to the community. Often she went into their houses and nursed them in their family situation. She made do, both in the homes and in the infirmary, with what equipment was available. She was never in the position of having all the available modern equipment that her voluntary hospital colleagues frequently had and the policy of deterrence often deprived her of even the rudimentary necessities.

The Poor Law nurses, until the 1930s, formed the large bulk of British nurses. They outnumbered the voluntary hospital nurses by about 2:1 and at times by a higher proportion than that. The voluntary hospital nurses were judged by those of them who worked in the London Teaching Hospitals and, because of this, they were given an élitist status in the nursing profession. Although the London Teaching Hospital nurses may have deserved this, and although there were many provincial voluntary hospital nurses who were equally worthy, their standard (even in London) was very variable and there were those who were certainly not worthy of the status. The Poor Law nurses were not judged by the equivalent criterion, that of the great, separate Infirmaries. They were not really even judged by the standard found in the rural workhouse infirmaries. They were judged not so much by their own professional standards but by an historical one passed by folklore through the generations and also by their association with the despised Poor Law. But in the face of this, they gave a service to the lowest elements of society as well as to other sections. They were stimulated by their disadvantages to raise the standard of nursing in the infirmaries to an acceptable level. Between the 1860s and the 1880s there were frequent criticisms of bad nursing in the infirmaries, but after that period, once paid nurses (whatever their training) had taken over in the infirmaries, there were few, if any, further complaints about their nursing. Certainly there were frequent complaints about a lack of nurses, lack of nursing facilities, lack of amenities and the lack of comforts for the patients but, after Dr Edward Smith's report, there seldom appeared a frank complaint about nursing. In their task therefore the Poor Law nurses were successful, and they became more successful with the passage of years as more facilities were made available to them.

The Poor Law nurses worked against incredible odds: they were subject to lay officials who were frequently petty both in outlook and in understanding. They were never given a chance to advocate their cause but had to plead or report through another person with a different professional understanding. They lacked accommodation, facilities, equipment and staff. They worked in an environment that was not only unsuitable but often actually hostile. They were supervised by officials who were also hostile to them, employed diverse and conflicting standards, outlook and goals. Often they worked in professional isolation. They were socialised by a professional culture whose primary goal was the 'recovery of the patient' but they worked in a situation where the attainment of this goal was invariably impossible. They had to devise new goals and seek new ways of rewarding themsleves (Coser 1963). In this they also succeeded. They were the first geriatric nurses and, for many years, they were the only ones.

In seeking to improve their own training and standards they forced upwards the standards of their medical officers and institutions. Quietly they refused to accept the dominance of the Master and Matron over the sick wards, they refused to accept the petty tyrannies of the workhouse in the infirmaries and they refused to accept the drabness of the workhouse wards for their sick wards. They insisted on adequate standards of linen supply, diet and treatment for their patients. They ousted lay authority from the sick wards and infirmaries, instituted a decent standard of cleanliness and care for their patients (even if it was not always wanted) and forced many infirmaries to employ more doctors, a higher standard of medical attention and a wider intake of patients. In order to be able to maintain (and after 1919 to retain) their nurse training schools, the authorities had to achieve certain minimum standards, employ a minimum of resident medical staff and take in a certain number of surgical and gynaecological cases. If the authorities wanted to attract and keep nurses they had to provide acceptable accommodation, working standards and a nursing structure.

Many authorities recognised the effect of the nurses on their patients and the community. It was said that the nurses were an accepted link between the authorities and the community, that they taught the poor to make more of their resources, to live a healthier life and to mitigate the effects of illness. In the *Poor Law Officers' Journal* (1911) there was a discussion on the social value of the nurses who went into the homes of the poor. It was said that they cared for the sick, advertised the importance of health and hygiene, were a refining influence in the homes; they promoted the speedier recovery of the sick and a shorter period of convalescence and prevented complications. They took a feeling of empathy and unity into the poor areas, helped to build a bridge between the poorer classes, offered a different point of view to 'the other side', especially during the early part of the 20th century when social conflict and industrial strife were prevalent. It was said that these nurses fostered a 'divine discontent' amongst the poor at their social conditions and helped them to adopt a better way of living. It was to be admitted that many of these district nurses were not employed by the Poor Law authorities but many of them were, and it was not unknown (it was officially encouraged) that the nurses from the smaller workhouses spent part of their time working in their patients' homes.

The Poor Law nurses organised the care of the sick in the infirmaries: before their advent there had been no system of care, and treatments ordered by the medical officers were carried out (if they were carried out at all) indifferently, irregularly and incompetently. Once the nurses were installed, the care of the sick was given more regularly and conscientiously and with great dedication. When Agnes Jones took over the male wards at Brownlow Hill Infirmary, the Visiting Physician wrote that there was a marked improvement in the standard of nursing, the reliability in carrying out the doctors' orders, in the demeanour of the patients and their comfort and order (*LGB Annual Report* 1865). This infirmary had never been short of medical staff, nor of sympathy and goodwill from the vestry. It was probably one of the best run and most generously administered infirmaries in the country: there was a medical committee comprised of eminent doctors from the Royal Liverpool Infirmary and several resident medical officers, but they could do very limited work for the patients – even with ample numbers of pauper nurses – until the paid nurses took over the wards. After the pioneer paid nurses were installed, a remarkable change overtook the wards. Once 'competent trained nurses' had displaced the pauper nurses it became possible to recruit probationers 'who were intelligent and of good character'. Police were no longer required to patrol the wards at night in order to preserve the peace. A similar experience was reported from the Chorlton Infirmary a year or two later when the pauper nurses were displaced by an organised nursing staff.

It is not too improbable therefore to suggest that what Florence Nightingale did for the troops in Crimea, the Poor Law nurses did for the sick poor in the workhouses. Miss Nightingale herself accepted that the conditions at Brownlow Hill (as described by Agnes Jones) were at least comparable to the conditions she had met at Scutari.

In the 20th century, there were few nursing leaders as there had been in the late 19th century. It was easier to be a national figure in the 1880s before the social structure of the country and national life had become more complex. Nonetheless the Poor Law nurses did throw up several prominent nurses of some considerable stature who fought hard to raise both the standards and the status of Poor Law nurses and who made a considerable contribution to the profession before and after the birth of the General Nursing Council in 1919.

It is no more valid to measure the quality of British nursing by the standards of the London voluntary hospital nurses than it is to remember the Poor Law nurses in terms of the early pauper nurses. In 1929 the Poor Law nurses formed the bulk of British nurses and the credit that was given to British nurses (and it was considerable in those days) must be given in fair measure to them.

In making this historical study, certain themes relating to the development of the Poor Law Nursing Service have emerged which it may be of interest to discuss.

As nurses became established in the workhouses and infirmaries the use of trained nurses also became established. This phase coincided with the great advances in scientific medicine and the medical officers became more interested in the employment of trained staff who enabled them to practice more effectively. The period also was marked by increasing opportunities for women in the labour market and a greater demand for nurses in other fields than in hospitals or infirmaries. There was competition for the employment of trained nurses and this led to an improvement in employment conditions, an improvement in the sick wards and a demand by many medical officers for advances in medical work and improved staffing in order that their particular workhouses should be more attractive to the nurses. The regulations laid down by the LGB for nurse training schools also stimulated an improvement in the medical staffing situation.

The evidence from many infirmaries, specifically Brownlow Hill, also shows that improvements in nursing enabled better medical attention to be given. Where poor nursing was all that was available, medicines were not given or were given indiscriminately or left to the other patients to dispense. Sometimes a ration was left for the patient to take himself. Where dressings were not done or diets not given, the medical officers lost interest and felt they were wasting their time. In 1866 Dr Robert Gee, a Consultant Physician of the Royal Liverpool Infirmary who was also in attendance at Brownlow Hill Infirmary wrote (*LGB Annual Report* 1865–6) that the trained nurses there were uniformly kind to the patients under their charge and added 'the medicines, stimulants, etc. have been carefully administered, and the other numerous but less agreeable duties have been faithfully and efficiently attended to. There has been no disorder or irregularity but a sense of comfort, order and quiet pervades the whole department. I believe further that every patient leaving the wards has been more or less morally elevated during his location there. The impression I have formed of the value of paid nursing, after no little experience of the character and results of pauper nursing, may be inferred from my earnest desire to see the system introduced into all the parochial hospitals in the kingdom.'

It will be helpful to recall that the philosophy of medicine, until the last 15 years or so of the 19th century, was one of amelioration. Scientific medicine had not reached the stage of allowing the philosophy of cure until after Koch's discovery of bacteria in the 1870s. If amelioration was the goal of medicine then good nursing was effectively the only tool of the doctors. If nursing was not available, the doctors were ineffective.

In contrast to the impetus which the nurses gave to medicine at that stage there was the impetus which scientific medicine was able to give to nursing. Lister's aseptic methods allowed the nurses to adopt better techniques for dressings. Burdett (1893) wrote that the cost of hospitals had increased partly owing to the increase of surgical dressings used by the nursing staff in the employment of aseptic techniques. But the adoption of these techniques by the nurses had helped to achieve a reduction in the surgical death rate from a range of 25–40% to about 4%. This is a remarkable achievement and was a real factor in encouraging further advances in surgery, there was therefore a hand-in-hand progress by both the surgeons and the nurses: if the nursing of the more advanced surgical cases had not also advanced, the mortality rate of postoperative cases would have been such that the surgeons would have hesitated to operate and the patients would have hesitated to submit to those operations. The demand for hospital-based treatment would not have increased as it did.

During the last few years of the 19th century and the early part of the 20th century science and social conditions stimulated the growth of specialism in medicine. This also found a response in nursing. There had been an earlier tendency to specialise in the sense that ward sisters were prone to remain in their wards for many years and were able to learn the ways of those doctors who had their patients there so that these ward sisters tended to drift into a specialist position as the doctors developed more restricted areas of work. Specialist hospitals also developed and the nurses within those hospitals assumed a deeper understanding of areas of nursing related to ear, nose and throat work, skin diseases, eye conditions or nervous diseases, etc. We have seen in the last chapter how specialist medical work provoked specialist nurses who thereupon provoked the acquisition of new specialist departments which presumably allowed more special cases to be accepted for treatment.

Thus it is not strictly true to say that nurses developed in the wake of the development of medicine. The movement of science allowed doctors and nurses to generate their separate skills concurrently, each either stimulating or enabling the other profession to take further steps. There were occasions when one profession took the lead and occasions when the other profession was the initiator but both depended on each other. Certainly the medical profession could not implement and practice medical advances without the support and progress of nursing using its own particular skills and knowledge. The lessons of the Crimean War, the war in Egypt in 1885 (when Florence Nightingale observed that the mistakes of the Crimean War had been repeated) and the deficiencies in nursing in the early Poor Law Infirmaries should not be forgotten.

At this stage it must be observed that the sources from which the details of this study were derived were principally official and semi-official documents or reports. The bias of the study is, therefore, more in a social, political and administrative direction and the evidence tends to show that the development of the Poor Law nursing service was more influenced by these factors than by any other.

There is very little evidence which points to the doctors' taking the lead in demanding the provision of nurses for the care of their patients. To Louisa Twining can be given the credit for the initiative and she was strongly and actively supported by other philanthropic ladies up to the turn of the century. It was they who shaped public opinion, they who importuned the Government, and travelled around the country recruiting nurses, training them and persuading Guardians to employ them. The doctors were divided; some supported her call for nurses and some resisted. In 1861 Joseph Rogers and Richard Griffin, both influential members of the Poor Law Medical Relief Association gave evidence to the Select Committee on Poor Relief (*Parl. Papers*, 1861, Vol. IX) but confined themselves to a discussion on the remuneration of the medical officers. On the other hand, Louisa Twining spoke at length of the need for well-trained and well-paid nurses.

In 1866 at the enquiry into the Paddington Workhouse (*Parl. Papers* Vol. LXI) the nurse, Jane Bateman, complained about the mismanagement of the sick and lack of support from the Master. In his evidence, the medical officer said that he did not consider Jane Bateman to have justifiable cause for her complaints and, he felt, paid nurses were unnecessary.

In the same year at the enquiry into the Rotherhithe Workhouse Infirmary, it was said that the medical officer had no use for paid nurses. Nurse Bateman's complaints were found to have been substantiated.

In the enquiry into the Strand Workhouse, the complaints were similar but the enquiry became much more complex. Joseph Rogers was one of the principal witnesses. He said that he had complained about the pauper nurses and had asked for paid nurses but admitted that he had never done so in writing. He did not make much of this aspect and did not give the impression that he had fought very hard for better nurses. Most of his evidence was about the administration of the workhouse, the Guardians and his remuneration.

Also in 1866 Dr Edward Smith (*Parl. Papers* Vol. LXI) discussed the use of pauper nurses and felt that there was a need for paid

nurses but thought they ought to be employed as supervisors of carefully selected pauper nurses. In 1867 (*Sessional Papers* Vol. LX) he
thought that paupers ought to be able to look after the sick in the
rural workhouses: 'it would be very easy to convert these women
into paid nurses'.

The pressures of the philanthropists became generalised and turned
into a public demand for an improved medical system as the working
classes were enfranchised at the end of the 19th century. The working classes became more vocal and better organised and the political
parties became more dependent on their vote. The social conscience
of the few was assumed by succeeding Governments as a social policy
in their quest for popular votes. The rise in the cost of medical care
and the increasing demand for hospital treatment made more sections
of the community dependent on some form of subsidised medicine.
The increasing importance and affluence of the working classes
established higher expectations and the assumption by the Government of a responsibility for health care followed. Social pressures
and economic expediency forced the municipalisation of the
Poor Law infirmaries and, ultimately, their nationalisation in
1948.

But if social pressure had demanded a Poor Law nursing service
it is equally fair to say that the rate of growth of the service was
dependent on economic and political factors.

The development of the Poor Law nursing service was only in-
termittently tolerated or encouraged (it was never refused) by the-
Government as it tried to maintain a balance between the progressive pressure groups (progressive in the sense that they wanted the
nursing service to be extended) and the conservative groups. When
social pressure was such that it was greater than the resistance of the
conservatives, there was progress. This was the case in 1865 when
Timothy Daly died and the press took up the issue after which the
PLB issued a general circular advising the employment of paid
nurses. Again in 1913 when war was anticipated, and the voluntary
hospitals were no longer able to cope with the demand for hospital
treatment; there had been steady and mounting criticism in the
Commons at the lack of effective action since the 1896 *British Medical
Journal Report* and after the 1905 Royal Commission.

At other times, as in 1902 after the Departmental Committee had
reported, the Government did nothing as there was no stimulus to
do anything. When it was faced with a situation in which it had to

take action it tended to look back to previous reports and act on them irrespective of whether or not they were still relevant.

The outstanding example of the relevance of politics to the nursing profession was the delay occasioned by the Government to any legislation for State Registration and, when the Act was passed in 1919, the difficulties made by the Government for the attempts of the General Nursing Council to establish a mandatory training syllabus. The Government was frightened by the clumsy actions of the Central Midwives Board after 1902 when they procrastinated for so long in licensing the infirmaries to train midwives. Whatever the motives of the CMB were, there is no doubt that they distinguished between the Poor Law infirmaries and the voluntary sector and succeeded in embarrassing the management of the whole of the Poor Law nursing service.

If the CMB could assume such authority and sanctions over para-governmental establishments which were only part of the Poor Law medical service, any Nursing Board set up by an Act for the registration of nurses could take similar powers but to a potentially more dangerous extent, since the Nursing Board could virtually paralyse the entire system of medical relief. The Government therefore did nothing to help any of the pre-1914 Bills. There is no evidence to show that they took active steps to put down any of these Bills, but that was never necessary: they simply did not support them or did not give them time in the House of Commons.

After the 1914–18 war, women were given the vote, there was a considerable amount of sentimentality in the country for nurses, and the vast number of discharged VADs who were liable to take up work as untrained nurses presented the Government with a very serious problem. Political pressure was such that a Bill had to be introduced and Dr Addison presented his own. Abel-Smith (1960) has said that after the GNC had been set up 'nearly every major decision in implementing the Nurses' Registration Act was taken by the Minister or the House of Commons' but he does not explain why. This observation is substantially true and it is suggested here that the reason for this was the Government's anxiety to protect the position of the Poor Law Nurses and the Infirmaries and then, later, to maintain a balance between the Poor Law sector and the voluntary sector on the GNC.

The mandatory syllabus of training was not authorised by the Minister of Health because at first many of the smaller infirmaries could not have fulfilled its requirements (nor, for that matter, could many of the smaller charity hospitals). A minimum educational standard for all candidates could not be accepted because it would have reduced the number of recruits. The Ministry of Health did not allow the GNC to employ inspectors of nurse training schools until 1945, because of its aversion to 'irresponsible' officials since the 1902 Midwives Act.

The Government had learned its lesson well but it is questionable whether the reasons for its apparent recalcitrance were ever appreciated by the profession. It is therefore doubtful that nurses learned from this the lesson that social reform (or nursing reform) which requires legislation or Government support is influenced by public attitudes and relies upon political and economic criteria.

Similarly, the advances made through the years depended on the economic climate: if the country was flourishing (as in the 1870s and 1880s) more nurses could be employed and more infirmaries could be built. As quickly as there was a set back in the economic situation so there was a period of stasis in the progress of the nursing service. It was only on the occasions of a critical shortage of nurses (there was always a shortage) that their conditions of service and salaries were improved.

But, whatever the state of the economy, there was never a time when the country invested anything in the nursing profession. Neither the Government nor, with a few exceptions, the local authorities (be they Guardians or Councillors) ever felt a need to invest money in training schools for nurses in any way commensurate with investment in medical schools. Where training schools were set up they were established for the most part as a means of providing cheap labour for the sick wards. The probationers were not paid a salary because, it was said, they were being trained free of charge. In 1902 it was acknowledged at the Departmental Committee (*Parl. Papers* Vol. XXXVIII) that there were about 400 probationers at non-training schools where there was overt and dishonest exploitation of their labour, and that everywhere probationers were used as assistant nurses during their training. Probationers were cheaper to employ than assistant nurses and were therefore preferred. It was cheaper to set up a mockery of a training school so that probationers could be recruited than it was to employ assistant nurses. In 1932 *The Lancet Commission* found that student nurses were hospital workers: they attempted to cost the difference in outlay if non-student nurse labour were employed and found that an approximate estimate was 47% extra at Guy's Hospital (£130 per student nurse over three years) and £37 per student nurse over three years at the London County Council hospitals. The comparison was made against the cost of employing assistant nurses. Burdett (1893) had found that fees paid by probationers amounted to 0·69% of the total income of London general hospitals and 0·70% for the provincial general hospitals. This frank exploitation would not have been reprehensible if the probationers had been given a student status and a proper professional education as was afforded to the medical students, but that was not done and the training schools enjoyed the best of both worlds whilst the patients and the public condoned the system.

This neglect of investment in the nursing profession was similar to the neglect in the establishment of a nursing infrastructure for the hospital service, the refusal to establish a Poor Law Nursing Service and the omission of a nursing department in the Ministry of Health. The country simply took their nurses for granted: they exploited their sense of vocation, neglected their professional education, overworked them, underpaid them, applauded them at times of crisis and undermined them in normal times. In this way a generalised image of nursing was established: a picture of repression, abuse, exhaustion and underprivilege which, not surprisingly, deterred would-be recruits, parents and school teachers. When alternative occupations for women became more plentiful, the country should not have been surprised to find that it was short of nurses. There were plenty of warnings about this accelerating situation; every report on nursing that was published from the end of the 1914–18 war has discussed the shortage of nurses, the dilution of nursing care and the increasing problem of recruiting candidates of an acceptable quality. It was the exception to the rule if any notice was taken of any of these reports. When the public complain of the quality of nursing care they must begin to realise their own responsibility in this problem and demand that the sick are nursed by trained nurses.

Another theme which presented itself from the evidence thrown up by this study was the consistent failure on the part of the Government to recognise the need to provide an infrastructure for the staffing (by nurses) of the country's infirmaries. The Government was also blind, for many years, to the need to establish a coherent medical structure. It did so in the end, but half-heartedly, slowly and in an unplanned way. It appointed a Medical Inspector (Dr Edward

Smith) in 1865 and eventually, at the end of the century, there were two medical inspectors working for the Local Government Board. But they did not appoint a nurse to the Board until the end of the 19th century when the appointment was as a Lady Inspector with a primary responsibility for looking at Poor Law schools; it did not adopt the general policy of appointing Lady Inspectors until 1911. Because these inspectors had general duties they also became involved as inspectors for infirmaries and female patients. It was therefore only inadvertently that the Lady Inspectors were involved in nursing until 1913. It was convenient to employ nurses as Inspectors but this qualification was not mandatory. A Medical Department grew up by evolution rather than by planning but even when it had established itself neither the doctors in that Department nor the Board felt any need for nursing representation in it. They simply assumed that doctors were able to establish criteria for nursing and to control, manage and train nurses. As the doctors at the Department were not able to make a complete tour of all the infirmaries inside of four to six years (there were only two of them even by the time of the 1905 Royal Commission) they continued on the assumption that the local medical officers could control the nurses in situ. The local medical officers were neither in full-time employment at the infirmaries nor of the highest quality. How the authorities ever thought that these medical officers could fulfil their delegated responsibilities for the nurses was not described. The Poor Law nurses were therefore left to do what they wished, or saw fit to do as their professional dictates demanded. In the separate Infirmaries the position was slightly different: there, there were several nurses, a Medical Superintendent of some professional calibre and in full time employment, a trained Matron and a nursing structure. But the nursing hierarchy, as has already been said, stopped at the Matron who was obliged to report through the Medical Officer. If the Medical Officer was sympathetic the Matron had considerable scope but if not, she was very limited and often worked in considerable difficulties. In any event, the Matron's constructive potential ended with the infirmary and went no further. It was no wonder therefore that standards of nursing and employment conditions varied so widely from one infirmary to another.

On the whole, with one or two notable exceptions, the Matrons and the nurses were much more concerned with establishing a social status for themselves than a political one. They were brought up in a period when women were naturally subservient to men. Florence Nightingale emphasised the nurses' dependency on the doctor (whatever her writings may have stated, her actions made this dependency clear) and the two philosophies syncretised and enforced a subservience to the medical officers which did a disservice to both professions. The dependence of the nurses on the medical officers for such matters as employment, promotion and even certification until well after the Registration of Nurses Act in 1919 only made the dependency more absolute.

The structure was lacking which might have allowed the nurses a voice in the development of their own service and profession but what system did exist actively militated against any voice being raised if a nurse wanted to keep her job. This position persisted well past 1948 and was not alleviated until the reorganisation of the nursing structure resulting from the Report of the *Committee on Senior Nursing Staff Structure* in 1965.

This position allowed a 'Third World' in the health care system which gave an imbalance to the three legs of administration: the administrators and the doctors developed professionally and politically but the nurses were left as an 'undeveloped race'. They now have the structure and the opportunity to make up for the lost years but they have first to neutralise persisting attitudes, and to resocialise mature members of the profession.

In spite of their disadvantages, however, the nurses did not capitulate entirely. Whereas the doctors and administrators were able to deal directly with planning and decision-making and the nurses were not so enabled, they found a method of making the best of whatever decision was thrust upon them. They became adept at avoiding direct confrontations, especially with the doctors, and developed the technique of establishing practices indirectly, by circumlocution. Where their efforts failed they could withdraw quietly without too much upset but where their efforts succeeded the results could be institutionalised and, with time, become formalised. Thus, the status of the Superintendent Nurses vis à vis the Matrons and later the Masters of the workhouse was clarified after years of quiet struggle.

The lack of structure of the Poor Law nurses should be contrasted with the complete structuring of the nursing service under the LCC. The latter authority first appointed a Matron-in-Chief then absorbed the Poor Law nurses. There was mobility within the service so that nurses could move from post to post without the loss of service or superannuation rights: nurses could broaden their experience without moving out of the LCC employment; there was some in-service training, there was a good support organisation with the appointment of ward orderlies (before any other authority in the country), there were ward clerks and a genuine attempt to identify and remove non-nursing duties. The nurses had a route for promotion, standard conditions of service and salary ranges and they were given a status which no other authority had given them previously. There were enormous problems to be overcome but the organisation of an LCC nursing service was successful and enabled the Council not only to hold on to its staff but to increase it during a period of the 1930s when there was a critical shortage of nurses throughout the country. The LCC was willing to initiate novel regulations and conditions for its nurses such as non-residence and, as far as their policies could show, they were very fair employers although at the same time retaining a discipline and insisting on a correct standard of behaviour. They gave incentives to their probationer nurses, tried to generate a hospital and a service ésprit de corps and, in personal emergencies, they were very generous with support. The one rule they would not relax, until the 1939–45 war made it necessary, was to allow the employment of a married nurse. In the beginning, from 1929 until the ensuing war, they centralised authority and delegated very little. The war forced a decentralisation of authority, such as the selection and employment of nurses by the hospital matrons, and after the war much of this decentralisation was allowed to continue.

Another theme that emerges from the study is the persistent confusion in the meaning of the word 'nurse'. This confusion allowed pauper nurses, assistant nurses, trained nurses, certificated nurses and qualified nurses and, for many years, 'existing nurses', all to be called 'nurse'. The bitter arguments during the 1860s as to whether or not a nurse should receive any training seemed to centre around this confusion of terminology and the subsequent arguments and discussions about status, duties and responsibilities, education and training, culpability, nurse:patient ratios, salaries, conditions of service, etc. have all been bedevilled by the same confusion. The interesting point to be observed is that the Government, doctors, nurses, Guardians and general public did not (and still do not for that matter) understand that there was this confusion.

When South wrote his paper in 1857 maintaining that the nurses 'required little teaching beyond poultice making, bed making and

H

hygiene' he was talking about the ward maids rather than the ward sisters but, although he made that point indirectly, the distinction was not understood. In later years, since the functions of the nurses were never clearly identified, the confusion continued and there were references to the numbers of patients supervised by nurses (the *British Medical Journal Report* of 1896) but no mention was made of the number of assistant nurses who were also available and giving what is now termed 'bedside' care. In the 1902 report there was a similar confusion with no distinction being made between trained nurses and probationer nurses when nurse:patient ratios were discussed, nor was there any clear indication given of the ratio between trained nurses and probationer nurses (with the exception of McVail's report to the Royal Commission). In fact all the reports written during the 100 years period have been equally confused. The nurse: patient ratios quoted through this period have therefore little real meaning except to underline the confusion in terminology. The one thing that does arise from this confusion is the astonishing realisation that patients really never have been nursed by trained nurses.

In the 19th century, Florence Nightingale trained her nurses to teach and to supervise. They were sent, after their training, into other hospitals where they assumed control of a large number of untrained nurses and instituted what order they could. They also started training schools and employed probationer nurses who worked in the wards learning to be nurses. As soon as they were trained, these nurses left and took up posts as private nurses, ward sisters, matrons or went into the Army or Colonial Nursing Services. The Poor Law admitted in 1902 to having little further use for the nurses it had trained except in the rural infirmaries. Most infirmaries tried to avoid the employment of trained nurses as they were too expensive; they preferred probationer nurses or assistant nurses. The expansion of nursing was such that the trained nurses always had supervisory posts available for them in hospitals. In the 20th century, this practice continued: the Wood Committee (Ministry of Health 1947) found that staff nurses, who were trained nurses actually giving bedside care for part of their time on duty, were not really trained but were, like the junior housemen, working for a reduced salary during a period of internship. These staff nurses were the nearest that the hospitals got to affording trained nursing care for their patients. Trained nurses have therefore always been employed by hospitals (except in very particular circumstances) in a teaching or supervisory capacity. Thus the criticisms frequently made of the Salmon Structure (that it took away the experienced nurse from the bedside) is without foundation because the trained nurse never seems to have been employed to give bedside nursing care as a primary function.

Medical historians have been able to describe consecutive medical paradigms as their profession developed. They have identified the eras of alleviation, public health and hygiene, the period of the bacterial theory of disease, the era of biochemical medicine, the era of social medicine and the era of behavioural diseases. Historians have never attempted to identify the equivalent nursing paradigms. Indeed it is questionable whether the indigenous function of the nurse was ever described until lately. There has been a significant lack of any stated nursing philosophy until recently and succeeding generations of nurses have been trained without any clearly stated objectives.

Florence Nightingale had three objectives: to help the patient become well; to help the patient die comfortably; and to keep the individual well. In the course of time three separate arms of nursing grew up each, apparently, seeking to attain one of the three objectives. The Public Health nurses or Health Visitors had as their objective the last one. The voluntary hospital nurses took the first one and the Poor Law nurses were left with the second.

The voluntary hospital nurses accepted their objective from the doctors whose primary goal was the cure or recovery of their patients. This goal was also the goal of the hospital and there was therefore accord. There still is accord because there are still acute cases which can be cured or helped towards recovery, but difficulties arise when there are irreversible cases for whom the doctors can do nothing and who are relinquished to the nurses who are then left without an acknowledged goal. In the days of the Poor Law infirmaries, these cases were discharged to them.

The Health Visitors had a recognised goal in the days of transmitted diseases, the days when maternity and infant mortality rates could be influenced by good hygiene and feeding. However, when those days passed, the Health Visitors slowly lost their objective and have not been entirely successful in finding a new one.

The Poor Law nurses, left with the chronic sick, the aged and infirm, never lost their objective but, as trained nurses, their work was removed from them, since, it was generally agreed, these cases did not need skilled nursing care. These nurses were in some danger of alienation however as they gradually assumed the values of the voluntary hospitals and as the infirmaries began to take on more and more acute cases. Public values placed more strength on the curing of cases than on the care of the long-term sick, the old and the infirm and in order to be accepted as socially desirable, the Poor Law nurses had to assume those public values. Thus, the public unthinkingly relegated their geriatric patients to the untrained nurses and the inferior institutions. They did this even as the pattern of disease was changing from the curable to the incurable and as the demographic trend was being confirmed and the older people in the country began to out-number the younger age groups.

Whereas the doctors were relatively slow to appreciate the implications of these changes it seems that the nurses failed completely. They did not, and have not adjusted their values and similarly they did not and have not adjusted their education of student nurses. It is only recently that nurses have been heard to distinguish their paradigm (care) from that of the doctors (cure) but many have not yet sufficiently convinced themselves of this distinction to be able to discuss 'the extended role of the nurse' in any direction but towards the discarded routines of the doctors. Only a few voices are heard trying to steer nurses towards a better understanding of their own role, a better and deeper recognition of their intrinsic skills and the development of indigenous nursing theory. For so long nurses have unthinkingly accepted medical values for themselves without realising that doctors and nurses have different goals and values which are sometimes conflicting. Doctors are advancing along the high technology route; nurses must realise that they must take a divergent route if they are not to abandon the care of their patients.

Another change which urgently needs to be considered by nurses (and perhaps by the doctors also) is that health care is no longer dispensed by the hospitals and staffs as a charity. The National Health Service is paid for out of taxation and is not reliant on charity (as were the voluntary hospitals) nor on rates (as were the infirmaries). With the advent of the Welfare State, everyone in the country has been taught almost from childhood that he has a right to 'free' medical care. Attitudes to hospitals have therefore changed a great deal in the past 30 years; patients enter hospital without any feelings of receiving charity: they are going into a hospital for which they have helped to pay; their taxes are contributing to the salaries of the doctors and nurses. It is therefore no longer reasonable for any nurse to expect to receive the automatic gratitude from her patients that she might have had one hundred years ago. The patient is the tax payer and the doctor and nurse are the public's employees. The relationship between the patient and the nurse is now quite different. This changed situation does not remove from the nurse her personal right to respect from the patient but respect for her profession must now be earned on an individual basis and can no longer be expected as an automatic right. Every nurse can carry a lamp but she will have to keep it polished for herself.

The distribution of morbidity shows a predominance in the geriatric group. There is little that medical science can do to cure these patients but there is a great deal that nurses can do to care for these people. It may be that an alternative nursing force is necessary, as it was in the days of the Poor Law nurse, in order to provide one type of nurse for the acute patients and another type for the long-term patient. It may be that the incipient reorganisation of nursing education proposed by the *Committee on Nursing (Cmnd. 5115,* 1972) will generate enough nurses who are trained to care for the long-term patients. History has shown how the aged and infirm were relegated and how the Poor Law nurses who looked after them were rejected: it may be that we can learn one lesson from history and avoid a similar mistake.

The effects of war on nursing are not so easily identified. It might have been imagined that war would enhance nursing, expand it and be an impetus to growth. In many respects these did happen. The Crimean War was the impetus required to start Florence Nightingale's reform of nursing. This reform showed itself in the Poor Law infirmaries and was an important aspect in the reform of Poor Law nursing. Amongst other things, it provided a standard by which the infirmary nurses could be measured. The Boer War did not seem to have very much direct effect on the Poor Law nurses: its effect was much more indirect. Many nurses left their civilian posts for war service and this created a serious shortage which was noted by the 1902 Departmental Committee but which did not evoke any official reaction. The overall response in the country was to be more mindful, for a while, of the need for a common standard of nurse training. During the 1914–18 war the Poor Law nurses looked after cases that they had never before nursed, they were supplied with equipment they had not previously enjoyed, worked with a quality of staff they had not met before and, often, in establishments different from their Poor Law institutions.

The new work broadened their experience and taught them new techniques and a new set of values (the learning was not only one way: the Poor Law nurses were well thought of for their better bedside care and skill in handling awkward patients). They learned to use new and more complicated equipment and many of them began to specialise. This would not have been possible under normal circumstances as specialism for either doctors or nurses was precluded by the method of staffing in the infirmaries: the resident medical officer had to be a generalist and gross classification of patients was difficult enough without the further classification demanded by specialisms. They must have begun to realise their deprived pre-war position when the military authorities insisted on something like one nurse for eight patients compared with the Poor Law ratio of 1:40. Undoubtedly they realised the meanness of their salaries and allowances by comparison with the army nurses and their own colleagues who had been 'requisitioned' with their institutions by the War Office and who, consequently received better rates. There was a great deal of feeling about this discrepancy and the LGB was forced to make adjustments. If they worked with the military authorities they would have met a different kind of doctor and nurse even from the voluntary hospitals. In these instances they had a greater opportunity to absorb their values and it may not have been without significance that many Poor Law nurses started to specialise after the war as was seen in the last chapter. They had had an opportunity to learn and they had absorbed new values. There was therefore a considerable widening out for the Poor Law nurses both professionally and socially. The end of the war however found the service very short of nurses. Many of them had had a taste of better things and did not return, some had been killed overseas and the shortage of labour during the war had interfered with recruitment and training. The war therefore had been professionally broadening but had reduced the quantity of Poor Law nurses. Financially it had benefited them but only temporarily as the post-war conditions tended to level off their salaries.

The war of 1939–45 appeared to have had a similar effect on the nurses in the LCC service. It brought an element of rationalisation to the training methods, since the LCC opened up area Preliminary Training Schools. It also introduced the employment of married and part-time nurses. Both wars forced a greater financial investment in hospitals and gave the nurses better equipment and more of it. Whereas before the 1914–18 war the policy of deterrence had deprived the nurses of ward and nursing equipment, irrespective of staff shortages, the wars brought a considerable influx of apparatus in order to improve the care given to patients, specifically the wounded troops, and in order to make the best use of what nurses there were: a reversal of attitude.

To sum up therefore, it has appeared that scientific and medical developments had some impact on the Poor Law nursing service by broadening out their work but that wartime needs tended to disburse these effects more quickly and more universally than would otherwise have been the case. Nursing also had a considerable impact on the way in which the medical officers could function and develop and the two professions must be seen to have an interdependence.

Economic conditions had more effect on the infirmary environment than on the nursing service itself as investment in the nursing service was never seen to be intrinsically desirable, only expedient in terms of short-term gains. Long-term losses were never considered.

Political considerations were of two orders, political influence on nursing and the political power of the nurses. The former was accepted as having had a much greater influence on the development of nursing in general and of the Poor Law nurses in particular than has previously been recognised but that in the end political direction for nursing depended on social considerations and pressure groups. As for the latter, it has been seen that the Poor Law nurses neglected to seek it; in the early days power was inherited by the social position of the nursing leaders who concentrated on achieving a professional status for nurses. When those leaders had gone the nurses were left with the strongly ingrained ethos of 'gentility', deprived of power and too genteel to seek it. By the time they woke up to their powerless situation the structure of the country had become so complex that mere stature (social or personal) on the part of their leaders was inadequate and the power-organisation that had been evolved around the medical service precluded the nurses from achieving it by depriving them of any voice in decision making.

In the end, it was social developments that had the greatest effect on the development of the Poor Law nursing service. At first the philanthropists shaped the service, subsequently the movement of social reform and the rising voice of the lower classes forced the development of the service and, at the last, public demands to break up the Poor Law resulted in the 1929 Local Government Act and the municipalisation of the Poor Law infirmaries and their nurses. It was a persisting demand for the abolition of the Poor Law, a new phase of social reform and the continuing financial inviability of the voluntary hospitals that finally resulted in the National Health Service, the nationalisation of hospitals and the ultimate absorption of the residual Poor Law nurses.

REFERENCES

Abel-Smith, B. (1960), p. 113.

Burdett, Sir Henry (1893). Chapter VIII; Chapter VII.

Committee on Senior Nursing Staff Structure (Salmon Committee), 1965. HMSO London.

See Coser, R. L., 'Alienation and the Social Structure'. In *The Hospital in Modern Society*, Ed. Friedson, E. (1963). London, The Free Press of Glencoe, Collier-Macmillan. p. 231.

LGB *Annual Report*, 1865, p. 67. See Appendices 1 and 2. Ministry of Health, *Working Party on Recruitment and Training of Nurses*, 1947.

Poor Law Officers' Journal, 1911, Vol. XX, pp. 316, 933, 1003.

Report on the Mismanagement of the Sick Poor, 1866. Parliamentary Papers, Vol. LXI, 495 f.

Report of the Departmental Committee on Nursing the Sick Poor In Workhouses, 1902. Parliamentary Papers, Cd. 1366, Vol. XXXVIII, pp. 5–7.

Report of Dr Edward Smith to Poor Law Board on Metropolitan Infirmaries and Sick Wards, 1866. Parliamentary Papers, Vol. LXI, 170.

Report of Dr Edward Smith to Poor Law Board on 48 Provincial Workhouses, 1867. Sessional Papers, Vol. LX, 325.

APPENDIX 1

FITTINGS FOR THE SICK WARDS 1868

The fittings should be such as are usually provided in the wards of General Hospitals, and amongst them the following:

The bedsteads should be of iron, with iron laths, of modern make and in good order. The length should be 6 feet 2 inches, and the width 2 feet 8 inches, except for the bedridden, the lying-in cases, and women with children, for whom the width should be 3 to 4 feet.

A palliasse of straw or other material, or a layer of cocoa fibre matting, to lie upon the laths.

The beds, whether of feathers, carded flock, cut straw or chaff, to be properly made, kept in good order, and sufficiently full. In some Unions, however, hair or wool mattresses are found to be better.

Two sheets, two or three blankets, and a cheerful-looking rug.

One half the number of bedsteads to have a raising rack.

Separate bed rests.

Spittoons.

A pottery urinal to each bed and special pottery urinary bottles for the use of bed-ridden men.

Medicine glasses and feeding bottles.

Stone or metallic feet and chest warmers.

Air or water beds.

Mackintosh sheeting to be used to all lying-in beds.

The same with funnels for dirty cases.

Square and round mackintosh cushions with depression in the centre to prevent bed sores.

Mackintosh urinals to be worn by men who pass their urine involuntarily.

A locker with shelves for the use of two inmates, or a bed-table similar to that recommended by Dr Acland of Oxford, an example of which may be seen at the office of the Poor Law Board.

Arm and other chairs for two thirds of the number of sick.

Short benches with backs and (for special cases) cushions.

Rocking chairs for the lying-in wards.

Little arm-chairs and rocking chairs for children's sick wards.

Tables.

Pottery wash-hand basins for those who are washed in bed.

Fixed lavatory basins for others, or washstands with fittings.

A sufficient number of roller towels, and one small towel to each person who is usually washed in bed.

A proper supply of both combs and hair brushes, to be kept clean and in good order, in each ward.

Sealed night stools.

Gas, where practicable, to remain lit during the night.

Bells to the nurses room.

Jackets with long sleeves, for lunatics.

It may be desirable that an inventory of the furniture, fittings, and medical appliances supplied should be fixed in some conspicuous place in each ward.

Poor Law Board
June 1868

(Taken from Poor Law Board *Annual Report* 1868–69)

APPENDIX 2

TABLES OF NURSING POSTS SANCTIONED BY THE LGB FOR ENGLAND AND WALES 1871–1913

	MAB			LGB	
	M	F	LA*	M	F
1871	—	—	—	114	770
1872	10	432	—	143	821
1873	16	432	—	145	840
1874	1·5	540	—	150	862
1875	18	602	—	160	906
1876	23	695	—	164	918
1877	3	533	—	167	925
1878	23	735	—	171	962
1879	24	793	—	171	1000
1880	N/A	N/A	873	173	1020
1881	N/A	N/A	951	177	1039
1882	N/A	N/A	1146	176	1063
1883	N/A	N/A	1016	175	1101
1884	N/A	N/A	991	176	1119
1885	DISCONTINUED			2319†	
1886				2381	
1887				2451	
1888				2522	
1889				2604	
1890				2720	
1891				2806	
1892				2994	
1893				3138	
1894				3239	
1895				3639	
1896				3874	
1897				4106	
1898				226‡	4427§
1899				236	4709
1900				445	4999
1901				254	5795
1902				264	5410
1903				268	5627
1904				273	5779
1905				274	5894
1906				278	6094

* Male, Female, Lunatic Attendant
† 'Nurse or attendant on lunatic.' No separate figures given.
‡ Superintendent Nurses.
§ Nurses or Assistant Nurses.

	LGB	
	Superintendent Nurse	Nurses or Assistant Nurses
1907	279	6258
1908	279	6543
1909	280	6645
1910	286	6991
1911	286	7187
1912	285	7367
1913	282	7624

Discontinued because of wartime restrictions and difficulties.

APPENDIX 3

SYLLABUS OF TRAINING FOR PROBATIONERS AT PORTSMOUTH WORKHOUSE INFIRMARY, 1902

HANDED IN BY DR KNOTT

PARISH OF PORTSMOUTH WORKHOUSE INFIRMARY
SYLLABUS

First year probationers' lectures from October to middle of May.

All subjects contained in the St John Ambulance books; first aid, and nursing course, home hygiene, Murche's physiology (elementary animal), taught by diagrams and on the body (children being utilised), the roller bandage, application of splints, prevention of bed sores, treatment of patients brought in with bed sores, regional anatomy.

Junior probationers were allowed to attend P.M.'s when convenient.

Incubation periods and time for quaratine after recovery of the various contagious diseases, diets, washing helpless patients, what to observe and report to the medical officer.

Urine testing.

Ward duties – housekeeping.

(First year probationers were examined in all the above subjects.)

Feeding of children.

SYLLABUS

Second Year Probationers

Lectures from October to middle of May.

In addition to first year's books, Miss Lückes and Miss Oxford's books were used.

Preparations and doses of opium, aconite, hydrate of chloral, prussic acid, perchloride of mercury, arsenic, acetate of lead, etc., phosphorus, belladonna, pil. hydrargyri, pot. iodid; all poisons, in fact. What to observe and report to the doctor when patients were taking the above drugs and they were not agreeing with them.

Disinfectants, deodorants, antiseptics, how used.

Feeding of infants.

Signs of pain in children: head, stomach, lung.

How to deal with a case of uraemic convulsions, haemoptysis, haematemesis, in absence of doctor.

Household duties, urine testing, food stuff values.

SYLLABUS

Third Year Probationers

Lectures from October to middle of May.

Regional anatomy, all subjects of first and second year; same text books.

Dispensing, elementary, how to put up a simple mixture, lotion, ointment, or pill.

Night duty in female imbecile wards to give opportunities for feeding, keeping clean, and managing lunatics.

Delirium, acute mania, mania a potu, proper use of restraint jacket after being ordered by medical officer.

Hysteria as apart from mania, general paralysis of the insane, idiocy, imbecility.

Preparation of operating room, antiseptics, sterilisation of dressings, instruments, nurses' hands, operation table, patient, how to prepare, chloroform ether.

Different kinds of instrument, names and uses.

Diseases of children, intussusception, signs of urgency of such a case, and report to medical officer.

Ophthalmia neonatorum, danger of, to patient and nurse.

Pneumonia, pleurisy, pleuritic effusion, instrument for aspiration, how used, ascites, paracentesis abdominis, various forms of Bright's disease, erysipelas, dangers of, necessity for isolation.

Diets in all diseases.

Acute rheumatism, complications, what to observe, dyspnoea, orthopnoea, hip joint disease, acute synovitis, bursitis, white leg, thrombosis, embolism, aneurism.

Precautions to observe in nursing all the above.

Vocabulary of medical terms.

Dressings of all kinds, skin grafting.

How to keep catheters clean and aseptic when the doctor wants them.

Sick room cookery, clothing, bedding, ward discipline.

How to train her juniors, how to take charge when relieving the sister.

Not only were the probationers trained in their several years as far as possible up to the syllabus, but opportunities were always taken to teach the juniors as well as seniors what to observe at the bedside, respect to senior officers, respect to their own position, tact, self-abnegation, truthfulness, devotion to their calling, care of their own health.

The first year probationers get one lecture and one demonstration weekly.

Second third year, two lectures, also lecture from matron – uses and names of instruments.

Third year, reading easy prescriptions, detection of poisonous doses, antidotes; this course is additional to their lectures, and supplementary to the lectures of the medical superintendent.

This is carried out by the assistant dispenser.

(Taken from Report of the *Committee on Nursing the Sick Poor in Workhouses*, 1902, Appendix XXVI)

DR McVAIL'S TABLES OF NURSE: PATIENT RATIOS AND PROBATIONER: TRAINED NURSE RATIOS, 1905*

	NURSE:PATIENT RATIOS EXCLUDING MATRONS AND ASSISTANT MATRONS	PROBATIONER: TRAINED NURSE RATIOS
Teaching Hospitals		
The London Hospital	2·1	1·8
Guy's Hospital	2·4	1·2
St George's Hospital	2·4	1·4
St Mary's Hospital	2·5	Not given
Western Infirmary, Glasgow	3·1	Not given
Royal Infirmary, Newcastle	3·3	Not given
General Hospital, Birmingham	3·4	Not given
Royal Infirmaries, Edinburgh,	3·7	Not given
Glasgow	3·7	1·9
Non-Teaching Hospitals		
Leicester Royal Infirmary	3·1	Not given
Sussex County Infirmary	3·1	Not given
Salop Infirmary	3·8	5·2
Derbyshire Royal Infirmary	3·8	4·0
Bradford Royal Infirmary	3·8	Not given
Halifax Royal Infirmary	4·1	3·0
Cumberland Infirmary	4·5	5·0
Kent and Canterbury Hospital	4·7	4·5
Sunderland Infirmary	4·7	
Poor Law Infirmaries		
King's Norton Union	10·4	3·8
Pontypridd Union	10·9	0·7

* It has been observed that some of the early statistics were incorrect or inaccurate. These tables were copied verbatim from the evidence but are not clear in their meaning. The only way in which the nurse:patient ratios can be given a sensible interpretation is to assume that the heading should be reversed in order that it may read 'Patient:nurse ratios'. The figures will then relate to the numbers of patients (i.e., 2·1 patients) per nurse. The second column of figures seems to be correctly entitled, that is to say, there were 1·8 probationer nurses per 1 trained nurse (The London Hospital).

Hope Infirmary, Salford Union	10·6	5·7
Prescot Union	10·1	2·7
Hull Union	16·7	1·5
Camberwell Union	7·2	0·9
Edmonton Union	14·8	2·3
Enfield Infirmary, Edmonton Union	22·2	0·6
Whitechapel Union	13·0	3·9

(Taken from *Royal Commission on the Poor Laws* 1909 Minutes of Evidence, Appendix Vol. XIV, Dr McVail's evidence)

BIBLIOGRAPHY

PRIMARY SOURCES

Acts: Poor Law Consolidation Act 1927 (17 and 18 Geo. 5 C. 14)
      Poor Law Act 1930 (20 Geo. 5 C. 17)
BMJ Report on Nursing and Administration of Provincial Workhouses and Infirmaries, 1894–96.
Departmental Committees
    Nursing the Sick Poor in Workhouses 1902 Cd. 1366, vol. xxxviii.
    To Consolidate the Orders of the Poor Law 1913, Cd. 6938, vol. xxxviii.
Health, Ministry of
    Annual Reports 1919–33.
    On the State of the Public Health 1920–33 (Chief Medical Officer's Annual Reports).
    Hospital Surveys, London Region, 1945, HMSO.
    Hospital Surveys, North West Region, 1945, HMSO.
Inter-Departmental Committee on Nursing Services, 1939 (The Athlone Committee) HMSO.
Ladies Public Health Society (In Union with Manchester and Salford Sanitary Association), *Annual Reports* 1902–4.
The Lancet Commission on the Recruitment and Training of Nurses.
    Correspondence and Editorials, *The Lancet* 1930, Vol. 2.
    First Interim Report, *The Lancet* 1931, Vol. i.
    Final Report, Comments, *The Lancet* 1932, Vol. i.
        Follow-up, *The Lancet* 1932, Vol. ii.
        One Year After, *The Lancet* 1933, Vol. i.
    Final Report (Supplement) The Lancet Ltd., London 1932.
Local Government Board
    Annual Reports 1871–1918.
London County Council
    Annual Reports 1915–37.
    Annual Report of Medical Officer of Health 1938–48.
    Special Committee on Health Administration in London 1917.
    Central Public Health (Staff) Sub-Committee, Minutes 1930.
Manchester Nurse Training Institute
    Annual Reports, 1866, 1868, 1881.
Parliamentary Debates
    Official Records 1846–1932.
Poor Law Board
    Annual Reports 1848–70.
Poor Law Commission
    Annual Reports 1847.

Reconstruction, Ministry of
  *Local Government Committee on Transfer of Functions of Poor Law
  Administration in England and Wales.* (Maclean Committee) 1917 Cd.
  8917, Vol. XVIII.
Reports
  The Poor Law Report 1834 (Ed.) Checkland, S. G. & E. D. A.,
  Pelican Classics, London, 1974.
  Mismanagement of Sick Poor, Parliamentary Papers, Paddington
  Workhouse 1866, Vol. LXI, 4951.
  Rotherhithe Workhouse Infirmary 1866, Vol. LXI, 523 f.
  Strand Workhouse Infirmary, 1866, Vol. LXI 556 f.
  Report of Dr. Edward Smith on Metropolitan Infirmaries and Sick Wards,
  1866, Vol. LXI, 176 f.
  Report of Dr. Edward Smith on 48 Provincial Workhouses 1867–8, Vol.
  LX, 325 f.
Royal Commission on the Poor Laws, 1909 Cmnd. 4499.
  Majority Report Vols. I, II.
  Minority Report Vol. III.
  Minutes of Evidence Vols. 1–37.
Select Committees
  On Poor Relief 1861–4, Vol. ix.
  On Registration of Nurses 1904, 1905, Cd. 281.
  On the General Nursing Council 1924–5, 167, Vol. vii.
  On Nursing Homes (Registration) 1926, 103, Vol. vii.
Working Party *On Recruitment and Training of Nurses* (Wood Committee)
  1947
  Majority Report, HMSO.
  Minority (Cohen) Report, HMSO.

SECONDARY SOURCES

Abdellah, F. G. Evolution of Nursing as a Profession. *International Nursing
  Review,* 1972, 19. No. 2, 219–38.
Abel-Smith, B. *A History of the Nursing Profession.* Heineman, London, 1960.
  The Hospitals 1800–1948. A Study in Social Administration. Heineman,
  London, 1964.
Ackernecht, Erwin H. *A Short History of Medicine.* The Ronald Press, New
  York. 1955.
Anderson, G. An Oversight in Nursing History. *Journal of the History of
  Medicine,* 1948, Vol. 3, 417–26.
The Association for the Improvement of the Conditions of the Sick in
  Workhouses. Deputation to the President of the PLB, 14 April, 1866.
Atkinson, A. B. *Poverty in Britain and the Reform of Social Security.* Cambridge
  University Press. 1970.
Ayers, Gwendoline M. *England's First State Hospitals.* Wellcome Institute of
  the History of Medicine, London 1971.

Baly, Monica, E. *Nursing and Social Change*. Heineman Medical Books, London 1973.

Bendall, E. R. D. & Raybould, E. *A History of the GNC for England and Wales*, 1919–69. H. K. Lewis, London 1969.

Bickerton, T. H. *A Medical History of Liverpool*. John Murray, London 1936.

Blythe, Ronald. *Akenfield*. Allen Lane, London 1969.

Bostock, J. *Sketch of the History of Medicine*. Sherwood, Gilbert & Piper, London 1835.

Bowman, Gerald. *The Lamp and the Book*. Queen Anne Press, London 1967.

Brain, Lord W. R. *Doctors Past and Present*. Portman Medical Publishing, London 1964.

Bruce, M. *The Coming of the Welfare State*. Batsford, London 1972.

Bruce, M. (Ed.). *The Rise of the Welfare State*. World University Press, London 1973.

Burdett, Sir Henry C. *Hospitals and Asylums of the World*, Vol. III. J. & A. Churchill, London 1893.

Cottage Hospitals. The Scientific Press, London 1896.

Carr, E. H. *What is History?* Pelican, London 1968.

Christy, Teresa. Problem Forum on Historical Research. *A.N.A. 8th Nursing Research Conf. March 1972*.

Clarke, Edwin (Ed.). *Modern Methods in the History of Medicine*. Athlone Press, University of London 1971.

Cole, Margaret. *Beatrice Webb*. Longmans Green, London 1946.

Coleman, R. & Daley, W. A. The development of hospital services with particular reference to the municipal hospital system of London. *Proceedings of Royal Society of Medicine*, 1942. Vol. 35, 741–52.

Cope, Sir Zachary. Florence Nightingale and her Nurses. *Nursing Times*, 1960 Vol. 56, 597–8.

Dolan, Josephine A. *Nursing in Society, an Historical Perspective*. W. B. Saunders, London 1973.

Dray, William H. (Ed.). *Philosophical Analysis and History*. Harper & Row, London 1966.

Eckstein, Harry. *The English Health Service*. Harvard University Press, Cambridge, Mass. 1970.

Epidemiological Society. *Transactions of the Epidemiological Society*, 1863, 1875–82.

Finer, S. E. *The Life and Times of Sir Edwin Chadwick*. Methuen, London 1952.

Ford, P. G. & Marshallsay, D. *Select List of British Parliamentary Papers*. Irish University Press, Shannon, Ireland 1970.

Forsythe, Gordon. *Doctors and State Medicine*. Pitman Medical, London 1973.

Frazer, W. M. *A History of English Public Health*, 1834–1939. Ballière Tindall & Cox, London 1950.

Freidson, Eliot (Ed.). *The Hospital in Modern Society*. Collier-Macmillan, London 1963.

Garrison, Fielding H. *An Introduction to the History of Medicine*. W. B. Saunders, London 1929.

Gelfand, Michael. *Philosophy and Ethics of Medicine*. E. & S. Livingstone, London 1968.

Hector, Winnifred. *The Work of Mrs. Bedford Fenwick and the Rise of Professional Nursing*. Unpublished thesis 1970.

Mrs. Bedford Fenwick. Rcn Research Series, London 1970.

Hodgkinson, Ruth. *The Origins of the NHS: The Medical Services of the Poor Law*. 1834–71. Wellcome Institute of the History of Medicine, London 1967.

King, Lester S. *Medical Philosophy* 1836–44. John Hopkins Press, Baltimore 1968.

Lederman, E. K. *Philosophy and Medicine*. Tavistock Publications, London 1970.

Lees, Florence. One Hundred Years Ago. *Queens Nursing Journal*, issues June to November 1974.

London County Council. *The LCC Hospitals – A Retrospect*. Staples Press, London 1949.

Longmate, Norman. *The Workhouse*. Temple Smith, London 1974.

McKeown, T. & Lowe, T. *An Introduction to Social Medicine*. Blackwell Scientific, London 1968.

McLachlan, G. & McKeown, T. (Ed.). *A Symposium of Perspectives: Medical History and Medical Care*. N.P.H.T., Oxford University Press 1971.

Major, Ralph A. *A History of Medicine*, Vol. 2. Blackwell Scientific, London 1954.

Marsh, D. *The Changing Structure of England and Wales*. Routledge & Kegan Paul, London 1965.

Marwick, A. *War and Social Change in the 20th Century*. Macmillan Press, London 1974.

Moorman, J. R. H. *A History of the Church in England*. A. & C. Black, London 1954.

Moss, R. & Thomas, H. Greenwich and Deptford Union Workhouse Infirmary. *British Medical Journal* 1966, Vol. ii, 1587–9.

National Association for Providing Trained Nurses for the Sick Poor. *Report by the Sub-Committee of Reference and Enquiry*. 1875.

Plotkin, Stanley A. The Crisis at Guy's. *Guy's Hospital Gazette* 1961, *75*, 45–50.

The Poor Law Officers' Journal, 1906–30.

Powell, Sir G. A. *The Metropolitan Asylums Board and its Work*. 1867–1930, MAB, London 1930.

Poynter, F. N. L. (Ed.). *The Evolution of Hospitals in Britain*. Pitman Medical London 1964.

Rogers, Joseph. *Reminiscences of a Workhouse Medical Officer*. T. Fisher Unwin, London 1889.

Rose, M. E. The Relief of Poverty 1834–1914. *Economic History Society*, MacMillan, London 1972.

Rosen, G. Social Variables and Health in an Urban Environment – The Case of the Victorian City. *Society for the Social History of Medicine*, March 1973, *10*, 9.

Rumsey, A. W. *Essays in State Medicine*. John Churchill, London 1856.

Ryder, J. & Silver, H. *Modern English Society 1850–1970.* Methuen, London 1970.

Schröck, Ruth A. For the Love of Money. *Nursing Times Occasional Paper* 20 June 1974.

Seelig, M. G. *Medicine, An Historical Outline.* Williams & Wilkins, Baltimore 1925.

Sheppard, Francis. *The History of London, 1808–1870: The Infernal Wen.* Secker & Warburg, London 1971.

Shyrock, Richard Harrison. *Medicine in America, Historical Essays.* The Johns Hopkins Press, Baltimore 1966.

South, John F. *Factors Relating to Hospital Nurses 1857.* London.

Statistical Society of London. *Report of the Committee of Beneficent Institutions: The Medical Charities of the Metropolis.* John Wm. Parker & Son, London 1857.

Stern, W. M. *Britain Yesterday and Today.* Longmans, London 1962.

Stocks, Mary. *A Hundred Years of District Nursing.* Allen & Unwin, London 1960.

Thompson, Flora. *Lark Rise to Candleford.* Oxford University Press, London 1949.

Titmuss, R. M. *Social Policy, History of the Second World War.* HMSO. London 1952–72.

   Problems of Social Policy. Ed. Abel-Smith, B. and Titmuss, K., Allen & Unwin, London 1974.

   Essays on the Welfare State. Unwin University Books, London 1963.

Trevelyan, G. M. *English Social History,* Longmans, London 1961.

Twining, Louisa. Workhouses and Women's Work. *The C of E Monthly Review,* Longman, London 1858. A Paper on the Condition of Workhouses read to the National Association for the Promotion of Social Sciences, Birmingham, October 1857.

   Workhouses and Pauperism. Methuen, London 1898.

Wakeman, H. O. *An Introduction to the History of the Church of England.* (Revised Ollard, S. L.) Rivingtons, London 1914.

Walton, R. G. *The Place of Women in the Development of Social Work (1860–1871).* Unpublished thesis 1972. Manchester University.

Webb, Sidney & Beatrice. *The State and the Doctor.* Longmans Green, London 1910.

Williams, K. Ideologies of Nursing: Their Meanings and Implications. *Nursing Times Occasional Papers,* 8 August 1974.

Wolstenholme, G. E. Florence Nightingale: New Lamps for Old. *Proceedings of Royal Society of Medicine.* 1970 Vol. 3, 1282–6.

Woodham-Smith, Cecil. *Florence Nightingale 1820–1910.* Constable, London 1950.

Young, A. F. & Ashton, E. T. *British Social Work in the Nineteenth Century.* Routledge & Kegan Paul, London 1956.

Young, Pauline V. *Scientific Social Surveys and Research.* Prentice Hall, London 1966.

INDEX